8209

─ TENZING NORGAY AND THE SHERPAS OF EVEREST ─

Tenzing Norgay

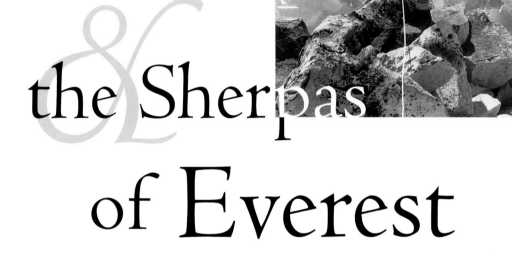

the Sherpas

of Everest

Tashi Tenzing

with Judy Tenzing

RAGGED MOUNTAIN PRESS / McGRAW-HILL
Camden, Maine • New York • Chicago • San Francisco
• Lisbon • London • Madrid • Mexico City • Milan
• New Delhi • San Juan • Seoul • Singapore • Sydney • Toronto

Ragged Mountain Press

A Division of The **McGraw·Hill** Companies

Library of Congress Cataloging-in-Publication Data

Tenzing, Tashi.

  [Tenzing and the Sherpas of Everest]

  Tenzing Norgay and the Sherpas of Everest / Tashi Tenzing with Judy Tenzing.

        p.   cm.

"First published in Australia in 2001 by HarperCollins Publishers under the title Tenzing and the Sherpas of Everest"—T.p. verso.

Includes bibliographical references.

  ISBN 0-07-138180-5 (hbk. : alk. paper)

  1. Mountaineering—Everest, Mount (China and Nepal)—History. 2. Tenzing Norkey, 1914– 3. Mountaineers—Nepal. 4. Sherpa (Nepalese people) 5. Everest, Mount (China and Nepal) I. Tenzing, Judy. II. Title.

  GV199.44.E85 T46 2001

  796.52′2′095496—dc21   2001004183

Design by Dede Cummings

Page layout by Janet Robbins

North American edition editors: Jonathan Eaton, D. A. Oliver, and Molly Mulhern

Illustration on title page by Robert Beer from *The Encyclopedia of Tibetan Symbols and Motifs*, courtesy Shambhala Publications, Inc. Other art credits can be found on page 293.

Title page: photo of Tenzing Norgay on the summit of Chukhung Peak, 3 April 1953.

For Pem Pem,
my amala

An extraordinary woman who lived through extraordinary times
and experienced all the highs and lows of Everest

●

and for the new generations of Tenzings who represent the future of the Sherpas
Pasang, Kinzom, Dechen, Deki, Nikhil, Tashi Phinzo, Syaza,
Pema and Dechen, Karchen, Norbu, Khenrab, Vrinda,
Norkila, Tshering Dolkar, Pasang Tshering, Phinzo Tashi, Lhakpa,
Tshering, Kunzes Tsedol, Riwu Dorje, Riggyal Motup,
Kesang Deki, Phurpi Yangzee, Karmi Diki, Nima Kanchi,
Tashi Sera, Rigzin, and Tenzing Thinley

CONTENTS

⬤

Acknowledgments   *ix*

Foreword by His Holiness The Dalai Lama   *xiii*

Foreword by Sir Edmund Hillary   *xv*

A Note on Sherpa Names   *xix*

Introduction   *1*

— Chapter 1
THE MOUNTAIN AND ITS PEOPLE   11

— Chapter 2
THE HIMALAYAN CLUB AND THE TIGER MEDAL   25

— Chapter 3
THE FIRST TIGERS OF THE SNOWS   37

— Chapter 4
TENZING'S EVEREST DREAM   61

— Chapter 5
EVEREST 1952   85

— Chapter 6
EVEREST 1953   107

— Chapter 7
TENZING AFTER EVEREST   141

— Chapter 8
MY QUEST FOR EVEREST   179

— Chapter 9
OTHER TENZINGS ON EVEREST   217

— Chapter 10
THE NEW LORDS OF EVEREST   239

— Chapter 11
MORE THAN MOUNTAINS   253

— Chapter 12
CHANGE AND THE FUTURE   261

Sherpa Ascents of Everest 1953–2000   271
Brief Bibliography   287
A Note from the Writer   289
Art Credits   293
Author Biography   296

— Maps
OVERVIEW MAP OF THE REGION   *xxii*
THE SOLU KHUMBU   6
MOUNT EVEREST   95

ACKNOWLEDGMENTS

WE WOULD first like to thank our children, Pasang Gyalpo and Dechen Lhamu, for whom everything in life for the last year has been addressed in terms of weeks and months AB—After the Book. Now, at last, we can go rollerblading together! We would also like to thank our dear friends and families who have tolerated our long silences and unreturned phone calls while we have typed our way, many times, over, up and down the slopes of Everest.

We thank our *amala* (mother), Pem Pem Tshering, whose incomparable memories of the days before and after Everest '53 inspired chapters of this book and whose love for her family and the Himalaya so honors her Sherpa people; and her sister and our aunt, Nima Tenzing Galang, whose wonderful recollections and honest approach to those times helped us keep it all in perspective.

For bullying and badgering until we approached a publisher with our manuscript I thank Coralie Younger, and for the support our book received and their unerring enthusiasm for this story we thank John Ferguson, Jesse Fink, and Alison Urquhart of HarperCollins*Publishers* Australia.

For their invaluable assistance and time while this book was being researched we most sincerely thank the following: Annelies Sutter—Aunty Sutter (Switzerland); Major Charles Wylie—Uncle Wylie—and Sheila Wylie (England); Annette Lambert—Aunty Lambert (Switzerland); George and Mary Lowe (England); Maria Feuz—Aunty Feuz (Switzerland); George Band (England); Mrs. Leon Flory (Switzerland); John and Eileen Jackson (Wales); Ernst Hofstetter (Switzerland); Michael Ward (England); Arnold and Silvia Glatthard (Switzerland); Michael Westmacott (England); the late Dolf Reist (Switzerland); Jean-Jacques Asper (Switzerland); Tony Streather (England); Norman G. Dyhrenfurth (Austria); Amy Warring of the Swiss Foundation for Alpine Research, Zurich; the wonderful women of the British Alpine Club, London; Joanna Wright of the Royal Geographical Society, London; Audrey Salkeld (England); Ed Douglas (England); Sir Christian Bonington (England); Dr. Samden Lhatoo (England, but whose heart will never leave the Himalaya); Brian and Jane Pullee of the Pen-Y-Gwryd Hotel (Wales); the National Geographic Society, Washington, D.C.; the American Alpine Club; Paul Stuber (formerly of Rolex, Switzerland); and the late John Hunt, Lord Hunt of Llanfair Waterdine, for his support for and after our 1993 Everest attempt.

In Darjeeling: our *amala*, Pem Pem Tshering, and *pala* (father), Dhendup Tshering; Dorjee and Doma Lhatoo; Nawang Gombu; Jamling Tenzing Norgay; Rabindranath Mitra; Ang Tshering; Ang Phuri; Ang Nimi; Topgay Sherpa; and Pasang Phutar.

In Kathmandu: Elizabeth Hawley; Glen Tulip; Phintso Ongdi and International Trekkers; Razzu Tuladhar (song specialist); Pertemba Sherpa; Gary McCue; Jamyang Wangmo; Tony Parr; Bikrum Pandey of the Himalaya Centre; Tendy Sherpa; Sonam Gyalchhen Sherpa of Sherpa Sewa Kendra; and Babu Chiri Sherpa (Takshindo).

In Khumbu: Ani Mingma, Lhakpa Sonam Sherpa and family (Namche); Ani Kantha and family (Pheriche); Ang Dorje Sherpa (Samde); Yangee Sherpa and family (Lobuche); Kami Temba and family (Thamey); Ani Pem Phuti and family (Samde), Dorjee Sherpa (Thamo); and Apa Sherpa (Thamey).

In Dharamsala: His Holiness The Dalai Lama, Tenzing Gyatso, for his kindness to the Sherpas and to the Tenzing family, and for the respectful foreword to this book.

In Delhi: Rita Gombu Marwah.

In San Francisco: Norbu Tenzing Norgay.

In New Zealand: Sir Edmund Hillary—Uncle Hillary—for his lifelong devotion to the Sherpas and his most appropriate and warm foreword; and Colin Monteath of Hedgehog House Photographic Library, Christchurch.

In Sydney: Rod Pyne and Michael Pyne for their literary advice and moral support; Sonam and Tseten Tshering for their advice, translations, and child-minding; Clare Forte for encouragement and faith in dark days; Basil Mourtos for photographs and support; Adrian Seaforth of Austral photo library; Bunty Avieson; and Therese Norgard of the Hyde Park Club, Sydney.

We would also like to thank Tim and Elsbeth Cunningham of Geneva for the honor of allowing Tashi to release some of the ashes of the late Leon Flory (Swiss Everest Expedition, spring 1952) over Mount Everest in May 2000.

This book is in loving memory of Judy's mother, Mrs. Kathleen Mary Pyne (née Cleary), who gave her daughter Tenzing's autobiography when she was very young, thus nurturing the seeds of a lifelong passion for the Himalaya. Kathleen passed away during the writing of this book.

Finally, I would like to thank my dear wife, Judy, whose hard work, passion for the Himalaya, and love and repect for the Sherpa people and our family brought this project to fruition.

FOREWORD

•

by His Holiness The Dalai Lama

I<small>N TIBET</small>, mountains are often considered the abodes of deities. Because of this, many people tend to go round the foot of mountains on pilgrimage. In fact, Tibetans have generally shown little interest in scaling the peaks that surround them, perhaps out of deference to these presiding deities. However, I think there is also a more practical reason. Most Tibetans have to climb far too many mountain passes to have any wish to climb higher than they must. When the people of Lhasa, for example, sometimes climbed for pleasure, they chose hills of a reasonable size and on reaching the top would burn incense, say prayers, and then relax with a picnic.

However, setting ourselves a clear goal and a firm determination to achieve it are two of the most powerful elements in accomplishing whatever we wish. There were many examples of this in Tibet. Great scholars often tell of their youthful ambition to study in the great monastic universities and earn their degrees, and, no matter what hardship they faced, they never gave up. Likewise, there are many tales of yogis who resolved never to leave their caves until they had gained the feat of meditation.

I believe that the achievement of Tenzing Sherpa, who accompanied Edmund Hillary on the first ascent of Everest, the world's highest mountain, in 1953, is a similarly inspiring story. For conquering a mountain peak requires not only great physical stamina, but also the possession of great courage, loyalty and trust, a concern for your companions greater than the natural urge for self-preservation. These are qualities I believe he possessed in abundance. Even today, many years after the event, adults and children alike marvel that Tenzing and Hillary were able to reach to the highest point on earth. It has become a standard of human success.

Tenzing Norgay and the Sherpas of Everest tells the story of Tenzing Sherpa and several members of subsequent generations of his family and their relationship to Everest. This is an admirable example of what cooperation and teamwork can accomplish.

THE DALAI LAMA
AUGUST 2001

FOREWORD

*

by Sir Edmund Hillary

THE SHERPAS of the mighty Himalaya are a remarkable group of people. Mostly small in stature they are amazingly strong and tough with an outstanding ability to perform effectively in the thin air at high altitude. When I first met them fifty years ago their life was a harsh and uncomfortable one, which they dealt with in remarkably philosophical fashion. They had an outstanding sense of humour even in the most unpleasant conditions and a strong community spirit, which gave them a remarkable combined strength. They were devout Buddhists with strong cultural beliefs and these qualities carried them through all the challenges that their tough environment presented to them.

In the early days they grazed their yaks at high altitudes and drove them over high alpine passes to trade in Tibet. But they had no interest in just climbing mountains. In the 1920s the first British expeditions attempted the ascent of Mount Everest and they employed groups of Sherpas as high-altitude porters. Few of the Sherpas at that stage had any climbing skills but their strength and ability to acclimatise made them formidable load-carriers. With their agreeable temperaments they proved excellent expedition companions.

As the years passed the skills of the Sherpas greatly increased and they achieved worldwide renown in the international mountaineering community. My first Himalayan expedition was to Garhwal in 1951 and we recruited four Sherpas from Darjeeling. Our *sirdar* was Pasang Dawa Lama—a formidable personality and a strong climber. Later that year we joined up with the famous mountaineer Eric Shipton to carry out a reconnaissance of the south approaches to Mount Everest. His sirdar was the amazing Ang Tharkay Sherpa—a warm and friendly personality with a fiery nature when action demanded it. Ang Tharkay was one of the really great Sherpas and I regarded myself as very fortunate to have his friendship.

I didn't meet Tenzing Norgay until the beginning of our 1953 British Everest Expedition but already his reputation as a skilled and forceful climber was widely known. I was very impressed on my first meeting with Tenzing. Tall and strong with a flashing smile he spread an aura of firm confidence. But perhaps his unique quality was his absolute determination to try and reach the summit of any mountain he was climbing—by no means a common attitude amongst the Sherpas in those days.

I soon learned to respect Tenzing's strength and skill and when we formed a team on Everest I believe we became a strong and energetic couple. We both had substantial motivation and confidence and this drove us to our ultimate success on top of the world. At this stage of our lives we were not really close friends (as Lambert and Tenzing had been) but mainly a well-balanced climbing team. It wasn't until nearly thirty years later when I was New Zealand High Commissioner to India that I saw a great deal of Tenzing and we built up a warm and enduring friendship.

Every great Sherpa sirdar had his own particular qualities and strengths. Dawa Tenzing had remarkable dignity and influence and reigned over my expeditions for a number of years. When I commenced my programmes of building schools and medical facilities, Mingma Tshering Sherpa proved an outstanding leader for our Himalayan Trust activities for almost twenty years.

And the Sherpas didn't only just excel in the mountains. With the establishment of schools in Solu Khumbu, many of the Sherpas blossomed in different fields—Ang Zangbu Sherpa became a senior pilot on a giant 747 jet; Pertemba Sherpa was not only an amazing climber but established his own trekking agency with great efficiency; Kami Temba qualified as a medical doctor; Mingma Norbu supervised all the Himalayan activities of the World Wildlife Fund; Lhakpa Norbu earned a doctorate at the University of Seattle; and Ang Rita Sherpa directed the widespread activities of the Himalayan Trust in Solu Khumbu.

Tenzing's family too have excelled in many fields. A number of them have climbed Mount Everest, some are teachers and company executives, and some run their own trekking agencies. Given the opportunity there is little that the Sherpas cannot achieve. For a tiny group of people from the wild and remote areas of the Himalayas the Sherpas have proved they are capable of dealing not only with extreme heights but they can successfully tackle many of the major challenges of the Western world too.

Ed Hillary

SIR EDMUND HILLARY
AUGUST 2001

A NOTE ON
SHERPA NAMES

T O THE UNINITIATED, Sherpa names can seem confusing and
even arbitrary. Yet some understanding of the Sherpa clan name
system is almost essential to a deeper appreciation of the roles
played by the great Sherpa climbers in the history of Himalayan mountaineering.

Sherpa naming is complicated further by the fact that, unlike
its kindred tongue, Tibetan, the Sherpa language has no written form.
It is closely related to Tibetan, and most Sherpas can grasp Tibetan
when the need dictates, yet Tibetans have difficulty comprehending
Sherpa. What hope, then, can the foreign linguist have?

It is best, I feel, to keep explanations succinct and as logical to
the Western mind as possible, sacrificing the nth degree of scholastic
rigor in favor of a working simplicity. With that in mind, the word
Sherpa refers to a clan of Tibetans who long lived in the southeastern
reaches of Tibet, along the Himalayan border with Nepal, and most of
whom migrated south into the high Nepalese valleys of the Solu
Khumbu, stretching south from Everest, starting between four and five
hundred years ago. *Shar* means "east" and *pa* means "people"—hence,

TENZING FAMILY TREE

Tenzing's Birthplace: Moyey, Tibet

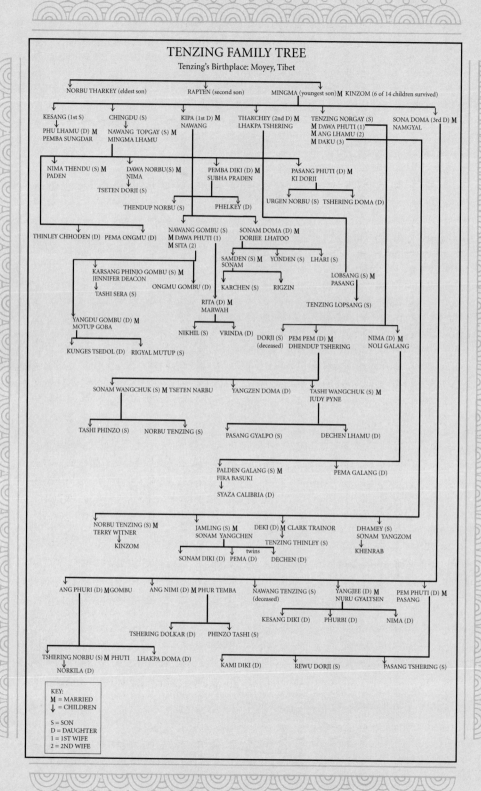

KEY:
M = MARRIED
↓ = CHILDREN

S = SON
D = DAUGHTER
1 = 1ST WIFE
2 = 2ND WIFE

people from the east. In the early 1900s, as the Sherpas proved their great physical aptitude for Himalayan exploration and mountaineering, foreign sahibs began to use the term *sherpa* to refer to any high-altitude porter, or load-carrier, even though the porter in question might in fact be a Tamang from central Nepal or a Rai from the south. This appellation broadened in subsequent years to cover almost any Himalayan local who worked as a mountain guide or porter. Most—but by no means all—such guides and porters were in fact ethnical Sherpas.

Turning to Sherpa family and given names, it may be expeditious to use that most famous Sherpa name—Tenzing Norgay Sherpa—as a point of departure. Tenzing's full name was really Tenzing Norgay Bhutia (since he was born in Tibet and hence was technically a Tibetan migrant to Nepal and India—hence a Bhutian). However, since he was in fact a Sherpa—a man from eastern Tibet—he more easily took on that name, as did his Khumbu clanspeople. Indeed, most people in Solu Khumbu have the last name of Sherpa—Pasang Kami Sherpa or Ang Rita Sherpa. This system works without problem in their homeland, since all Sherpas are able to differentiate among same-name Sherpas by identifying their villages, parents, brothers, or sons. The method is sometimes long-winded, but it has worked for ages and encourages conversation between travelers. Only since the coming of Western institutions—such as English school enrollments, passports, and the like—has the need for a more definitive and less confusing system developed. Tenzing was, and is still, known in Nepal and India as Tenzing Norgay Sherpa. Tenzing and Norgay were his first and middle given names, since all Sherpas have dual names, one of which is often the name of the day on which they were born. Thus, Monday is Dawa, Tuesday is Mingma, Wednesday is Lhakpa, Thursday is Phurba, Friday is Pasang, Saturday is Pemba, and Sunday is Nima. Ang, meaning "young," sometimes becomes the first name, as in Ang Norbu or Ang Dawa. Though Sherpa was Tenzing's clan name, his descendants have sometimes taken on the names of Tenzing or Norgay as family names in order to make life in and travel to the West less complicated. Most Sherpas today, however, retain the clan name Sherpa as a family name, whether they live in the Himalaya or abroad.

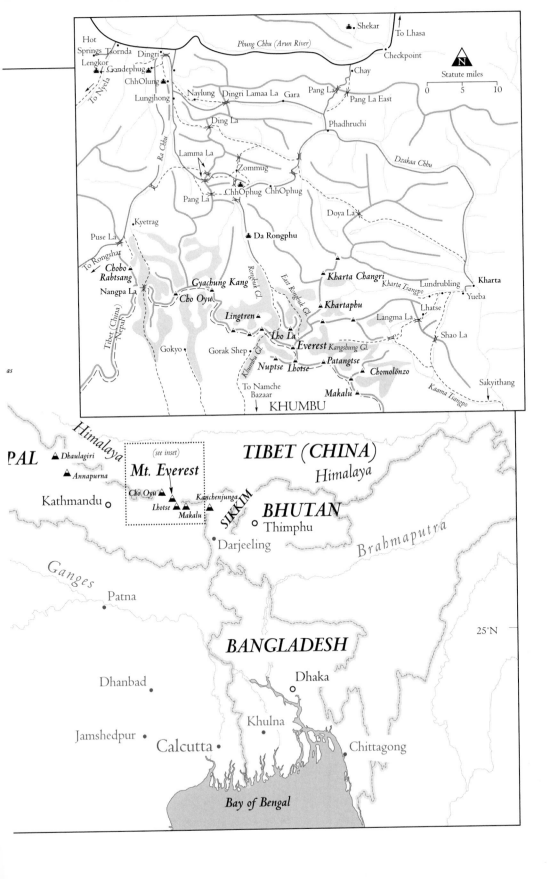

INTRODUCTION

I AM A SHERPA, a man of the mountains of the eastern Himalaya. I am the grandson of that most renowned of all Sherpas, Tenzing Norgay, Man of Everest, Tiger of the Snows. I am proud of my heritage and my people and I draw immeasurable strength from my family and my Tibetan ancestry.

I believe that the peaks of the Khumbu region of Nepal belong to my Sherpa people. Our spirits dwell in them, and our devotion to them is deep and eternal. Before foreigners came to the Himalaya and discovered this greatest of mountain ranges, we lived in harmony with these towering giants. While they sometimes demanded sacrifice, they always offered us a livelihood, however meager, and protection from the world beyond their icy flanks.

Like my late grandfather, I am passionate about climbing and about mountains, in particular one mountain—Chomolungma, Everest. This great peak is like a member of my family, and I have always felt a special relationship with her. Yet she has not always been kind to me and my family; indeed, she has tested our deep faith in her to its

Taweche (20,889 feet) and Cholatse (21,129 feet) towering above the Sherpa village of Pheriche, in the Khumbu region of Nepal.

limits. Seven times my grandfather Tenzing tried to reach the summit. Only once did she permit it. She was more lenient with me, for I reached the top on my second attempt, but she yielded only after exacting the ultimate price—the life of a much-loved family member.

I invite you to travel back in time and up the icy slopes to summit Chomolungma with me. It is 23 May 1997, and my Sherpa people and our Tibetan kin are celebrating Buddha Purnima, the birthday of Lord Buddha. It is 6:50 A.M., a clear, blue, still morning. From this height—8,850 meters—we can see clearly the curve of the earth below, a view at once terrifying, exhilarating, and humbling. Directly above us is the deep midnight blue of the outer spheres of our planet's atmosphere. Chomolungma's characteristic plume of frozen moisture trailing off to the east in the jet stream is for once absent, and we are privileged with a 360-degree view of the world at our feet. More than the intense cold and the thin, oxygen-starved air that surrounds us, it is the vista that takes our breaths away.

For fifty miles in all directions, I can see clearly the Tibetan Buddhist world in which I have spent my life—yet now it seems more grand and powerful than it ever has before. We can look down the massive north face of the mountain to the fabled Rongbuk valley of eastern Tibet, where the East and West Rongbuk glaciers meet before sweeping westward onto the high, wild Tibetan Plateau toward Lhasa. Gazing downward, we can imagine the old expeditions under Bruce and Ruttledge, tiny ants in the distance, wending their way from the north across this vastness toward their holy grail, the summit on which we stand.

Beyond the western horizon lies Mount Kailas, that most sacred of peaks for my people, and to the north the vast plains of this ancient land stretch as far as the eye can see into China proper.

In the distant south, beyond the great wall of the Nuptse ridge, lie the interconnected valleys of Solu Khumbu—the home of my Sherpa people for the last four centuries or more and the heart-home of my grandfather and myself. In one of these valleys, on the wide field of Tengboche, just visible in the mists below, stands the great monastery whose lamas have blessed Everest expeditions from the time teams have approached the peak from the south. Burned to the ground in 1989, this revered monastery has risen from the ashes grander and

View from Everest looking south over the Nuptse ridge.

stronger than before, and provides a fitting altar at the feet of the great peaks of the Everest basin. Hidden from view but only a ridge south of Tengboche, in a protected horseshoe-shaped valley, is Namche Bazaar —the Sherpa "capital" of the Everest region and an age-old stopping point on the trade routes from Tibet to the southern plains.

Still farther south lie the emerald vales of the middle Himalayan hills, and beyond them the dusty, golden expanse of the vast plains of southern Nepal and northern India. It was from those broad plains in what was then British India that explorers emerged to marvel at the size and grandeur of these forbidden peaks to the north.

To the east we can see Kanchenjunga ("Five Treasures of the Snows"), India's highest peak and third in the honor roll of the world's greatest mountains. This grand massif stands sentinel over my childhood home in Darjeeling; in my grandfather's heart it was second only to Everest. Out of sight but clearly visible in my mind is the long, forested ridge that lies beneath Kanchenjunga's southern ramparts, and on which my hometown nestles. There my mother, Tenzing's daughter Pem Pem, is even now doing continual *pujas*, or prayers, for my summit climb, and I can almost smell the sweet brew of her Darjeeling tea.

East down the Kangshung face of Chomolungma and a little north, we overlook the old monastery of Ghang-La where my grandfather was born, and the nearby village of Moyey where he spent his early years. I can only imagine how he felt as he stood on this summit forty-four years ago looking toward these places. For him the emotion could only have been heightened by the immensity of that first great ascent.

Down the north face, somewhere on a scree slope beneath the northeast ridge, lie the remains of George Leigh Mallory, the legendary Himalayan climber who made his gallant attempt on Everest in 1924 only to disappear into clouds beneath the summit. Somewhere below that same old route lies his comrade in that ill-fated quest, Andrew (Sandy) Irvine, whose camera may hold one of Everest's greatest secrets—whether one or both of these men actually reached the summit of Everest on that early attempt from the north.

To the west, past the great peak of Cho Oyu, I strain to see where my ancestors trod that ancient path over the 18,753-foot Nangpa La pass between eastern Tibet and the Khumbu—some laden with their meager worldly belongings, some with only the clothes they wore in their escape from an impoverished and sometimes brutally oppressed life in Tibet. In my mind's eye I can see my uncle Nawang Gombu as a young monk, making his way by dark of night and in the bitter cold of a Himalayan winter out from Da Rongphu monastery and over the Nangpa La in only his monk's thin robes.

Three weeks' march southwest of us is Kathmandu, the bustling capital of Nepal and the place in which I will formally celebrate my success in a few days' time. Of course now it is but a few days' walk south from Everest to the tiny airstrip at Lukla, from which we can fly to Kathmandu, but in my grandfather's day there was no alternative to the long trek from Everest to the edge of Kathmandu town. I smile as I look down to the villages of my family in Khumbu, each one waiting

View from Everest looking southeast, with Makalu center and Chomolönzo to its left. In the distance, left, is Kanchenjunga.

with *kadas* and blessings for my success. Sharing this with them is as important to me as my ascent, and I know I will tread carefully on my descent, for they are walking with me, step by step.

How different this Sherpa world is from the isolated Himalayan kingdom that opened its doors to the world in 1950. Then these remote, arid valleys were inhabited by Bhutias (migrants from Tibet) and their yak herds whose only contact with the outside world was with traders plying the old route between Tibet and the ports of India. Everest has changed everything—and nothing. Certainly villages such as Namche Bazaar and Tengboche have grown in size and affluence, and this main route in to the great mountain has become as familiar to hundreds of Westerners as it has always been to the Sherpas. The trappings of modernization are there, as well: neon lights, communications systems,

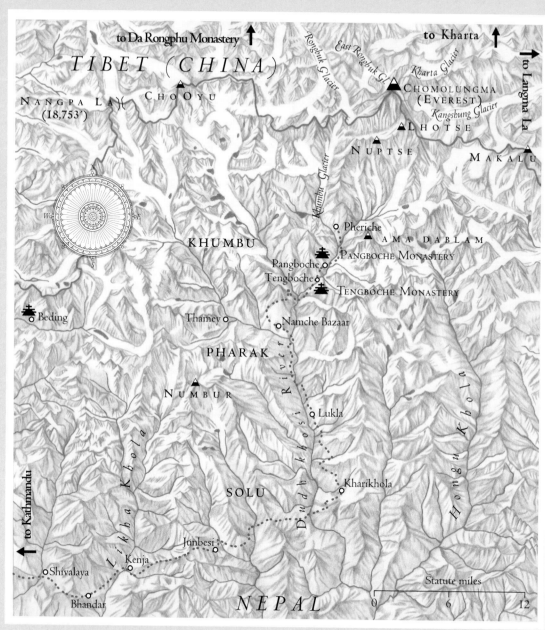

to Da Rongphu Monastery ↑   to Kharta ↑

→ to Langma La

TIBET (CHINA)

NANGPA LA)(
(18,753')

CHO OYU ▲

△▲ CHOMOLUNGMA
(EVEREST)

Rongbuk Glacier   *East Rongbuk Gl.*   *Kharta Glacier*

Kangshung Glacier

▲ LHOTSE

△ NUPTSE   ▲ MAKALU

Khumbu Glacier

○ Pheriche

KHUMBU   ▲ AMA DABLAM

🛕 PANGBOCHE MONASTERY
Pangboche ○
Tengboche ○
🛕 TENGBOCHE MONASTERY

🛕 Beding   Thamey ○   ○ Namche Bazaar

Dudhkhosi River

PHARAK

▲ NUMBUR   ○ Lukla

Hongu Khola

○ Kharikhola

SOLU

Likha Khola

to Kathmandu   ○ Junbesi

Kenja ○

○ Shivalaya

Bhandar ○   NEPAL

Statute miles
0   6   12

△ Mountain Peaks   ···· Trail

🛕 Monastery   )(**Pass**

○ Towns and Cities

The Solu Khumbu region.

advertising, and rock music. Life was unquestionably hard in the old days of isolation and subsistence farming, and the opportunities that came with foreign climbers have brought previously unimaginable prosperity to these high, wild valleys. Where once we lost our people to illness and poor harvests, we now have modern medical facilities, schools, and food aplenty. That which we once held so true, however—a deeply ingrained sense of tradition, cultural strength, and the family and social structure that bound all of this together—is now being slowly dismantled by the intrusion of a new world that offers so much excitement, comfort, and variety to our young people.

Yet we Sherpas are a tough people—we adapt well and quickly—and I am confident we will survive this transformation with our culture and our ancient values intact. I believe little has changed in the Sherpa heart, for whether I meet my family and friends at Everest Base Camp, in Kathmandu, or in San Francisco or London, the bond of Sherpa kinship and tradition runs deep and strong. Here, on the summit of Chomolungma, I feel as close to them as I ever have—and I know this will never change.

Let us take the luxury of one last look around this great circle of snows and mist, emotions and histories. It is time to head down the mountain. The climber who lingers is forgetting to fear Chomolungma, and that would be foolish indeed.

⁂

The story of Sherpas on Everest is a story of great strength and courage, both physical and spiritual. Engaged in a quest that was alien to them—foolhardy and pointless—the Sherpas of the pioneering Himalayan expeditions were faithful, strong, and reliable climbers and load-carriers. They were the backbone of any mountaineering expedition, the success of which relied largely on their ability to function well at the great altitudes to which they were naturally adapted. Due to barriers of racial attitude and language, however, as well as their own lack of ambition in this mountaineering world, Sherpas were not seen as central players on the Everest stage.

My grandfather changed this image completely. He was illiterate and spent his childhood and youth unexposed to any world other than that of his own people. Yet in him burned a desire and a dream that was alien to his own race: that of climbing Chomolungma. He didn't know how he would do it, but he felt he possessed the power and the will to succeed. The advent of the big Everest expeditions paved the way for this extraordinary dream to become a reality. He was absorbed by what had previously been an alien quest, and it changed the course of his life—and through him the terms of Sherpa existence—irrevocably.

Tenzing Norgay and the Sherpas of Everest is both about my Sherpa people and for them. It is about those great old Sherpa climbers of the early days of Everest exploration who held no dreams of glory or summit success, but who climbed bravely and selflessly for decades to help others in their own quests. It is for my family, who have achieved much in the field of mountaineering and in other more diverse fields. It is for the young Sherpas who today wear the laurels of Everest success as easily as any foreign climber. Indeed, Sherpas currently hold most of the major records on Everest:

- First person to reach the summit: Tenzing Norgay with Edmund Hillary, 1953
- First person to climb Everest twice: Nawang Gombu, 1963, 1965
- Most number of summits: Apa Sherpa, eleven
- Fastest ascent time: Babu Chiri Sherpa, Base Camp to summit in 16 hours, 56 minutes on 21 May 2000
- First third-generation member of one family to climb Everest: Tashi Tenzing, 23 May 1997

But this book isn't only about climbers—it's also about doctors, porters, teachers, businesspeople, nomads, hoteliers, holders of elite administrative posts at home and abroad, traders, and yak herders. It is written to give all Sherpas the recognition and credit they have so long deserved. It is written to remove the veil of anonymity they have worn for most of the last hundred years. It is written to expose their weaknesses and problems and explain the challenges they have faced and still encounter.

The Sherpa village of Khumjung, between Namche Bazaar and Tengboche on the Everest approach route, with Ama Dablam ("Mother's Box") towering above.

Primarily it is written to honor the Sherpas, a people of great strength and spirituality, intelligence, and good humor, and a people whose loyalty and personal integrity have earned them a reputation worldwide to equal that of the great mountain beneath which they dwell—Chomolungma, Everest.

CHAPTER 1

THE MOUNTAIN
AND ITS PEOPLE

E VEREST. The highest point on earth, the Third Pole, the "ultimate challenge"—at least to the Western world.

When the West's obsession with this peak began, the Sherpa
people knew nothing of surveying, the poles, or the global significance
of this big pyramid of rock at the head of one of so many massive
Himalayan valleys. It was just another towering peak like so many near
it, stretching into the distance as far as the eye could see. It was not
even a particularly important peak spiritually. Then and even today,
the Sherpas believe that the Himalaya is the abode of the gods, but ask
a Sherpa which is the most sacred summit in the world and he or she
will point you to 6,714-meter Mount Kailas in western Tibet (where
Lord Shiva abides) or to Khumbila in the Khumbu region of Nepal, the

Everest by moonlight from the Khumbu Glacier, with the southeast ridge descending left to right and the South Col lower right.

sacred peak of the Sherpas. Everest is revered, there is no question, but no more so than many other peaks in this vast range. Height, technical difficulty of climbing, and the kudos rewarding a successful summit mean little or nothing to most Sherpas. Had Europeans not come to seek out and reconnoiter these mountains in the latter part of the nineteenth and early twentieth centuries, there is little doubt that Everest would not have been climbed to this day; it would have remained simply a big mountain among many big mountains.

As we know, however, Everest *was* "discovered" by the West and everything changed—for the world, for the region, and most significantly, for the Sherpas, the inhabitants of the valleys beneath its southern flanks.

The word *Sherpa* (pronounced *shawa* in the Sherpa language, an eastern Tibetan dialect) should be clarified, as it is so often misunderstood. It is derived from two words, *shar* meaning "east" and *wa* (or *pa*) meaning "people belonging to." Thus *Sherpa* or "people from the east."

We Sherpas are descended from the nomads, agricultural laborers and traders of southeastern Tibet. My people are tough—mentally and physically—and extremely canny in business dealings. Toward the end of the fifteenth century our ancestors began to migrate south, over the high Himalayan passes and into the valleys beneath the eastern Himalayan peaks of the kingdom of Nepal. (Nepal was not then a single political entity, but a group of powerful and warring kingdoms.) There they found land for tilling and herding, which, though harsh, was more hospitable than the high (4,000- to 5,000-meter) Tibetan Plateau from which they had come.

The reasons for the migration are complex. One was the spread of Islam from Mongolia, which affected the politics of Lhasa, Tibet's capital, and created strong ideological disparities between central Tibetans and those of the remoter regions in the far east and west who were devout followers of the old Nyingmapa Buddhism, introduced into Tibet around 750 A.D. by Padmasambhava, also known as Guru Rimpoche, the great "lotus-born" Indian saint, and then, much later, into the Khumbu. There were other reasons, too: the desire for more arable land and a more benign climate, both of which were offered in the remote and sparsely inhabited valleys south of Everest; and, most important, freedom from the oppression of harsh feudal lords who employed the poorer classes to work in their fields and tend their yak herds. As time passed, traders and herders visited Tibet from the Khumbu with tales of valleys and rivers where few people lived and where life could be vastly safer and more promising.

So they came, over the high and wild Himalayan passes with their families and worldly belongings and, most crucially, their herds of yaks, those extraordinary high-altitude beasts of burden that once formed the mainstay of life for these communities and that, to this day, continue to play an important role in the life of the Sherpas. Initially the Tibetans settled in the valleys immediately south of Everest, now known as *Khumbu*, where the villages are at altitudes from 4,000 to 4,500 meters with even higher summer grazing pastures. This area extended from the snowline of the peaks of Everest, Cho Oyu, and Makalu down to the Dudh Khosi River beneath the large village of Namche Bazaar (known in the Sherpa language as *Nawche*). Namche became a major trading post in the trade route that then developed between Tibet and India. It is today the most wealthy and prosperous center in the upper Everest region.

As more eastern Tibetans migrated they began to settle farther and farther south, into the middle Khumbu region known as Pharak (around Lukla and its adjoining valleys) and south into Solu Khumbu (*Shar Khumbu* in Sherpa)—a region extending from below Lukla to Phaphlu and also known as *Shorong* to the locals. The lush and heavily forested Solu valleys, with villages at 2,600 to 3,300 meters, were rich in wildlife and timber and inhabited by a small clan descended from the Mongols called *Dongphus* (related to the Rai people who today dwell in the far southeastern valleys of Nepal). The intermixing of the Shorongs and the Dongphus resulted in a race of Sherpas quite distinct in appearance from their upper Khumbu relatives. They are shorter, darker, and stockier in build, while the Sherpas of the Khumbu are still very eastern Tibetan in appearance—often taller and fairer, with sharper facial features.

These Sherpa communities lived an isolated and undisturbed existence for centuries, rarely venturing far from their villages, except for those in trade with Tibet and India. They grazed their yak herds in the high summer pastures, often above 5,000 meters, during the warm months and grew potatoes and barley in small terraced plots of land near their homes. Life was hard, but they knew no other. Some had migrated south in search of wealth and land, many had suffered under

The Chumbi Valley in remote southeastern Tibet. The long trek from Darjeeling to Everest's northern approach took the early British expeditions through these lush and heavily forested valleys.

the feudal landlords of Tibet; all found this new life a welcome release from serfdom and tenant farming and the endless battle for survival on the high Tibetan Plateau. They had little or nothing to do with the Hindu, caste-based politics of Kathmandu and controlled their local affairs according to the laws and cultural traditions of their Tibetan ancestors, remaining culturally and ethnically close to their trading partners in southeastern Tibet.

Life carried on in this way until the late nineteenth and early twentieth centuries, when a mountain in the eastern Himalayan range came to the notice of the surveyors of what was then British India. Even then, these measurers and calculators were working from India and from the Tibetan side of the Himalaya, as Nepal, under the rule of the Shah dynasty since the mid-eighteenth century, had long been closed to all foreigners (and would remain so until 1950). The Sherpas had no concept of the changes that the "discovery" of this peak would have on them and their future.

The highest peak on earth was first observed in 1847 by J. W. Armstrong of the Great Trigonometrical Survey of India, which had been headed by Sir George Everest from the 1820s to the 1840s. Located about 150 kilometers west of Kanchenjunga (the third highest peak in the world), it was sometimes visible from Darjeeling, the old hill station to which the British of Calcutta, originally the capital of British India, would retreat in summer to escape the suffocating heat of the Indian plains. Then labeled Peak B, it was much overshadowed in majesty and appearance by Makalu (then known as Peak XIII) to its southeast. In late 1849 and early 1850 the mountain, which had been renamed Peak H and finally Peak XV, was observed from six different stations along the Indian plains using a surveyor's 24-inch theodolite.

Andrew Waugh had by then succeeded Everest as Superintendent of the Great Trigonometrical Survey, and his chief surveyor, Mr. Radhnath Sikhdar, calculated their findings. When the final results were tallied in 1852, they showed that this Peak XV was indeed the highest in the world. The six stations showed heights for the peak ranging from 28,990 feet to 29,026 feet, giving an average of 29,002 feet—remarkably accurate given the distance from which the measurements were taken.

Word went back to the Royal Geographical Society in London, and Peak XV was renamed Mount Everest, after Sir George Everest.

Instantly, passions were ignited among explorers and mountaineers throughout the world, though for political reasons, the first Everest expedition would not be attempted until 1907. In the century and a half since 1850 the peak has been measured time and again, most recently in 1998 when Boston's Museum of Science and the National Geographic Society sponsored an Everest expedition with the express purpose of accurately measuring the peak using GPS equipment, which is unaffected by atmospheric refraction and the gravitational pull of the mountains themselves, factors that would certainly have affected the earlier readings. The result was an estimate of 8,830 meters, or a whisker under 29,000 feet. The 1998 team was impressed by the closeness of their measurements to the accepted 1954 calculation by Mr. B. L. Gulatee of the Survey of India—29,028 feet or 8,848 meters.

There are variables, of course: snow cover on the summit, the accuracy of other measurements used to calculate the summit point. However, the 1998 results are now universally accepted, and with K2, the world's second highest peak, coming in at 28,250 feet by the same methods of measurement, Everest's summit reigns supreme as the highest point on earth.

As the Great Trigonometrical Survey of India progressed into the late nineteenth century, British botanists, ethnographers, missionaries, and adventurers followed the geographers into the Himalaya. Darjeeling was the center of this activity in the eastern Himalaya, activity that created opportunities for local porters (load-carriers) and guides. While Hindu Nepalis traveled to Darjeeling for the "coolie" or manual labor wages they could earn in road and construction crews or on tea plantations, Tibetans and Sherpas were superior high-altitude porters. Lured by the promise of wages, Sherpas began making the difficult trek east from the Khumbu. Many went seasonally, but by some accounts hundreds lived in Darjeeling by 1900.

The growing Western obsession with Everest was a mystery to the Sherpas and Tibetans. Yes, their mountain was large, but so were Makalu and Cho Oyu, and they had heard of similarly large mountains on the western side of Nepal in the Annapurna Ranges. They showed no interest in this developing knowledge and measurement but were most curious about the strange men from the West who began to come to see the peak; curious about their clothes, their tons of equipment and para-

The view south up the Rongbuk Valley toward the north face of Everest (top right), taken during the 1924 British Expedition.

phernalia, and their cameras, and bewildered by their fascination with a high, cold, dangerous place where the gods lived and where men should not venture. To the Sherpas the mountains were sacred places; some of them were of supreme spiritual significance. The deities who controlled human lives and dictated fortunes lived in these mountains, and disturbing them was never entertained by the Sherpas and Tibetans who lived at their feet.

Sherpa Buddhism has a very strong base in the ancient Bon (or animist) traditions of Tibet, which promote the protection and reverence of many features of the natural world. The Buddhist lamas, who were often consulted before an expedition set out, told the Sherpas never to set foot on a mountaintop, as the deities would be displeased and calamity would befall their communities. Such beliefs were and are common in traditional societies worldwide; we Sherpas are no exception. Indeed, Ang Tshering, who in 2001 was the sole surviving Sherpa member of the 1924 British Everest Expedition in which George Leigh Mallory and Andrew Irvine died, said he was afraid when the British began climbing the peak; he was afraid for them, and afraid for the effect their trespassing on the mountain might have on his people. Asked if he had had the desire to try for the summit he replied, "No, the Lamas at Da Rongphu Gompa [monastery] told us we were not to climb the mountain." And they did not.

This mountain was not known as *Everest* to the Sherpas or Tibetans; it was called *Chomolungma* and, as far as is known, this name had been used by Tibetans as long ago as 750–800 A.D. It is often said (indeed, even by many Sherpas) that Chomolungma means "Mother Goddess of the World." However, this translation does not precisely fit the Sherpa language, traditions, and view of life and spirituality. More accurately, the name of the mountain is *Jomolangma*, after the minor female deity Jomo Miyolangsangma, who resides there. *Jomo* means "lady" and *langma* is the shortened form of *Miyolangsangma* (Tibetans traditionally shorten long names). Hence, Lady Langma is the shortened name for the goddess and the name of the mountain. Jomo Miyolangsangma belongs to a group of deities known as the Five Sisters of Long Life, who, it is believed, dwell on various peaks along Tibet's southern border.

The supreme goddess of this group is Tashi Tsheringma, who resides alternately on Gauri Shankar, a stunningly beautiful peak west of Ever-

Northeast ridge of Everest from Lhakpa La, 22,500 feet, taken during the 1921 British Expedition. The north face of the mountain is at right. From the North Col (lower right), the north ridge climbs steeply.

est, and Mount Jomolhari, a major sacred peak in the nearby kingdom of Bhutan. In the Himalayan spiritual hierarchy, then, Jomolangma does not rank highly.

It is also noteworthy that in Tibetan Buddhism, which is also Sherpa Buddhism, the concept of a monotheistic deity or supreme god/goddess does not exist, making it even more unlikely for this idea of a "Mother Goddess of the Universe" to be accurate. However, we Sherpas do not set great store in what we consider unnecessarily complex matters such as this and seem to happily accept this image of the universal mother goddess. Our spiritual beliefs and values give us strength. We do not question them.

Everest has yet another name—Sagamartha—which is a word from ancient Sanskrit, a language used only by religious teachers and very highly

Alexander Mitchell Kellas (far right, top photo), a British research chemist who first visited the Himalaya in 1907, held the Sherpa people in high regard. These photos were taken en route to Langpo Gap, in Sikkim.

educated people in South Asia. This name was given to Everest by the Nepali government after the mountain was established as the highest on earth. In Sanskrit, Sagamartha means "Head of the Sky," but these words would not be used by the average Nepali. It seems the Sanskrit name was merely given to fit the mountain's newfound fame and image.

By the early 1900s, the quest for the summit of Everest was on, although the Sherpas who lived and worked beneath the mountain were totally oblivious to it. Slowly but surely they would be drawn into the ensuing race. At first there was no "race" at all, for Britain controlled access to Everest by virtue of events and politics in the region. Tibet was closed to all foreigners until Britain forged a way in with the Young-husband Expedition of 1903–04, which entered Tibet from Darjeeling with a large force of Indian troops and made its way through to Lhasa. The ostensible goal was to strike diplomatic accords with Tibet, but the mission became an invasion in fact if not in name, and seven hundred Tibetans were killed. The Dalai Lama fled to China, and the eventual agreement thus lacked weight, but the British did win the right for future exploration and climbing teams to enter Tibet, establishing an irreversible pattern of passage for the Raj. Access to Tibet was via Darjeeling, in British India. Nepal was completely cut off from the outside world until its borders opened in 1950 when, in response to the Chinese invasion of Tibet, political change in Kathmandu, and the vision of King Tribhuvan, Nepal turned to the West and started admitting foreign visitors. So, in reality, without the express permission of the Raj, one could not access Everest until the 1950s. This was an enviable position for British mountaineers, and they were quick to respond. Major Charles Granville Bruce attempted to organize the first Everest expedition in 1907, but the resentful Tibetan government (and their sympathizers in the British government) denied permission, so the first Everest expedition would not take place until 1921.

Sherpa participation in the Himalayan climbing stage was accelerated by the high-altitude explorations of Alexander Mitchell Kellas, who was born in Scotland in 1868. Kellas had been a keen hill walker from a young age and went on to earn a doctorate in chemistry in 1897. He lectured in his subject from 1900 onward, but his teaching was punctuated regularly with long and adventurous forays into the Himalaya, his first being in 1907 to Kashmir and Sikkim. In 1909 he made the first of many treks

Kellas's journeys to the peaks of Sikkim in 1907–11 confirmed his beliefs that Sherpas functioned well at altitude. These photos show the first Sherpa guides looking into Tibet from the summit arête of Chomiomo, 1907.

from Darjeeling. His passion for the mountains was matched only by his fascination with high-altitude physiology, and Kellas was the first person to study and research seriously the effects of high altitude on the human body. From his early expeditions he took note of the strength and adaptation of the locals to high-altitude work and exertion.

Because he usually traveled and climbed without other Europeans, Kellas began to seek out locals to assist him in carrying loads, cooking, undertaking tests for heart rate and breathing at altitude, etc. He quickly realized the value of the local people to forthcoming climbing and reconnaissance expeditions and began to educate his fellow climbers about their natural climbing skills, their inherent ability to acclimatize to high altitudes, and their phenomenal mountain endurance. He also began to train the Sherpas as mountaineers and high-altitude porters. Indeed, Kellas stated that one of the purposes of his attempt on Kabru in Sikkim in the spring of 1921 was to train Sherpas for the forthcoming Everest reconnaissance expeditions. His estimations of their potential contribution to Himalayan mountaineering proved uncanny. When he died in Tibet on the 1921 Everest Reconnaissance Expedition,[†] he was buried on a rocky hillside above Khampa Dzong with a view to the three peaks he alone had climbed—Pauhunri, Kangchenijau, and Chomiomo.

In his recollection of the sad event, the great British climber George Mallory wrote:

> I shan't easily forget the 4 boys, his own trained mountaineers, children of nature, seated in wonder on a great stone near the grave while Bury read out the passage from the Corinthians.[††]

Those four nameless "boys" were the beginning of a tradition that would lead to one of the greatest achievements in adventure and exploration in human history—the ascent of Everest. An unidentified porter also died on that 1921 reconnaissance—and that too became something of a tradition. By 1990, 43 of the 115 climbers who had died on Everest were Sherpas.

[†] There is speculation that Kellas died from a lethal combination of exhaustion, heart failure, and complications—including diarrhea—resulting from dysentery.

[††] Letter from Mallory to George Winthrop Young, 9 June 1921, Everest Archives, Royal Geographical Society, London.

~ CHAPTER 2 ~

THE HIMALAYAN CLUB
AND THE TIGER MEDAL

●

BY THE EARLY 1920S Darjeeling had become the base for most Himalayan exploration and mountain reconnaissance. This most English of Indian towns was abuzz throughout the summer months, when *sahibs* (the Hindi term for "boss" or "master") and their *memsahibs* (the sahibs' wives) packed up their goods and chattels and headed for the hills to escape the stifling, sauna-like conditions of the Indian plains. Many Brits resided permanently in Darjeeling—as army officers, government administrators, tea plantation managers, traders, and other functionaries of the British Empire—and the new era of Himalayan exploration brought an added dimension to life in the hill town. In addition to the endless stream of balls, dinner parties, polo matches, and afternoon teas there came the arrival of large parties of Britain's upper-middle-class adventurers, for whom the unexplored wilds of the

Darjeeling bazaar, photograph taken by Captain Noel at the start of the 1922 British Everest Expedition.

Above: Darjeeling street scene, 1922. Below: Darjeeling in 2000, with the Himalaya beckoning in the distance. The main peak of Kanchenjunga (28,168 feet), the world's third highest mountain, is at center.

Sherpas carry their loads up the Rongbuk Valley in Tibet on the 1933 British Everest Expedition.

Above: During the 1922 British Everest Expedition, both Sherpas and Tibetans carried loads. The Sherpa at left wears his hair in the traditional single braid. Right: As early as 1921 the Sherpas and Tibetans displayed their aptitude for technical climbing.

Sherpas on the North Col, 1922.

Himalayan Range were proving irresistible. And, of course, there was Everest, now recognized officially as the highest point on earth, just visible on a clear day some hundred miles to the northwest, completely unexplored and most certainly unclimbed. Holding all the aces in the Everest game, since the only practicable route in to the north side of Everest was to enter Tibet from Darjeeling, the British set about this quest with Bruce's long-delayed Everest Reconnaissance Expedition of 1921, followed by a climbing attempt in 1922 and Mallory and Irvine's attempt in 1924.

By the time of these first serious attempts on Everest, the Sherpas were gaining a reputation as top-notch high-altitude porters, due in no small part to Alexander Kellas's praise. The first high-altitude porters had been Tibetans, but more Sherpas than Tibetans journeyed to Darjeeling, where the jobs were handed out. The trek from Khumbu was hard, but the journey from Tibet was much harder. The Sherpas were in the right place at the right time and demonstrated a great ability for the work.

It was a lucrative profession. Previously a Sherpa without land or capital could not hope for much more than a meager level of prosperity—even after a lifetime of hard work. Working regularly as a porter, a Sherpa could earn enough in one season to buy a small piece of land or invest in some trading business.

High on the Himalayan slopes, Sherpas carried loads of up to 75 pounds, and sometimes more for extra pay. It was also quite common on an expedition for every sahib to bring a Sherpa orderly, or attendant, who would help carry his personal belongings and fulfill camp duties such as laundry, cooking, and serving tea. The Sherpas were generally enthusiastic, energetic and good-humored and quickly gained a reputation for being first-rate mountaineers as well as wonderful companions. After his 1934 reconnaissance of Nanda Devi, the British climber and explorer Bill Tilman wrote of the Sherpas:

> For nearly five months we had lived and climbed together and the more we saw of them the more we liked and respected them. That they can climb and carry loads is now taken for granted. But even more valuable were their cheerful grins, their willing work in camp and on the march, their complete lack of selfishness and their devotion to our service. To be their companion was a delight, to lead them an honour.

The price paid by my Sherpa forebears for the sahibs' approbation was high from the first. Seven Sherpas died in an avalanche in the Everest attempt of 1922. In the 1924 attempt that took the lives of two sahibs (Mallory and Irvine) and two non-Sherpa porters, four Sherpas were pinned by a blizzard for three days and came close to death. They were severely hypothermic and in deep shock when rescued. At least twenty Sherpas would die in Himalayan expeditions of the 1930s, though not on Everest. But the rewards justified the risk. Sherpas have always carried wood, water, and other loads through our mountainous, roadless homeland with its steep foothills and rope bridges that beasts of burden can't cross. More affluent Sherpas would (and still do) hire others to carry loads for them. If one was already resigned to a life of load-carrying, why not do it for better pay at high altitude? It was dangerous, but it was also, potentially, the way to a better life. As time went by and the Sherpas began to learn mountaineering techniques, they became more involved in finding routes, selecting camps, cutting steps, and fixing (setting up) climbing ropes.

By the 1920s, the old Tea Planters' Club in Darjeeling had become the recruitment center for Sherpas. Thousands of Sherpas were living more or less permanently in Darjeeling by then, having made the two-week, hundred-mile trek southeast from the Khumbu to take odd jobs in the hope of a big team arriving and needing porters. Sahibs would

Blessing of the 1933 British Expedition before its start in Darjeeling.

stand on the rotunda and view prospective applicants, who would wait in the street below clutching their expedition books or any letters or references they may have had from previous expeditions or employers. This rather haphazard method of selecting local expedition staff began to change when, on 17 February 1928, the Himalayan Club was formally inaugurated by the British, with branches in Bombay, Calcutta, and Darjeeling. The first president was Field Marshall Sir William Birdswood, then Commander-in-Chief of the Indian Army. The idea of such a club had in fact been debated as early as 1866, when Mr. F. Drew and Mr. W. H. Johnson formally suggested it to the Asiatic Society of Bengal. It took another sixty years, however, before two British officers, G. L. Corbett and Major Kenneth Mason of the Survey of India, decided in 1927 on an afternoon stroll in the old hill station of Simla to work to establish the club. Thus the Himalayan Club was born. Its professed aim was to promote science, literature, and general knowledge pertaining to the Himalaya, the Karakoram, and Hindu Kush mountain regions. Its primary role, however, was to assist Himalayan exploration and travel by publishing detailed descriptions of routes and formalizing the system of recruitment, selection, and wage-setting by which expeditions staffed Sherpa porters and guides.

The Honorary Local Secretary of the Himalayan Club in Darjeeling was responsible for keeping a written record (often a rather vague affair!) of each Sherpa with his contact information and expedition experience. With the quasi-military efficiency that characterized even the most nonmilitary colonial activities of the time, each Sherpa porter was given a book that was stamped and signed at the end of every expedition by the expedition leader and Himalayan Club Secretary. When word of a new expedition went out, the Sherpa would go to the Tea Planters' Club, book in hand, and present himself or herself for work. (*Sherpani*, Sherpa women, portered loads to the bases of mountains in the prewar years but were seldomly involved in high-altitude carrying or mountaineering before the 1970s. Not that they weren't tough enough. Indeed, John Jackson, a reserve member of the 1953 Everest expedition and member of the first successful expedition to Kanchenjunga in 1955, recalls a Sherpani in 1955 carrying a full load to base camp and then, right there on the glacier, promptly giving birth to a child! Yet even today the high-altitude work is done mostly by men.)

There were of course some well-known and respected Sherpas who were contacted directly for an expedition, but without this book it was generally very difficult to get a chance on a team. When Tenzing stood beneath the rotunda in 1935—with Eric Shipton standing above—he was without a record book, and it was purely by good fortune—and perhaps that famous smile—that he was selected.

When Sherpas and the sahibs were negotiating for and then working together on expeditions, the language barrier was not insurmountable. Many of the early sahibs spoke Hindustani, which was often sufficient to communicate basic points. British climbers Tilman and Shipton had been around long enough to acquire basic Nepali. For their part, many Sherpas seemed to have an aptitude for language, and in very little time could bridge the remaining linguistic gap.

Wages for Sherpas were set by the Himalayan Club (unofficially) in consultation with the expedition leader and were a constant source of conflict between the sahibs and their Sherpa porters. In the early days of expedition work the Sherpas were generally quite satisfied with the amounts paid by the foreigners, since most had always lived from what the stingy soil produced and were unaccustomed to having cash. By the late 1920s, however, with their reputation as high-altitude porters estab-

Sahibs and Sherpas gather to make business arrangements, 1922.

lished, they began to demand better pay and equipment for their hard and often dangerous work. It must be said also that there was a perception among the Sherpas that these Western expeditioners were incredibly wealthy, which, in comparison, was quite true. The Sherpas had never seen such equipment, clothing, and technical gear, and never in such quantities. By today's standards, the mountaineering kit of the early Western climbers was primitive, but it was a far cry from the hand-crafted boots and traditional wraparound *chuba* that Sherpa and Tibetan men wore. And we Sherpas are quite wily businesspeople! Some of the old campaigners relate with a wry smile that they soon came to appreciate the power they had over the sahibs when it came to wage negotiation. They played the game to the hilt.

Yet, in general, conditions in the early years of mountaineering for the Sherpa staff were less than satisfactory. To appreciate this fully, one has to understand attitudes of the time, both sahib and Sherpa. India was the "jewel in the crown" of the British Empire and had been so for over two centuries. The social hierarchy that had developed over this time was deeply entrenched. The British were accustomed to having servants and the servants were accustomed to serving them. Dissatisfaction with this arrangement in India—socially and politically—was only beginning to surface.

Unlike the Indians, the Sherpas had not grown up in an imperialistic society and did not automatically accept the British as superior. True, many Sherpas had suffered severe oppression in Tibet, but most who came to Darjeeling in the 1920s and 1930s were from the Khumbu region of Nepal and had lived a relatively class-free existence. They were like the Americans who went West in the 1800s, or the Mexicans and Guatemalans who today face hardship, failure, and deportation in their search for wages in America. They accepted that the sahibs had financial superiority, but the Sherpas could be quite forceful when they perceived an injustice. In 1933, when Pasang Phutar from Darjeeling and four Sherpa colleagues were recruited to accompany Bill Tilman into the jungles of Sikkim in the eastern Himalaya on a reconnaissance trip, they were left to fend for themselves on the return leg of the trek. Tilman set out to walk back to Darjeeling alone and gave the five Sherpas three days to carry the remaining gear back. Tilman traveled light, moved quickly, and was back in two days. The Sherpas, with their loads, made slow progress through the thick forest and heavy monsoon rains and did not return for five days. After the designated three days, Tilman lodged an official complaint with the Himalayan Club Secretary, commenting that the Sherpas were, in the words of Pasang Phutar, "probably lying about in the sun somewhere smoking *bidis*," cheap local cigarettes. The Sherpas arrived home in Darjeeling scratched, bruised, leech-bitten, and exhausted, and, on hearing of Tilman's complaint, vowed never to work with him again. (They later relented, however, accompanying him and his party to Nanda Devi in 1934.)

Himalayan climbing expeditions were suspended during the war years and the postwar Indian uprising. In 1951, however, the post of Himalayan Club Secretary was filled by Jill Henderson, who adopted a "motherly" approach toward the Sherpas. Henderson undertook measures that would offer some security for their families in the event of an accident or fatality, including a basic form of expedition insurance. Indeed in 1953, after Tenzing had left Darjeeling for Nepal to join the British Everest Expedition, Henderson and Tenzing's friend Ravi Mitra convened a special meeting of the club to discuss arrangements for his family and those of the other Sherpas should ill befall them. Tenzing was not aware of this until after the climb. Thankfully, there were no fatalities or serious injuries on that climb.

The Himalayan Club remained active after Henderson's term ended in 1955, but the focus of expedition recruitment had by then begun to move from Darjeeling to newly opened Nepal, a Hindu kingdom where Britain had no foothold and where the rules and regulations of the Himalayan Club were of little consequence. For the following decade or so Sherpas were still recruited from Darjeeling, as the depth of expedition experience there and the long-established bonds of friendship and loyalty between Western climbers and many Darjeeling Sherpas overcame the disadvantages of geography. Nevertheless, the Himalayan Society was formed in Kathmandu in the early 1960s to work with Sherpas there. Eventually the Darjeeling Sherpas were left to rest on their much-deserved laurels or move into mountaineering training and instruction.

The work of the Sherpa climbers and their contribution to the successes of the early expeditions were clearly appreciated by the leaders and members of the Western teams. The term "Tiger" was coined by the sahibs in the 1920s for those Sherpas who carried loads to the highest altitudes. The Sherpas were delighted with the appellation and felt honored by it. On Hugh Ruttledge's 1933 expedition to Everest, eight Tigers carried loads up to Camp VI (27,400 feet): the great Sherpas Ang Tharkay, Da Tshering, Nima Dorje, Ang Tshering, Kipa Lama, Pasang, Rinzing, and Tshering Tharkay.

The seventh expedition to Everest under Bill Tilman in 1938 finally established formal recognition of the highest-climbing Sherpas with the presentation of a Tiger Medal by the Himalayan Club. All six Sherpas —including my grandfather, Tenzing Norgay—who reached Camp VI (27,000 feet) on this climb were given the honor, and it was officially entered into their record books—the highest recommendation and honor a Sherpa mountaineer could be afforded by the sahibs and a source of great personal satisfaction to those who received it. Tenzing valued his Tiger Medal above all the other honors he received.

The fraternity of the "Tigers of the Snows" was thus established, and despite the subsequent political and cultural changes throughout the Sherpa community and the Indian subcontinent in general, this honor is still regarded by Sherpas as the ultimate mountaineering prize.

CHAPTER 3

THE FIRST TIGERS
OF THE SNOWS

•

WHEN DR. KELLAS first recruited Sherpas as mountain guides and porters in 1909, one of his objects was to study the effects of high altitude on humans. He was quick to appreciate the Sherpas' ready acclimation to high altitude and their physical strength and abilities in the harsh and unforgiving environment of the Himalaya. He extolled their good natures and cooperative attitudes. He found the Nepalese Sherpas superior to all other "coolies." But one wonders whether he could have been aware at this early stage in Himalayan mountaineering of the other qualities so many of my people possessed—qualities of far greater value than simply being able to carry heavy loads to great heights. The extremes of altitude, cold, and wind on those massive Himalayan peaks were a terrifying new experience to all who now ventured onto their slopes, Sherpas included.

A group of porters at Rongbuk in eastern Tibet, 1938 Everest Expedition.

When one listens to the stories of the old Sherpa Tigers in the 1930s—tales of courage, hardship, and sacrifice—it is extraordinary to consider that only twenty years before, the work of a mountaineer was unknown to these mountain-dwellers. For centuries they had lived and worked beneath the great Himalayan peaks but had never climbed them. The peaks were sacrosanct, not to be defiled by human activity. And yet, when called upon to join the Western expeditions, they proved able and willing expedition members, reaching heights of endeavor and self-sacrifice rarely seen in any society or profession. They did it for wages, of course, but also for honor, pride, curiosity, and something more—a yearning for a glimpse of the wide world that comes, perhaps, from our ancient roots as nomadic traders, a yearning my grandfather and other Sherpas sometimes expressed. One cannot imagine where Himalayan mountaineering would be without them.

Sherpas have been instrumental in setting up top camps on nearly every major peak: Everest, K2, Kanchenjunga, Nanga Parbat, Nanda Devi, and many others. In Mallory's 1924 Everest expedition, after disastrous storms and in horrendous conditions, fifteen Sherpas were still fit and willing to carry loads as far as the North Col and even beyond in order to give the climbing team its best chance of success.

On K2, during the 1939 American Expedition, three Sherpas—Pasang Kikuli, Pasang Kitar, and Phintso Sherpa—offered to climb 7,000 feet from Base Camp to Camp VII in a raging storm to attempt to rescue American climber Dudley Wolfe, who was alone and ill. They reached the camp and found Wolfe too weak to make the descent. There being no room for the Sherpa team at this camp, they told him they would down-climb to Camp VI for the night and return to help him descend the following morning. The next day the three set out from Camp VI at first light but were never seen again. Like Wolfe, they died on the mountain.

Then there is the story of Gaylay Sherpa, second orderly (personal attendant) to team leader Willy Merkl on the 1934 German expedition to Nanga Parbat. Gaylay chose to stay and die with the failing German rather than leave him alone on the mountain.

Another Sherpa legend was Lewa, who was with Smythe, Shipton, and Holdsworth on Kamet in 1939. Despite severely frozen feet he climbed to the summit with the sahibs, helping with the arduous job of cutting steps and fixing ropes. Once on top of the mountain, his feet were so frostbitten that he had to be assisted down and later lost all his toes.

Mountaineering has changed, and so has Sherpa society and our homeland. That which is quintessentially Sherpa, however, has not. There are exceptions, of course, but many, many Sherpas still possess that deep strength of personal spirit, loyalty, and hard work that so endeared them to early climbers and still engenders such respect and worldwide acclaim today.

There are so many of the old Tigers of the Snows whose stories could be told—too many for one volume!—yet a select few paint a true picture of the old Sherpa, whether expedition *sirdar* (foreman), porter, or mountain guide. These characters are legendary in their own land but known to few abroad. Their wages were meager (old Ang Tshering recalls they were paid less than one rupee a day in 1924, plus rice and soup meals), the risks overwhelmingly great, and the personal rewards minimal. Their stories deserve to be shared with the world and given equal billing with other climbers in the annals of mountaineering history.

ANG TSHERING, 1908–

As I walk along the small road through Toong Soong Busti, the Sherpa quarter in Darjeeling, an old man with silvery hair and a kind face weathered by many years in the high mountains shuffles out from a small doorway. I stop to acknowledge him. He is a living legend in my eyes, though few know of him or what he has achieved in his long life. "Is that Tashi?" he asks, his eyesight not what it once was. "Yes, *Gaga* [grandfather]," I reply. He grips my hand tightly with the strength of a man who has spent his life climbing and with the warmth of one who shares my passion for the great peaks of the Himalaya.

Ninety-three years old in 2001, Ang Tshering is the only surviving member of the 1924 Everest Expedition on which British mountaineers George Mallory and Sandy Irvine perished. His sitting-room is a treasure-trove of memorabilia: photographs taken with Pandit Nehru, his Tiger Medal, and even a Medal of Honor of the German Red Cross. If you join him for tea and he is not too tired, he can tell you tales of the greatest years of Himalayan adventure and reconnaissance. Names such as Tenzing Norgay, General Bruce, Ang Tharkay, and Anullu Sherpa,

Right: 1924 Everest Expedition veteran Ang Tshering in 1954. Below: Ang Tshering with his mountaineering medals, Darjeeling, 2000.

Mallory, Dyhrenfurth, Nawang Gombu, Shipton, and Smythe casually punctuate his stories. Ang Tshering's memories span the entire era of Himalayan mountaineering.

Born in 1908 in the village of Thamey, in the Khumbu region of Nepal, Ang Tshering, like so many other Sherpa lads, grew up working fields and grazing yaks. He might have been content with a subsistence life had not Sherpa men begun returning from Darjeeling with stylish new clothes and reports of good money being made as porters on expeditions with sahibs. So, at the age of sixteen, he left home like so many others and walked to Darjeeling. With just ten rupees in his pocket plus a little extra made from collecting firewood, he managed to survive until the great Everest Expedition of 1924, for which—despite his total lack of experience—he somehow won a spot not just as a so-called local porter (carrying burdens on the approach march) but as one of the expedition's fifty-two high-altitude porters. His first journey into Tibet was wondrous for him, and he visited the great Da Rongphu Gompa, beneath Chomolungma's brooding north face, for a blessing from the Head Lama. The Lama's warning that the high peaks should never be climbed instilled great fear in Ang Tshering, and the loss of Mallory and Irvine confirmed his foreboding. He vowed never to be part of a summit party—a vow he would later break.

His memories of this expedition remain vivid, although he had little to do with the sahibs other than when climbing. He and the other Sherpas watched in amazement the antics of the foreigners; their food, clothing, and equipment; and, most of all, their cameras. He was astounded at the strength and determination of these men who seemed so "pale and weak" in appearance. Although Ang Tshering enjoyed climbing immensely and took every opportunity to supplement his natural abilities with advice from the sirdar, Gyaljen, and by watching the sahibs, he did not relate to the Western obsession with summits; still, he accepted the attitudes of the sahibs and was willing to do all he could to help them. He recalls that many of his Sherpa colleagues also found the British quest baffling and, while willing to fulfill their duties as porters, did not want to be part of a summit team. Sherpas of those years feared frostbite and avalanche above all else; it was best not to offend gods who had such weapons at their disposal.

After 1924 there was no expedition work for several years, so Ang

Tshering made ends meet by wood-cutting and rickshaw-pulling. "There were over a hundred rickshaws in Darjeeling in those days," he remembers. To a young man the whole scene was exciting, even glamorous, despite the punishing toll such work exacted on legs and back. Then, in 1929 and 1930, came two expeditions to Kanchenjunga, at 28,028 feet the world's third-highest peak and one of its most challenging. Kanchenjunga is clearly visible from Darjeeling, rising imperiously just a few days' trek to the north. Ang Tshering, tall, strong, and with previous expedition experience, joined both expeditions. His endurance, his skill in difficult snow and ice conditions, and his courage earned him high regard from both the sahibs and the Sherpas. In 1931 he accompanied Frank Smythe's team in an attempt on Kamet in the Garhwal Himalaya, and in 1933 was selected to join Ruttledge on yet another attempt on Everest's North Face. Appalling weather again defeated the team, but by the end of this expedition Ang Tshering had firmly established his reputation as a Tiger.

The 1934 German attempt on Nanga Parbat was planned with military precision, and the team's selection of thirty-five high-altitude porters from Darjeeling was carried out with great care and consideration. Ang Tshering was invited, and the group left Darjeeling for Srinagar in Kashmir in northwestern India. A forbidding peak, Nanga Parbat allowed them to cut and hack their way up to within a day's climb of the summit. Then came a storm such as only the Himalaya can produce: relentless gale-force winds, blizzard conditions, and mind-numbing cold. The story of the days that followed has become one of the great legends of Sherpa tragedy and endurance.

Camped at 24,000 feet (Camp VIII) the sahibs and six Sherpas saw the morning of 6 July dawn sunny and calm, but by nightfall everything had changed. The gale had become almost a hurricane, bending the tents double, and no meals could be prepared as no one could leave their tents. The cloud mass thickened on the following day, making midday seem like midnight, so the decision was made to retreat to Camp IV. But with zero visibility, no food, and immobilizing cold, their progress was dismal, and the great mountain began to pick them off one by one. Snow-blinded and frostbitten, the Germans and Sherpas were unable even to make Camp VII, and were forced to bivouac in the hellish conditions. Sherpa Nima Norbu died that night, and German Uli Wieland the next morning. Within forty-eight hours Sherpas Dakshi, Nima Tashi, and Nima Dorje II were also dead, soon followed by another German climber, Willi Welzenbach. After eight days in this maelstrom the last survivors, team leader Willy Merkl and Sherpas Gaylay and Ang Tshering, tried again to descend. They were all that was left of the group of three Germans and six Sherpas who had begun the descent. But the nightmare was not over. Before they reached Camp VI, Merkl's strength gave out completely; Gaylay opted to stay with him while Ang Tshering carried on to try to get help. In the 1935 *Himalayan Journal*, German Fritz Bechtold describes Ang Tshering's arrival in camp:

> From down below in Camp IV a man was seen pressing forward across the level saddle. Now and again the storm bore down a cry for help. The solitary figure reached and came down over the Rakhiot Peak. It was Ang Tshering, Willy Merkl's second orderly, who at length, completely exhausted and suffering from terrible frostbite, found refuge in Camp IV. With almost superhuman endurance he had fought his way down through storm and snow, a hero at every step.

Gaylay and Merkl did not survive. Their bodies were found together, perfectly preserved, four years later. All the evidence suggested that Gaylay had outlasted his leader but was unable to move. Ang Tshering, the sole surviving climber of the high-mountain team, had stayed alive by eating ice for nine days. On the recommendation of the German survivors, Ang Tshering was awarded the Medal of Honor of the German Red Cross, evidently the first occasion on which a Sherpa was awarded a foreign honor.

Ang Tshering spent almost a year convalescing in hospital and lost all his toes to frostbite. But the psychological damage was far worse than his physical injuries, for he now feared the high mountains and for many years chose to work only as a local town guide in Darjeeling. Yet with the passing of time the mountaineer in him reawakened, and when he was invited to join a team to climb Kamet under Major General Williams in the early 1950s, he agreed. Ang Tshering was in his forties, he had no toes, and he hadn't climbed for nearly fifteen years. Although he managed to get as high as 24,000 feet, Williams's entry into Ang's Himalayan

Above: Eric Shipton's 1951 Everest Expedition discovered this yeti footprint. Shipton placed his 13-inch (33 cm) ice ax next to the print to show its size. Some members of the expedition thought the footprint was authentic; others deemed it the result of a Himalayan brown bear pawprint that had melted and refrozen. Below: Michael Ward, a member of Shipton's climbing team, compares his footprints with those of the yeti.

Club book read, "He was nervous about frostbite and this height would appear to be his limit." Disappointed in his performance, Ang Tshering found work as cook on the 1952 autumn Swiss Everest Expedition (for which my grandfather was sirdar) and, a year later, an expedition to Dhaulagiri.

In 1954 a German-Swiss-British-American expedition that held great appeal to Ang Tshering came to Darjeeling. It was a quest to find the elusive yeti—the apelike creature of Himalayan legend and lore said to inhabit the high mountains and passes, descending only to steal food from the village fields in winter—in which most Sherpas still believe. Ang Tshering was asked to be *sirdar*, the foreman of the Sherpas. The sirdar selects the other Sherpas and is responsible for their performance and also for the overall logistics of the porters and all loads. It is a position of responsibility, conferring good pay as well as respect and prestige among the Sherpas. For Ang Tshering, this was a huge confidence boost and also rekindled his desire to go back to the mountains. No yeti was found, but Ang Tshering was awarded 100 rupees for being the first person on that expedition to find its footprint. He was later awarded medals by the German and British Alpine Clubs for his contributions to mountaineering.

With the success of Tenzing and other Sherpa climbers on various Himalayan peaks, Ang Tshering began to thirst for at least one summit, despite the vow he had made thirty years before. He had seen that some of the Sherpa successes were not accompanied by disaster, and he felt that he could overcome his fears just one more time. In 1959 he joined an Indian team under a Captain Kohli attempting Nanda Kot in Kumaon. Though he was included in the summit team as a climbing legend and sentimental choice, his toeless feet gave him trouble, and he retreated only 800 meters from the top. In 1960, his dream was finally realized with another Indian climb of Nanda Ghunti in the Garhwal Himalaya led by Sukumar Roy. On 22 October 1960, at the age of fifty-two, he stood for the first time on a Himalayan summit. He was overjoyed.

Another climb the following year brought him another summit—Markartha—but he was caught in an avalanche and this time took it as an omen, putting away his climbing boots for good. He devoted himself to raising his eight children, for his wife of twenty-five years, Pasang

Chokhe, had died in 1960. Today a grand old man of the mountains, Ang Tshering chants on his Buddhist prayer beads and sits in the sun, watching the world go by in bustling Darjeeling.

ANG THARKAY, 1907–1981

Ang Tharkay was a legend not only among the Sherpa people but among most of the pre- and post-World War II climbers from abroad. The nineteenth name on the Sherpa registry of porters at the Himalayan Club, which was established in Darjeeling in 1928, he was known as dignified, loyal, supremely capable, and eternally good-humored and tolerant. Mention his name to this day among the older climbers in Darjeeling, Britain, France, Kathmandu, Switzerland, and the United States and you will be greeted with a warm and knowing smile, for they all remember this remarkable man of the mountains and hold him in high esteem.

Ang Tharkay was born in 1907 in the tiny village of Khunde in the Khumbu region of Nepal, and he spent his childhood as all Sherpa children did in those days—tending yaks and tilling fields of barley and potato. From ages thirteen to fifteen he worked for other Sherpa families—cutting and carrying wood, watching cows, performing manual labor—to supplement his own family's meager income. His imagination fired by the mountaineering equipment and tales of a Sherpa friend returning from expedition work, Ang Tharkay resolved to find such work himself. His first expedition was in 1931, when he joined a Bavarian team on Kanchenjunga, but only later did he go to live in Darjeeling. He next joined Hugh Ruttledge's 1933 Everest Expedition and came to be referred to by the sahibs as the "great-hearted little Ang Tharkay." Although only five feet tall and cursed with slightly knock-knees, he was a powerhouse in the mountains. He was the first Sherpa to carry loads to 27,000 feet (Camp VI), and he did so with ease, without oxygen. He once took on the 80-pound load of a sick porter and carried it, with his own, equal load, up 400 feet at high altitude. He had immense fortitude and seemed fearless—entirely unfazed by avalanche or altitude.

The following year he climbed with Shipton and Tilman in their historic journey up the great Rishi Gorge, forcing a seemingly impossible route into the virgin Nanda Devi Sanctuary in India's Garhwal

Ang Tharkay at the start of Shipton's 1935 Everest Reconnaissance Expedition.

region. As sirdar, Ang Tharkay played a vital role, fixing ropes with Shipton up the final stages of the gorge and retracing his own steps many times to get his porters and Sherpas up the nightmarish final segments and into the sanctuary. Like Tenzing Norgay, he possessed both the climbing skills of an experienced sahib and the people skills to get the porters and Sherpa staff to do things they pointedly refused to do for others.

In 1935 Ang Tharkay joined two major expeditions: Shipton's Everest reconnaissance expedition (which climbed thirteen 20,000-foot peaks, more than any previous expedition) and Reggie Cooke's first ascent of Kabru North in Sikkim. Scolding himself for his colonial bias and knowing that Ang Tharkay could easily have summited, Cooke later noted that he "stupidly left him at Base Camp." In 1936 Ang Tharkay went again to Everest with Ruttledge, who described him as "probably the best mountaineer in the Sherpa community." There followed an attempt on Dunagiri in the Garhwal with Shipton, and work with Major Osmaston of the Survey of India, who was surveying and photographing the Nanda Devi Basin.

In 1937 Ang Tharkay again joined Tilman and Shipton, this time to explore and survey the Shaksgam region of the Karakoram between K2 and the Shimshall Pass. The next year marked the last major expedition on Everest until the early 1950s, and Ang Tharkay, as sirdar of a thirty-one member Sherpa team, was indispensable. At the age of just thirty-one he was one of the first twelve Sherpas to be awarded the Tiger Medal, acknowledging his accomplishments as an outstanding mountaineer. His natural climbing skills were matched by his organizational and people management skills, making him an ideal sirdar.

The war years were lean for Ang Tharkay as for all climbing Sherpas, but finally in 1950 came a great opportunity that would secure his name forever in the annals of Himalayan climbing. With Nepal only just opening up to foreigners after centuries of isolation, Frenchman Maurice Herzog was granted permission to attempt Annapurna I. The expedition was a success; it was the first of the world's fourteen 8,000-meter peaks ever climbed, and for his role as sirdar and climber, Ang Tharkay was awarded La Legion d'Honneur. A proud man, he felt that the French treated the Sherpas more as equals than did the British. Indeed, Herzog offered him the chance to join the summit team, an opportunity Ang Tharkay declined, to his later regret, because his feet were beginning to freeze. Accepting a subsequent invitation, he became the first Sherpa to travel to Paris and the West. The visit was at once exciting, eye-opening, and wrenching. While there he wrote an autobiography, *Memoirs of a Sherpa*, that was published in French in 1954. In this, the first Sherpa autobiography, he called himself a "poor little Sherpa," and the Khumbu a "miserable land." But the West confused him, and he was happy to return to his "miserable land."

In 1951 Ang Tharkay worked as sirdar on another of Shipton's Everest reconnaissance expeditions, which pioneered the now conventional route to Everest from the south but could not negotiate the Great Crevasse at the top of the Khumbu Icefall. Dr. Michael Ward, a Himalayan explorer, climber and physiologist, recalls an amusing incident in this expedition. The team inadvertently entered the remote Rongshar Valley in forbidden Tibet on an exploratory return route to Kathmandu, and they were detected by what Dr. Ward described as a "group of Tibetan levies armed with muzzle-loading guns with antelope-horn rests and brandishing swords." As the Tibetans approached,

Sherpas at Namche Bazaar, 1951. Ang Tharkay is standing second from right.

the shouting and verbal threats began in earnest. The Sherpas responded with equal vigor, Ang Tharkay, expedition sirdar, in the lead and thoroughly enjoying himself. He advised the British climbers to retire to a safe distance and let him handle the matter, which they willingly did. Twenty minutes and a good deal of shouting later, Ang Tharkay returned to report with a broad grin that all was settled, but that it would be necessary to collect seven rupees (roughly twenty U.S. dollars today) from the sahibs to pay the Tibetans off. It seems that they had initially asked for ten rupees, and Ang Tharkay had been horrified at this outrageous demand. The shouting had been the negotiations.

The following year he was sirdar for the British Cho Oyu team as they prepared for their Everest assault in 1953. In the spring of 1953, while another Sherpa was making history on Everest, Ang Tharkay went with the Swiss under the leadership of Leutenberg to reconnoiter Dhaulagiri in central-western Nepal. He was then part of the first successful expedition to Nun, and in 1954, at age forty-five, he was sirdar again on the American team to Makalu under Dr. William Siri.

This series of expeditions in the 1950s was an exhausting one for a middle-aged man, the more so since his role in most expeditions was split between sirdar and high-climbing Sherpa, with all the additional physical and mental stress this dual responsibility necessarily brings. Ang Tharkay was an extraordinary mountaineer by anybody's terms.

With the establishment of the Himalayan Mountaineering Institute (HMI) in Darjeeling with my grandfather's help in 1954, a new life unfolded for this old Tiger. He was deservedly chosen as one of seven Sherpas to go to Switzerland to be trained by the renowned Swiss mountain guide Arnold Glatthard as a climbing instructor. (Tenzing trained for three months with Glatthard first, then helped train the other six.) Glatthard later remembered Ang Tharkay fondly as an able and enthusiastic student whose natural abilities and already prodigious experience made him a joy to teach.

Ang Tharkay returned to Darjeeling and worked as an instructor at the Institute for over two years, into 1957. He then made use of his organizational skills as a road construction contractor in Western Sikkim. Despite his success in this field, he decided in 1962 to return to Nepal, the land of his birth. That year the mountains beckoned one last time, and he went as sirdar with the second Indian Everest expedition under Major John Dias. Ang Tharkay reached 27,650 feet on this climb, at the age of fifty-five. It was to be his last major expedition.

In 1966 he acquired a large parcel of land near Daman, a few hours south of Kathmandu, and there he spent his final years growing vegetables and keeping buffalo. He built a house in Kathmandu and established a trekking agency, but was happiest at Daman, in sight of the mountains.

He died of cancer on 27 July 1981. The British climber and explorer Trevor Braham, who had been accompanied by Ang Tharkay many years before on two journeys into Sikkim, wrote in memoriam:

> It was his enthusiasm and ability that provided the main driving force, and I learnt much about human relationships by watching the way in which he treated his men, and witnessing their respect and affection for him. He was a man of the highest integrity.

And finally, Eric Shipton writes of this legendary Sherpa in his book *Upon That Mountain*:

We soon learned to value his rare qualities which made him outstandingly the best of all the Sherpas I have known. He had a shrewd judgement both of men and of situations, and was absolutely steady in any crisis. He was a most loveable person: modest, unselfish and completely sincere, with an infectious gaiety of spirit. He has been with me on all my subsequent journeys to the Himalaya, and to him I owe a large measure of their success and much of my enjoyment.

PASANG PHUTAR, 1910—

When Pasang Phutar returned from an expedition to Masherbrum in the Karakoram in 1938, seven of his fingers were severely frostbitten and had to be amputated. At the age of twenty-eight his climbing expedition days were over—or so he thought. With the meager seventy rupees compensation he received (ten rupees per finger) he bought a pony and made a living taking tourists for pony rides around Darjeeling.

Fifteen years would pass before he went to the mountains again, but despite his handicap, the call of the high peaks was always inside him, as it had been from an early age.

Pasang's father was a trader who often went to Tibet selling butter, bringing back salt to sell in Nepal and India. It was an age-old profession, and Pasang often accompanied him from their home in Namche Bazaar, in the Khumbu, over the high and wild Nangpa La pass into Tibet. He loved the high mountains, and when the great expeditions began in the 1920s and 1930s he, like many others, deserted the trade of his forefathers and headed for Darjeeling to find work as a Sherpa porter. After surviving as a laborer for two years, he finally got his chance in 1931 with the German Paul Bauer's expedition to Kanchenjunga. The expedition was eventually abandoned, but not before one German and one Sherpa climber had fallen to their deaths. Pasang was deeply upset and questioned the wisdom of the profession he was pursuing. But young men forget, and in 1933, when Ruttledge's Everest expedition was looming, Pasang was one of the first to volunteer. The attempt met with terrible weather and was ultimately abandoned, but not until after Pasang and the other Sherpas had carried loads up to

Camp V at 25,700 feet. A new Tiger was recognized and would later be awarded with a medal.

Pasang's next climb was Kabru in Sikkim with Cooke (and Ang Tharkay) in 1935. Despite an epic ascent of the great icefall—it took them twenty days to scale this one section—Cooke succeeded in reaching the top of the virgin peak.

Pasang next joined Tilman on an expedition to Nanda Devi, in India, that would follow the route Shipton and Tilman had opened in 1934.

It was the first time Pasang had been out of the Darjeeling area since his arrival from Nepal. The local Dhotial porters pulled out in the upper reaches of the Rishi Gorge, where the going gets exceptionally tough, especially with the river in full flood, but the Sherpas carried the loads in relay, and after a marathon effort reached the holy mountain. But the journey in had taken its toll, and not even the extreme beauty of the Nanda Devi Sanctuary was enough to heal their weakened bodies and spirits. Pasang Phutar could not climb beyond Camp I, and only two Sherpas carried until Camp II. Tilman, great bear that he was, went on to reach the summit himself. The Sherpas were in awe of him and found him too tough to keep up with. Pasang recalls, "He was like a monkey. He could climb anything." Tilman was not a man to pander to them if he thought they could work harder. It took a tough Sherpa to meet his standards, but Pasang respected that.

The Masherbrum expedition of 1938 was a disaster for all concerned, with two of the British climbers suffering severe frostbite and no one climbing higher than Camp VII, at just over 25,000 feet. With seven of his fingers gone, Pasang could no longer climb, and his days of mountaineering were seemingly over.

Yet Pasang still dreamed of the mountains. He was a clever businessman and was making as much money from his pony and tourism as he ever had from mountaineering, yet in 1952, when the Swiss fielded an expedition to Everest, he could not resist—fingers or no fingers. As an added bonus, the walk in would take him back through the Khumbu, the place where he was born and raised. On Everest he climbed as high as the South Col, continuing with two other Sherpa porters and their sirdar, Tenzing Norgay, after another two Sherpas had turned back for fear of frostbite. To Pasang, who had already lost most of his fingers, how much more tangible must that fear have been? Unable to reach the South Col by daylight, forced to bivouac in the fearsome wind and cold, ill and exhausted, the Sherpas followed Tenzing to the South Col the next day, albeit reluctantly. In his autobiography, Tenzing writes of urging Pasang and the other Sherpas up to the Col: shouting, slapping, and pulling them up. Pasang responded with a heroic final push and finally got his load to the Col before collapsing, exhausted, and having to be helped back down the mountain. Pasang recalls that Tenzing climbed like a yak—ever upward with ever-increasing loads.

In 1956 the Japanese approached Pasang to be sirdar for an expedition to the 26,760-foot Manaslu in the Gurkha Himal (*himal* means "group of peaks"), east of the Annapurnas in central Nepal. His friend Gyaljen Mikchen had been to the peak with the Japanese two years before and had had a great deal of trouble with the local inhabitants at Sama, who believed that the previous expedition of 1953 had angered the spirits of their mountain. A subsequent avalanche destroyed a three-hundred-year-old monastery, killing three high lamas. Despite Gyaljen Mikchen's greatest efforts at mediation, the local villagers had physically blocked the foreign climbers from reaching the peak. Pasang forged on with the Japanese, and as the team neared Sama the villagers again turned out in force to stop them. Pasang took quick action, catching hold of the village headman, tying him to a tree, and holding him hostage until a deal had been struck. The Sherpas won out and the expedition was permitted to continue. Pasang climbed hard and reached 23,000 feet, but the pain in his hands from climbing fingerless was too great to bear, and he was forced down. Yet Pasang was content; he was climbing again, and that was what he loved. The summit was irrelevant.

Pasang joined several expeditions over the following few years. In 1958 he climbed Langtang with the Japanese, who succeeded in getting a team member to the summit. In 1959 he again went as sirdar with a Japanese team to Himalchuli, and followed that with yet another Japanese attempt on Langtang. Pasang enjoyed climbing and working with the Japanese since they treated him as an equal and a member of their team rather than as a porter. Certainly the authority and respect he commanded in his role as sirdar was not lost on them, and they followed suit.

Pasang ended his climbing career—this time for good—with an expedition in late 1959 to Cho Oyu with the French and then the first

Indian Everest expedition in 1960, a fitting note on which to end a long career in the mountains. Today he can be found most afternoons sitting on Chowrasta in Darjeeling, talking to old friends and watching the world go by. When asked why he climbed, he replies that he simply loved to do it. Today, he says, our Sherpa people are beginning to understand that some Sherpas have always climbed for the love of the mountains.

DAWA TENZING, 1907–1985

Many of the old Sherpas were impressed by the image and antics of the sahibs of the great expeditions. Not Dawa Tenzing. He was never tempted by the "bright lights" or material trappings that being a successful sirdar could bring.

Born in Khumjung village in the Khumbu, he was a veteran of numerous expeditions, notably the 1924 British Everest expedition and others with Eric Shipton and also Charles Evans of the 1953 British team. He was a tall, strong, imposing figure, and always wore the traditional turquoise earring and kept his hair in a single braid with red cord to one side of his head. He was a devout Buddhist, and despite sometimes seeming aloof had a wonderful sense of humor. Lieutenant Colonel Charles Wylie, a Gurkha officer and member of the 1953 British Everest team, recalls that Dawa Tenzing (or Da Tenzing, as he was known), the deputy sirdar of the 1953 Sherpa team, carried loads to the South Col after other Sherpas had given up, and handled the Sherpa team with confidence and professionalism when Tenzing Norgay was away on his summit bid with Hillary.

A renaissance Sherpa, Dawa Tenzing saw himself as a connoisseur of local tea. A Darjeeling tea planter donated a large quantity of tea to the 1953 expedition. After his first sampling Dawa proclaimed that the tea was "not very good." When asked why (for it was the finest Darjeeling blend), he replied that it could only be brewed three times, whereas the tea which he himself bought in the local bazaar could be brewed no fewer than nine times!

Despite his advancing middle age in the 1950s, Da Tenzing carried on his expedition work unchanged. He was on Makalu with Hillary in 1954, and in 1955 (then aged somewhere between forty-five and fifty years) was sirdar on Charles Evans's first successful ascent of Kanchenjunga,

Ever the proud Sherpa, Dawa Tenzing at home in Khumbu in his later years.

again carrying loads to almost 27,000 feet. In 1956 he was sirdar on the first Swiss expedition to climb Everest as well as a first ascent of adjoining Lhotse. He went on to Ama Dablam with Emlyn Jones, then was sirdar on Colonel Jimmy Roberts's successful first ascent of Annapurna II. A short foray to Kanjiroba Himal in western Nepal followed, before he returned to Everest in 1963 with the Americans, where, nearing the age of sixty, he again climbed twice to the South Col. His work on every expedition earned outstanding reports from the sahibs, and the success of the expeditions he guided and supported speaks for itself. He was a great Tiger of the Snows.

Yet Da Tenzing's climbing accolades were more than equaled by the depth of affection and respect with which he was held by all Western and Sherpa mountaineers. He became an international celebrity by remaining resolutely himself. On visits to Britain he was a great hit and cut a dashing figure with his braided hair and traditional Sherpa dress. Though he enjoyed traveling abroad, his head was never turned by what he saw. John Jackson, reserve member of the 1953 British Everest expedition and member of the 1955 British Kanchenjunga team, recalls once asking Da Tenzing what he thought of London. The Sherpa replied, "I don't think much of it. In that village no one has time to stop and talk to anyone else."

Comfortable in his own cultural skin, Da Tenzing sought none of the trappings of the West. When asked what he would most like to take home from England, he replied that he would like a good cow with which to improve his breeding herd in the Khumbu. On another occasion in England, George Band, of the 1953 team, took Da Tenzing and a Sherpa friend, Chunjup, to see the film of the expedition then showing in a London theater. When Da Tenzing saw himself and his friends on screen, he began loudly and animatedly pointing out each one. A stuffy gentleman seated behind Da Tenzing asked him and his companion to quiet down, and it was left to Band to explain to the interlocutor that he was addressing the very Sherpas they were all watching on the screen.

Despite Da Tenzing's austere manner, he liked a good joke. In 1963, in Britain with Tenzing Norgay for the tenth anniversary of the 1953 expedition, he was the guest of Emlyn Jones, another reserve for 1953. On entering his bedroom he found a large double bed.

"How many people do you think sleep in that bed, Da Tenzing?" said Emlyn.

"Five," Da Tenzing answered without hesitation, to which Emlyn shook his head. "Three?"

"Just two," replied Emlyn.

"Ooh," said Da Tenzing, "then they must be very fat."

Da Tenzing's life was not without tragedy, and one event in particular exacted a great toll on this man. In the 1970s his beloved son, Mingma, was killed in a climbing accident. Da Tenzing was also climbing at the time, but on a separate expedition, and was safe and well, but his wife was told that both Mingma and Da Tenzing had been killed. She was inconsolable, but in the typically reserved and stoic Sherpa manner kept her grief to herself. A few nights later, however, after dark, she went out into the biting cold of a Khumbu night and threw herself into a river. When Da Tenzing returned home, he found that he had lost both his son and his wife.

Although Da Tenzing continued his expedition work, his personal life was coming apart. When Tony Streather, a British climber and member of the 1955 Kanchenjunga team on which Da Tenzing had been sirdar, passed through the small village of Dewuche in 1976 en route to Everest Base Camp, he found the great Da Tenzing in a very poor state. It was not long after the loss of his wife and son and, in addition, he had been accused of stealing from a monastery. Anyone who knew Da Tenzing knew this to be impossible; the accusation stemmed from some kind of petty jealousy or personal feud. Yet Da Tenzing was deeply troubled by the affair and had given every cent he owned to the monastery, hoping this would settle the matter. He had no income, little food, and was living in poverty with his daughter, Ang Nisha.

Convinced he was going to die, he asked Tony Streather to take his beloved Tiger Medal and other papers to the Alpine Club. Streather, mindful of the effect such a handover would have, replied that while the club would be honored it was not yet time, and he should hold onto them.

Finally Da Tenzing's luck changed. His court case came up while Streather and his team were still in Dewuche, and one of the team members, a well-connected major in the Royal Nepalese Army, went with Da Tenzing and spoke on his behalf. There was not a scrap of evidence; the charges were dropped and Da Tenzing was cleared of wrongdoing. Streather then organized Da Tenzing's friends in Britain to raise monthly payments to him, a practice they managed to continue until his death seven years later. Knowing that Da Tenzing's pride would not permit him to accept charity, Streather convinced him that the payments constituted a pension to which his long and exceptional service to British expeditions entitled him.

But tragedy struck again. In February 1983, after a Buddhist pilgrimage to India with his second wife and a large party of Sherpas from Solu Khumbu, the bus on which they were returning to Kathmandu left the road and crashed into a deep ravine. Thirty-two people were killed, including another of Dawa's sons and that son's wife. Twenty others, including Da Tenzing and his wife, were seriously injured. Da Tenzing never fully recovered, having lost the use of his right arm, and died peacefully in his sleep two years later.

●

There are many more stories from the early days of Himalayan climbing and exploration of exemplary Sherpas who consistently gave of them-

Top: Da Namgyal, 1953. Middle: Noyce and Anullu, 1953. Bottom: Tenzing and Da Namgyal, 1953.

selves far beyond what was expected. They carried on their backs not just the supplies, but the hopes and successes of every great Himalayan expedition. They worked for wages, yet wages alone cannot explain their efforts. Their names are known to all Sherpas, but to few outside the mountaineering fraternity.

Da Namgyal, a shy and retiring Sherpa who possessed exceptional strength, was one of only three Sherpas to climb beyond the South Col of Everest in 1953. He climbed with John Hunt to 27,500 feet with a full load of stores. On that same historic expedition, Ang Nima carried a load to Camp IX, at 28,000 feet—the only Sherpa apart from Tenzing Norgay to do so.

Anullu, younger brother of the great Da Tenzing, was a veteran of many of the great expeditions of the 1950s. In 1953 he was the first Sherpa to the South Col, and he was a climber on the 1955 first ascent of Kanchenjunga, on Everest with the Swiss in 1956 and with the Americans in 1963, and on Ama Dablam, Annapurna II, and Makalu, among many others.

Phu Dorji summited Everest in 1965 with the Indian team after carrying as high as 27,930 feet, thus giving the summit team its best chance of success. He was back in Base Camp when he received a radio call from high on the mountain saying he could join the fourth summit team if he could return to the South Col in two days. The opportunity to summit came rarely to a Sherpa in those days, so he took his chance and made it to the Col in less than two days before forging on to reach the last camp, at 28,000 feet, the next day and finally the summit on 29 May 1965—a record for any climber in those days. Phu Dorji was killed in an accident in the Khumbu Icefall during a Japanese expedition in 1969–70, another Sherpa claimed by Chomolungma.

In 1953, one man would change the Sherpa world forever. His achievements would change the way his own people saw themselves and would make the word "Sherpa" commonplace around the world, even among those with little or no knowledge of the Himalaya or mountaineering. The changes he would set in motion would, in the end, leave him behind. The road to the future he would build for his people would prove too long for one person to walk in a lifetime. That person was Tenzing Norgay.

CHAPTER 4

TENZING'S EVEREST DREAM

✦

DURING HIS LIFE, Tenzing spoke little of his birthplace in Tibet nor of his early life there in a small, remote village near the great peak of Makalu and a day's walk from the east side of Everest. In his autobiography, *Tiger of the Snows*, he recalled a place called Tsa-Chu, meaning "hot springs or water," and being told by his mother of visits to the legendary monastery of Ghang-La—a revered pilgrimage site for Tibetans from the region. His remembrances of Tibet were a mosaic of legends and family recollections, seemingly independent of the oppressed, impoverished life his family actually led there.

Only after his success on Everest did his nationality become a matter of inexplicable curiosity and debate in the academic fringes of the Everest world. Like the Dolpopas and Manangis of western Nepal, Sherpas are ethnically, spiritually and linguistically Tibetan, yet they

Kedarnath, in the Garhwal region of northern India, west of Nepal—the first mountain summited by Tenzing Norgay, 1947.

have frequently moved back and forth across the Himalaya in pursuit of trade and, for many, migration. They have no concept of nationality—only of race and religion—so that when Tenzing moved permanently to the Khumbu, as had so many of his clanspeople, it never occurred to him that he was changing his nationality. Nor did it when he settled across the Indian border in Darjeeling. He needed no passport; indeed, Sherpas, Nepalis, and Indians still travel without passports between these countries, as do some Tibetan nomads who continue to cross the high passes to trade in the Khumbu, Sikkim, and Darjeeling. The question of nationality was and still would be, were he alive, irrelevant to him, as to all his Himalayan people. He was a Sherpa—that was all. In *Tiger of the Snows* he explains it simply and succinctly:

> In a way, Tibet is the home of my spirit, but as a living man I am a stranger there. Mountains are my home but one does not build his house and raise his family on a peak or glacier. Solu Khumbu was once my home but I am now only an occasional visitor. Today my home is Darjeeling.

The real story of Tenzing's early life makes his later achievements the more outstanding, for when Tenzing was born his family was living in servitude and poverty, and the future held little hope for him. By rough calculations and cross-references with the Tibetan calendar, one can place Tenzing's birth around 1914, the Year of the Hare in the Tibetan astrological system. His mother remembered that the season was late spring, although no date can be fixed. (Later in life Tenzing liked to say his birthday was 29 May—for obvious reasons!) He was the eleventh of thirteen children, and had six brothers and six sisters.

In Tibetan and Sherpa tradition the child is named by the lamas after prayer and consultation of the sacred scripts and histories. Tenzing was originally named Namgyal Wangdi by the lama of the small but highly revered *gompa* (monastery) of Ghang-La, the ruins of which still stand in the Rapchu Valley east of Kharta, beyond the Langma La. In a neighboring valley one passes the sacred lake of Tse-Chu, or "water of long life"—probably the place Tenzing remembered as Tsa-Chu in his autobiography. On the hillside above this holy lake is a small temple and a cave where Guru Rimpoche, Tibet's greatest saint, is believed to have meditated. Tse-Chu is drained by a small tributary of the Kama Tsangpo of eastern Tibet that eventually flows into the great Arun River of Nepal. Tenzing's mother had gone to Ghang-La monastery on pilgrimage from their home village of Moyey—a small hamlet near Yueba in the Kharta district of eastern Tibet—and Tenzing was apparently born at or near the gompa.

The members of the 1921 British Everest Reconnaissance Expedition described this region, and in particular the Kama Valley, as the most beautiful in the Himalaya (though they would later find that forbidden Nepal held even greater treasures). In *The Epic of Mount Everest*, Sir Francis Younghusband, legendary Himalayan explorer as well as agent of Britain's designs on Tibet, described it thus:

> The beauty of the Kama Valley lay in this, that it came straight down from Mount Everest which filled in all the upper part; that it ran directly under the mighty cliffs of Makalu, a mountain not 2,000 feet lower and even more beautiful than Everest; and that its fall was so rapid that while these two great peaks were in full view it had yet descended to altitudes where luxuriant vegetation was possible. From grassy meadows where cattle were grazing and gentians, primulas and saxifrages were in bloom, Everest could be seen only 15 and Makalu only 8 miles away.

Tenzing was not a strong baby and was prone to illness. His parents, Kinzom and Mingma, later took him to the Da Rongphu (Rongbuk) monastery at the foot of Everest's massive north face, where Kinzom's nephew, Nawang Tenzing Norbu, was Head Lama. (Nawang Tenzing later established the monastery at Tengboche in the Khumbu.) Nawang Tenzing consulted his texts and proclaimed that Kinzom and Mingma's child was in fact the reincarnation of a wealthy Sherpa who had recently died in Solu Khumbu. The name Namgyal Wangdi should no longer be used, he told them, so the boy was thus renamed Tenzing Norgay, meaning "wealthy or lucky follower of religion." Everyone was very happy with this change, and seemingly the toddler's fortunes changed with it. He became stronger and rarely suffered any illness after that time, unlike so may of his siblings, who did not survive childhood in the harsh conditions of Tibet.

Above: Tashi in front of Tenzing's family home in Moyey, Tibet, in 2000. Below: Tashi with some of the remaining members of the Tenzing family in Yueba, Tibet, in 2000.

Tenzing's early life was spent in the family village of Moyey. The sister villages of Moyey, Shingsha, and Khangdey lie less than ten minutes' walk apart, and all are presided over in spiritual matters as well as high religious practice by the Head Lama, Jimba Chota, of the Taboling Gompa, which stands high above their valley. The Lama, now seventy-eight years old, remembers Tenzing's mother, Kinzom, well; she was a tough, hard-working woman who lived an arduous life yet was always in good spirits and ready to help. She was as devoted to her family as she was to the beliefs and traditions of her people.

Tenzing's clan or family name was Ghang-La (his father's full name was Ghang-La Mingma) after the sacred monastery near which Tenzing was born. (Years later, when Tenzing bought his new home in Darjeeling after 1953, he would name it Ghang-La.) The small village of Moyey remains near the roadhead at Kharta and in it stands the house where Tenzing and his family spent his early years—a simple structure of wooden poles and stacked stones, something very common in the poorer villages of Tibet and the Himalaya. Some of Tenzing's family still reside in Moyey and nearby Yueba, although, until recently, they have been isolated by the remoteness of their valley and the fact that they are illiterate and have no means of communication.

On the high and wild Tibetan plateau, fierce winds, bone-numbing cold, and the constant dangers of grazing yak on the slopes of Himalayan giants continually threatened life and property. Indeed, Tenzing's sister Thakchey (or Chewi) lost her husband and only son in an avalanche while crossing a high pass. She alone survived, eventually to make her way to Nepal and Darjeeling, where she remarried and had one more child, a son, Lobsang (who tragically died at the age of forty after falling on the descent from his first summit of Everest in 1993).

To make life even harder in the old days of Tibet, a very powerful and long-established feudal system of life existed. The monasteries were concerned with the spiritual development of the Tibetan people and the study and preservation of Tibetan Buddhism, but were also involved politically in the well-established hierarchy of feudal lords and landowners—much as existed in medieval Europe, except that due to Tibet's isolation the system there continued much longer. These landlords were hard taskmasters, and if one's lot was to be subservient to them, life was indeed tough.

The local governor or *Dzongpen* ("Dyingpen" in some dialects) of the district of Kharta was one such taskmaster in the early 1900s. He owned vast tracts of land, and many local families had been bonded serfs to the Dzongpen family for generations. Tenzing's family were serfs, and suffered a great deal at the Dzongpen's hands. Tales of cruelty and torture were common—whippings, being tied naked outdoors in the fierce cold of a Tibetan winter, being buried in earth or rocks up to the neck for days.

In time Lama Nawang, the youngest son of the old Dzongpen and younger brother of the new Dzongpen, married one of Tenzing's older sisters, Lhamu Kipa. She had been an *anila* (nun) and he a monk. Their families were humiliated by the union, not so much because the pair had renounced their religious vows, but because Lhamu was a serf and Lama a noble. Consequently, the treatment of Tenzing's family grew more harsh, and an already onerous life became unbearable.

From over the high passes of the great Himalaya, word filtered in, as it had for hundreds of years, of a better place south of Chomolungma, in the Solu Khumbu region in Nepal. Traders spoke of high valleys sparsely populated by Sherpas who kept the same customs, traditions, and religious beliefs as their Tibetan brothers. So, one by one, Tenzing's family began to make their way over the great Nangpa La (a pass at 5,716 meters) west of Everest and into the Khumbu valleys.

One remarkable story of this diaspora is that of Nawang Gombu, the son of Lama Nawang and Tenzing's sister, Lhamu Kipa. His parents had left Tibet when he was only about five years old, but he had been sent back to the monastery at Rongphu to be trained as a monk in his early teens. It is a tradition in Tibetan families that at least one son be entered into a monastery; however, the life of a novice monk is extremely hard and the punishment for errant monks severe. If he were to make two hundred mistakes in his lessons, the young monk would receive two hundred whips from a bamboo cane, or worse. Gombu was meant to study at Rongphu for five years, but after one year had had enough. He and a fellow novice, Ang Tshering (a common name among the Sherpas), saved scraps of food over many months and finally, on a dark and bitterly cold Himalayan night, crept out of the gompa, scaled the monastery fence, and fled over the high Nangpa La

The Dzongpen of Kharta and wife, 1921.

into Nepal. The teens made the journey alone—an incredible feat for anyone, let alone two young, lightly clad boys with little food and no shelter. Nawang Gombu was later to make his own profound mark on Everest, becoming the first person to scale the mountain twice, in 1963 and 1965.

Family recollections are hazy, but it is accepted that Tenzing was between the ages of six and eight when he left Tibet with his parents for the Khumbu. At times they were pursued by the Dzongpen's men, but were offered shelter and given sanctuary by Sherpas below the passes who had long heard of the cruelty of this Tibetan lord. It was in this way that Tenzing's family came to enter Nepal and start a new life in the remote and relatively rich valleys south of Everest.

They did not own land but worked in the homes of other Sherpa families in the villages of Thamey Og (Lower Thamey), Thamey Teng (Upper Thamey), and Chanakpa, in the valley beneath the great peak of Cho Oyu, as well as in some of the other major Khumbu villages. Tenzing worked as a yak herder, taking the herds up as high as 18,000 feet in the summer months. The herders would go up in small groups for days at a time, carrying their food and sending a runner back to the village when the rice ran out. From the Thamey Valley floor you cannot see Everest, but from the high pastures and ridges above the valley it is clearly visible, towering over its neighboring peaks. It was during these relatively peaceful and happy years in Khumbu that Tenzing's Everest dream took hold.

Tenzing grew to be strong and sure-footed. Like all Sherpas he coped well at high altitudes, yet in Tenzing there developed something more, something almost alien to his race, and this was a passion for and ambition to climb mountains, specifically Everest. British explorers and mountaineers such as Dr. Alexander Kellas and General Charles Granville Bruce had begun hiring Sherpas to assist in their Himalayan reconnaissance work, and when some of these Sherpas returned to Khumbu after the Everest expeditions of 1921, 1922, and 1924, they brought with them exotic mountaineering clothing and gear as well as tales of heroism and great tragedy—the stuff dreams are made of to a young boy. "I remember I was very shy and stayed much by myself," Tenzing would later write in his autobiography. "While the other boys chased one another and played games with mud and stones, I would sit alone and dream of far places and great journeys." This Everest about which everyone spoke was Chomolungma, whose peak seemed close enough to touch when Tenzing grazed the yaks in the high pastures. It became the fixed point of his yearning, the symbol of a bigger, more exciting, less fettered life. He came to consider Everest "his mountain" long before he had the chance to join an expedition. He knew he could climb it.

Such dreams brought great mirth from his family, for whom the idea of scrambling up glaciers and high, dangerous ridges was pure madness. It was tough enough simply to survive, and they believed that life's energies were better invested in saving money to buy land and yaks. Yet Tenzing's dreams took him beyond the valley in which he grazed the yak of the Khumbu Sherpas to the distant places he heard about from Sherpas who had ventured farther afield in their quest for work and trade. They spoke of Kathmandu, Nepal's bustling capital, and of distant Darjeeling, the staging point for the British expeditions. The lure of the outside world proved too great, and at the age of thirteen he stole away to Kathmandu, still a rather primitive town but a world away from the Khumbu, its streets crowded with many people of exotic appearance and customs. It was six weeks before homesickness and a lack of funds drove Tenzing home to Solu Khumbu, but a seed had been planted.

Tenzing's family stayed in Thamey Teng, and in the neighboring village of Thamey Og lived a young *Sherpani* (Sherpa woman), Dawa Phuti. She was very pretty, had a great sense of fun, and, by all accounts, was extremely strong-willed. Her father was a prosperous Sherpa who had worked hard, owned a large herd of yaks, and had some small but successful business concerns in Khumbu. He had three daughters, Dawa Phuti being the eldest, but no sons. He arranged a match for his eldest daughter—as is the custom among the Sherpas—with a lad from a good local family who would help him in his work and provide for his daughter.

Dawa Phuti had already met Tenzing Norgay, however, and the two became inseparable. Dawa Phuti's father was not pleased, but was unable to convince his daughter that his own choice was far preferable to a poor Sherpa of no means or future prospects. At this time in the early 1930s, Tenzing heard that the Everest reconnaissance expeditions were resuming after a lull of several years, and portering work was becoming increasingly available in Darjeeling. He made up his mind to leave Khumbu and head for Darjeeling, a month's march over what were then some of the roughest trails in the Himalaya—poorly defined, winding through deep forest, and detouring around taboo tribal areas. Dawa Phuti was caught between her father's plans for her and her desire to follow Tenzing, but with characteristic determination she chose Tenzing. The young couple left under cover of night with a small group of other young people leaving home against their parents' wishes, and together made their way to Darjeeling. Tenzing and Dawa stayed at a place just outside Darjeeling called Alubari, where Tenzing obtained work herding cows and doing odd jobs. By custom they were considered married, though they had not yet observed a religious ceremony.

After a year-long absence, Tenzing and Dawa Phuti returned to the Khumbu to reassure their families that they were alive and well. Since they had not heard a word from him, Tenzing's parents thought he must have died, and we can only imagine what Dawa Phuti's parents thought. Despite her father's pleas, Dawa Phuti refused to remain in Thamey. After some time with their respective families, the two returned to Darjeeling and formally married in 1935. They took a small room beneath a house in Toong Soong, the Sherpa sector of Darjeeling, and lived a meager, quiet life. Some time later Dawa Phuti's father and youngest sister made the arduous journey from Thamey to Darjeeling via the Nangpa La into Tibet and over the Jelep La to Darjeeling to see that she was well cared for and happy. On seeing that she was, they accepted the marriage and returned to Khumbu via the route by which they had come—a remarkable exhibition of family devotion and caring. Dawa Phuti was a much-loved child.

Nineteen thirty-five was a landmark year for Tenzing, for at last his dream of going to Everest was realized. Eric Shipton, the famed British Himalayan explorer and mountaineer, was in Darjeeling recruiting Sherpas for another expedition to Everest. Tenzing was still without an Expedition Book (the expedition record book the sahibs required all Sherpa climbers and porters to keep), certificates, or expedition references, but he had purchased a stiff cotton khaki jacket in an attempt to look more mature and professional. He was still only twenty years old and was up against seasoned expedition veterans. He waited beneath the rotunda at the Tea Planters' Club—the place where expedition leaders would sit and survey the Sherpa applicants for expedition work—until there were only two more positions to be filled. He spoke no English, and when asked for his papers had to shake his head.

Eric Shipton was a perceptive man, however, and knew a strong climber when he saw one. And, it seems, that famous smile of Tenzing's worked its magic, for he was finally selected to go. This was a reconnaissance expedition only, yet Tenzing reached 22,000 feet with no difficulty. One of the highlights of the trip for him was a visit from

Eric Shipton recruiting Sherpas in Darjeeling in 1935. Tenzing is fourth from left. The 1935 British Everest Expedition would be Tenzing's first mountaineering expedition.

his father while they were camped at the Rongphu monastery in Tibet, beneath the north face of Everest. His father had heard about Tenzing's first expedition and had crossed the great Nangpa La to meet his son. Tenzing remembered this visit well, for two reasons: first because he had been so pleased to see his father again, and second because his father had arrived at the expedition camp with stories of his encounter with a yeti on the high pass into Tibet. Tenzing had always been fascinated by the Sherpa tales of yetis and firmly believed in their existence. Throughout his mountaineering life he constantly sought them and was determined to verify that these elusive creatures of the Himalaya were not simply Sherpa myth. In years to come his daughters Pem Pem and Nima would be regularly taken on yeti-finding forays onto the high ridges of the Khumbu, always without success and not always with a great deal of enthusiasm from the girls!

Not long after Tenzing returned to Darjeeling, Dawa Phuti gave birth to their first child, a son named Nima Dorje, and the family passed the winter with Tenzing picking up odd jobs around town.

Tenzing in Kashmir, 1947–48.

In 1936 Tenzing took part in two expeditions. The first was to Everest with Hugh Ruttledge and Eric Shipton, and Tenzing's selection was virtually assured after his work with Shipton in 1935. This was a large expedition, and its goal was not reconnaissance of Everest but a bid for the summit. It was not to be—horrendous weather forced them back time and again, and although Tenzing was among those to reach the North Col, a bid for the top was never a real possibility. Eventually defeat was conceded and the expedition headed home. The second project for Tenzing that year—although it involved no climbing—was with Major Gordon Osmaston of the Survey of India, who was heading out to survey the area around the great peak of Nanda Devi in the Hindu Kush mountains, in the Garhwal. The expedition wages were a boon for Tenzing and Dawa Phuti.

In 1937 Tenzing joined another expedition to the Garhwal, this time to 6,280-meter Bandar Panch (Monkey's Tail) with two British school-teachers, J. T. M. Gibson and J. A. K. Martyn from the Doon School in Dehra Dun, northern India, but no opportunities came for another crack at Everest. In the spring of 1938, however, Tenzing got another chance to climb on his mountain with an expedition led by Major Bill Tilman that included Eric Shipton, Frank Smythe, and Noel Odell—all old Himalaya hands. They mounted yet another bid for the summit, but were turned back again from their highest camp by weather and deep snow.

For Tenzing, as for all climbers, there followed a long, long wait for Everest. The Second World War and its aftermath would make the quest for Everest a low priority for Western climbers for some time, and the nearly six thousand Sherpas in Darjeeling would find precious little expedition and tourist work. Meanwhile, Tenzing had a growing family to support. In the autumn of 1938, Dawa and Tenzing's second child, Pem Pem, a daughter, was born.

In the spring of 1939, Tenzing was contracted by a Canadian, Beryl Smeeton, to accompany her and her husband, Miles, on a climb on Tirich Mir in the Hindu Kush range in Chitral, in what is now Pakistan. They did not succeed, but they climbed for the pure joy of climbing—a treat for any mountaineer and a great delight for Tenzing after his Everest epics. En route, Tenzing met a Major White of the Indian Army Scouts, who offered him work as an orderly in Chitral. Tenzing accepted and stayed on until the end of 1939, when news reached him of the death of his beloved son, Nima Dorje. Accounts and records are unclear, but it seems the child died from a severe case of measles, for which there was no vaccine in those days.

In early 1940 Tenzing headed home in deep sadness to take care of his family, which would soon swell with the birth of a second daughter, Nima Tenzing. With no prospects of an Everest expedition in the foreseeable future Tenzing decided, after some time, to take his wife and two daughters back to Chitral, where he had guaranteed work.

Everest seemed far away to Tenzing in Chitral, but having his family with him made life easier. Then, in 1944, everything changed. Dawa Phuti fell ill. The climate in Chitral is much warmer and more humid than in the hills of Khumbu and Darjeeling, and did not agree with her. She grew steadily weaker until she passed away late that year and was buried in a British cemetery in Chitral. Tenzing was in despair, both for himself and for his two young children. Single fathers were unknown in Sherpa society, and although Tenzing could find a nanny for the girls, what they really needed was a mother.

He would have to remarry, and Sherpa cultural norms required that his new wife be a woman of his own race, a Sherpani. So he packed the girls, aged four and five, onto a horse—one in each saddlebag—and crossed the mountains on foot to the railhead, where he gained free rail passage to Darjeeling by virtue of an old uniform of the Chitral Scouts that Major White had given him to wear on the journey. From Darjeeling he sent word to Dawa Phuti's family in Thamey, and they performed the necessary Buddhist burial rites for her at Mendey, a sacred cave high above the Thamey Valley.

Not long after Tenzing arrived home, he met a Sherpani whom he had known from his first days in Darjeeling and to whom he had once sold yak milk. Her name was Ang Lhamu, and it turned out that she was a cousin of Dawa Phuti. Tenzing's choice of a second wife, however, was not without drama, since some of his late wife's relatives in Darjeeling did not approve of him remarrying so soon. Tenzing was a quiet and well-mannered man but also a determined one, and in response to their complaints he sat outside his rented house sharpening his formidable *kukri* knife, quietly vowing to kill anyone who stood in the way of the wedding. When Tenzing and Ang Lhamu married in 1945, Pem Pem and Nima once again had someone to take care of them. To them, she became "Mummy." She was also a devoted wife and homemaker—welcoming everyone who came to their home in Darjeeling—and a hard worker who supported the family when Tenzing could not find employment.

Soon Tenzing was off again, this time to Tibet for an exploratory venture with the American Lieutenant Colonel H. Taylor. Then, in 1946, he returned to climb Bandar Panch in the Hindu Kush with Gibson and Martyn, but again failed to summit. The remainder of the year and much of the next brought hard times for everyone. India was on the brink of independence, and many foreigners were pulling up stakes and moving back to Europe, Britain, and the United States. Businesses folded and there was little work, a great deal of uncertainty, and no major Himalayan climbing expeditions. Yet 1947 was an interesting year for Tenzing. First there was a curious expedition to Everest with Earl Denman, a Canadian-born climber who had no permission to enter Tibet and little money to finance his climb. Moreover, he wanted to attempt Everest *alone*—or, at least on a very small scale, with only himself and one or two Sherpas. He wanted Tenzing to be one of them. The plan was madness from day one, but Tenzing must have sympathized with the power Everest had over this man. He too was under its spell, and the desire to go back, whatever the circumstances, was too great for him to resist. They made their way via secret routes into Tibet, and finally reached the mountain. Denman's lack of any experience of Everest, along with poor equipment and little or no food, doomed their quest, and after an exhausting, dangerous, and hopeless attempt, Denman admitted defeat and they packed up and made their way back to Darjeeling. It was a strange interlude in Tenzing's life, but the expedition intensified his dream of reaching the summit of Chomolungma.

There followed in 1947 an expedition that would establish for Tenzing a lifelong friendship with the Swiss. Quite the antithesis of Denman, the Swiss were organized, well-equipped, and experienced expeditioners. Climbing with them proved to be a great joy. Renowned Swiss climber André Roch came to Darjeeling to recruit Sherpas for a climb of several lesser 6,000-meter peaks in Garhwal, and Tenzing was the first to offer his services. He had heard of Roch from other Sherpas, and was keen to work with him. Once they reached Garhwal,

Above: Tenzing and the Swiss climbers with whom he reached his first summit, Kedarnath, Garhwal, 1947. (L to R) Tenzing, Alfred Sutter, René Dittert, and Alex Graven. Below: Annelies Lohner and Tenzing.

Kedarnath, 1947.

Top Left: X marks the spot of Wangdi Norbu's fall on Kedernath. Right, Top to Bottom: Tenzing led a party up to Norbu the morning after the accident. Bottom Left: Tenzing is at right.

Tenzing met the other Swiss members: Alfred Sutter, a businessman and keen climber; René Dittert, a jovial man who quickly endeared himself to all the Sherpas and with whom Tenzing later climbed on Everest; Annelies Lohner, a young, enthusiastic climber from Zurich and in that day one of the rare memsahibs in the Himalaya; and Alex Graven, a leading guide of the Swiss Alps.

The first peak attempted was Kedarnath—not technically difficult, but still high and challenging. Tenzing was appointed as a personal guide or attendant for Lohner, who was not part of the summit party. He was disappointed at not being permitted to climb for the summit, but his time in the high camp with Lohner cemented a friendship that lasted until his death. She was bright, cheerful, and very fond of all the Sherpas. Tenzing cooked for her and helped her with expedition tasks—organizing mail runners, preparing ration sacks, etc.—as much as he could. They kept each other company, although Lohner (later Sutter) remembers that when it was time for the Sherpas to commence their evening entertainment with games and cards, Tenzing would come to her holding her toothbrush and toothpaste—a subtle hint indeed!

The Swiss were aware of Tenzing's desire to attempt a summit, but they had a most experienced sirdar in Wangdi Norbu, an old Tiger of the Snows. Wangdi headed off with the first summit party, but the attempt ended in a terrible and bizarre accident that almost cost him his life. Sutter and Wangdi were roped together, but on nearing the summit ridge slipped and fell almost a thousand feet. Miraculously, Sutter was not badly hurt, but Wangdi suffered a broken leg and the others were too exhausted to carry him down. They hurriedly set up a tent around him and assured him they would be back at first light the following morning to rescue him. He was in pain, but was warm and in stable condition. Sadly, however, Wangdi misunderstood their meaning, and after they had gone and night set in he began to believe he had been left for dead. In desperation he tried to cut his own throat. When Tenzing led the rescue party back the next morning to bring his old friend down, he was horrified to find Wangdi covered in blood and at the point of death. Wangdi survived but never climbed again. Tenzing was asked to step in as sirdar, and thus given his first chance in a summit party. Kedarnath was Tenzing's first Himalayan summit, followed quickly by three other virgin peaks—Satopanth, Balbala, and finally

Above: The summit of Balbala, 1947. Below: The valley leading to Satopanth, 1947.

Kalindi. These climbs established between Tenzing and the Swiss firm bonds both in climbing and in friendship that would never be broken.

Having been recommended by the Himalayan Club, Tenzing spent 1948 on a remarkable journey into Tibet with Professor Giuseppe Tucci, an Italian scholar and internationally renowned expert on Tibetan art and literature. For almost nine months they traveled together across Tibet, collecting art, gathering information on monasteries and paintings, and seeking the meaning and translation of rare and ancient texts. Sherpas are Tibetan Buddhists, to whom religion is what one does when one *lives*, like breathing and eating. It is not a practiced aggregation of gestures and words for specific occasions, and it is not something one thinks about. The teachings of Lord Buddha and the rituals are not questioned—that is the work of the scholars and lamas in the monasteries. Consequently, it is hard for my people to understand when outsiders analyze their beliefs. Their faith is ancient and simple and is imparted to them from the moment they are born. Though they generally do not understand the Western fascination with their Buddhism, they have no resentment toward those from abroad who want to embrace and practice it. It was this way with Tenzing and Tucci. Tenzing was amazed by the professor's curiosity and knowledge but dumbfounded by the depths of his inquiry. From his journey with Tucci, Tenzing learned more about his own culture and religion than he would have thought possible, yet it never occurred to him to question or reassess his fundamental beliefs. They remained as strong as they had ever been—unquestioned and unassailable. All the same, it was an incredible journey through a land that was to change dramatically in the years to come, and that would never be the same again.

After his Tibet adventure, Tenzing was offered work instructing Indian Army troops in mountaineering and outdoor survival skills in the western Himalaya of Kashmir in the winter of 1948 and in Kulu in the winter of 1949. In Kashmir, a British officer, the commander of a Gurkha regiment and a keen climber, met Tenzing and photographed him at work. This was not unusual except that the officer was Major Charles Wylie, who would, three years later, work closely with Tenzing on the 1953 British expedition that summited Everest. Still later, Wylie would become a much-loved friend of the entire Tenzing family.

Finally, in 1950, Nepal opened its doors to the world. One of the first people to be granted expedition permission was Major Bill Tilman, with whom Tenzing had climbed in 1938. Tilman enlisted Tenzing for a three-month exploration of central-western Nepal. It was a difficult journey in many ways—especially in the steamy, leech-infested jungles in the southern reaches of the kingdom—but Tenzing trekked easily beneath many of the great peaks he had heard of but never seen, including Annapurna, Dhaulagiri, and Langtang. There followed another expedition to Bandar Panch later in the spring of 1950, and at last Tenzing managed to reach the summit. Sadly, Gibson, from the Doon School, who led the climb, failed for the third time to realize his dream of summiting.

Later in 1950 Tenzing was asked to join as sirdar a trip to explore the far reaches of the Himalaya—the Karakoram, western Tibet, and up into Russian Turkestan—led by a British Gurkha officer named Captain J. W. Thornley. It would have been a remarkable journey had politics and bad luck not dogged their every move. Refusal of their request to enter the Karakoram and the Soviet frontier areas was the greatest blow. By way of compensation the British thought they would walk to the base of Nanga Parbat, a mountain much feared by the Sherpas after great tragedies in both 1934 and 1937, and once there see if a chance came to climb it, as eventually it did. Against his better judgment, Tenzing joined them on the climb. When the route became increasingly dangerous and the other Sherpas turned back, Tenzing was torn between loyalty to the sahibs and his duty to his Sherpa friends and colleagues. As sirdar he was not expected to summit, and he chose to remain in the charge of the Sherpas, letting the sahibs carry on without him. Two men, Captain Thornley and Captain W. H. Crace, were last seen high on the mountain. They never returned. It was a sad end to what had been an expedition of discovery for Tenzing, but once again the gods had been with him and he was safe.

In 1951 there was another expedition to reconnoiter a route on Everest, this one led by Eric Shipton. Tenzing wanted to join it and would have been welcome, but he had committed to go to Nanda Devi with a French team—an expedition that was to end, like Nanga Parbat, in the loss of two climbers, Frenchmen Roger Duplat and Gilbert Vignes, high on the mountain. Tenzing himself, who was climbing a different route,

The eternal Tiger of the Snows on Nanda Devi, 1951.

reached the summit of Nanda Devi East, a climb he later described as "harder than Everest."

Then, in the same year, came yet another tragic climb on a small peak near Kanchenjunga called Kang—at 5,780 meters a Himalayan minor. Tenzing guided one other climber, a Swiss named George Frey, and all went well until Frey inexplicably slipped and fell to his death. Tenzing returned to Darjeeling jaded, saddened, and not a little afraid.

Yet his fortunes were about to turn, and the tragedies that had plagued him during 1951 were about to be replaced by the golden years of his climbing life.

CHAPTER 5

EVEREST
1952

✳

I F YOU WERE TO ENTER THE HOME of the late Raymond Lambert in Geneva, one of the first things you would notice is a beautiful teak Buddha in pride of place in the otherwise European sitting room. Draped with care around the Buddha's neck is an old red Indian cotton scarf—not in itself a remarkable item, but one that stirs the memories of climbers and armchair mountaineers alike. The scarf belonged to Lambert, and he wore it when he and his great friend Tenzing made the second of their two courageous attempts on the summit of Everest in the autumn of 1952. Before he left for home at the end of that climb, Lambert gave the scarf to Tenzing as a memento of enduring friendship. On 29 May 1953, Tenzing wore the scarf to the summit of Everest, thereby ensuring that Lambert would reach the great moun-

Everest, autumn 1952. Lambert and Tenzing making their way over the South Col. Makalu rises above the clouds in the background.

tain's peak in spirit, if never in fact. Later he returned it to Lambert, a token of the consuming dream and the special relationship they shared.

●

Their friendship had begun in 1952, in those heady postwar years when many things changed for Everest mountaineering. With the opening of Nepal to the world in 1950, the mountain could be approached from the south by means of a long trek through Solu Khumbu, my grandfather's homeland. Britain's monopoly of the peak effectively ended, for Nepal was an independent kingdom without exclusive ties to any one nation.

At first it seemed that the British would nevertheless be granted the first crack at Everest from the south. The first Westerners permitted access to the Solu Khumbu were an American, Dr. Charles Houston, and the British climber Bill Tilman, who together ventured up to Namche Bazaar, the unofficial Sherpa capital of the Everest region, in 1950. Once there, the two could not resist the temptation to press north as far as the Khumbu Glacier. Though they had no time to scout the great Khumbu Icefall that tumbles from the Western Cwm, both men deemed the southern faces impracticable for a summit attempt, as had Mallory many years before.

Later in 1950 the Himalayan Committee of the Alpine Club (successor to the old Everest Committee) and the Royal Geographical Society hurriedly organized a spring 1951 reconnaissance of the Khumbu Icefall to see if there might in fact be a route through it and onto the South Col. The leader was Eric Shipton, with the great Ang Tharkay as sirdar, and the climbers included Dr. Michael Ward, a London surgeon; W. H. Murray, a Scottish mountaineer; Tom Bourdillon (later a member of the Everest expedition of 1953); and Edmund Hillary and Earle Riddiford, two New Zealanders. An Indian geologist, Dr. Dutt, also accompanied them. The Swiss Foundation for Alpine Research asked if one of their mountaineers, René Dittert, could join Shipton's team, but the British denied the request, thus upsetting the Swiss. Shipton's team did force a route up through the icefall but were barred from the Western Cwm by two enormous crevasses cutting across the route. They retreated, their reconnaissance done.

Having laid the groundwork, British climbers—and most particularly Shipton himself—were confident of receiving a Nepali permit for a summit attempt in 1952, but they were wrong. The home ministry of Nepal's royal government granted climbing rights for both the spring and autumn seasons of 1952 to the Swiss. Bitterly disappointed, the British asked the Swiss to consider a joint effort with Shipton as leader. The Swiss refused, but offered to accept a group of British climbers as part of the Swiss team, hoping to procure Shipton's expertise. Offer followed counteroffer without resolution until the Nepalese intervened to say that the Swiss alone would attempt Everest in 1952, and the British could have Cho Oyu, Everest's 26,750-foot neighbor.

The Swiss sought out Tenzing to join the spring expedition, which was to be led by Dr. Edouard Wyss-Dunant, and he joyfully agreed. As sirdar to an Everest expedition, he would have a new world opened to him—a new route, new climbing companions, and a chance to spend time in his homeland among his people. How could he refuse? His daughters remember that for days after being asked to join the expedition he was uncharacteristically giddy with joy.

Tenzing knew only two of the Swiss team, René Dittert and André Roch, from their Garhwal expedition in 1947, but was sure he would like the other members as much as he did these two. The Swiss, like the Sherpas, are mountain people. They have no colonial history in the East, and politics, however obscure, should never be a part of any climb. Having no precedent for treating the local people in any other way, the Swiss treated them as equals. The British, on the other hand, as Lord Hunt explained in a frank media interview shortly before his death, "couldn't have been expected to know any better." Britain had ruled India and exerted considerable influence over much of central and south Asia—including the Himalaya—for two hundred years, and this attitude colored their treatment of Sherpas. Tenzing did not resent this state of affairs—it was simply the way things were—but he looked forward to climbing with the Swiss.

Normally the selection of climbing Sherpas, as opposed to general expedition load-carriers, was done by a sirdar and Western climbers together, but the Swiss left it to Tenzing alone to choose a Sherpa team capable of carrying loads to the South Col of Everest and beyond if required. Tenzing selected thirteen of the best Darjeeling Sherpas—

including Da Namgyal, Phu Tharkay, Pasang Phutar, Mingma Dorje, Ang Norbu, Ajiba, Dawa Thondup, Pansey, and Aila—and headed for Kathmandu to meet the Swiss climbers. He had to cajole some of the top Sherpas to go, as there had been disputes on Eric Shipton's 1951 Reconnaissance Expedition over wages and conditions, but his influence and the respect he commanded won out in the end.

When he and his fellow Sherpas reached Kathmandu in late March, the cream of Swiss and French climbers from around Geneva—René Dittert, André Roch, Ernst Hofstetter, Dr. Gabriel Chevalley, Leon Flory, Raymond Lambert, Jean-Jacques Asper, and Rene Aubert—were there to greet him. Dittert and Roch were thrilled to see him again, and conveyed warm wishes and prayers for success from the Sutters and Ernst Feuz from the 1947 Garhwal expedition. Tenzing and Raymond Lambert hit it off instantly, despite the significant language barriers— new to the Himalaya, Lambert spoke no Nepali or Hindustani and knew only one or two words of English. "See, I have brought a bear along with me!" said Dittert when introducing Lambert. The burly Lambert laughed and shook hands with Tenzing and all the Sherpas. The Sherpas were fascinated by his boots, which looked far too short for his feet and particularly for his imposing stature. Later they learned that he had lost all his toes to frostbite after being caught in a wild storm in Chamonix in the Swiss Alps in 1938. This handicap, however, did not affect his climbing at all, as the world was soon to discover.

●

The 155-mile march northeast to Everest was tough for the porters— some 170 in number—hired in Kathmandu to carry the tons of expedition equipment and supplies to base camp. The route cuts across the grain of the land, and each day's hike was the equivalent of climbing a small mountain with a full sixty-five-pound load. The route in to the north side of Everest, though difficult due to the long march from Darjeeling over the high pass into Tibet, was nevertheless much easier in its final approach over the relatively flat Tibetan plateau, where yaks could be used. The rope bridges and many of the steep trails of the foothills of Nepal were not suitable for beasts of burden, so everything had to be carried on a person's back. Today, helicopters and road transport have vastly changed this situation, but fifty years ago there was no alternative to human carriers.

Tenzing excelled in handling disheartened and exhausted Sherpas and porters. Like the great Sherpa sirdar Ang Tharkay, Tenzing walked with them, talked to them, bought them *rakshi* (rice wine) and tea at small teahouses along the way, and tended to them when they were ill or injured. He was a famous sirdar by 1952, highly respected by all who worked with him or knew of him. He was not a wealthy man but was comfortable and, above all, had prestige in an almost classless society. When such a man physically assists and keeps company with porters and local staff, it is an extraordinary boost to their morale.

Hard toil is also made easier by jovial company and a relaxed atmosphere in camp. René Dittert was a delight on this expedition, and the Sherpas loved him. They called him "Khishigpa," meaning "flea," since he never sat still. He joked with the porters, played tricks on the Sherpas, and generally broke the ice between the various groups. Ernst Hofstetter was also popular with the Sherpas, finding ways to joke with them that transcended language barriers. He later recalled complaining to them about the fact that he was losing his hair. In true Sherpa character they decided to have some fun, convincing him that smearing his scalp with yak fat would cause instant hair growth. Ernst tried it despite the dreadful smell. Realizing he had been had, Hofstetter got his revenge by leaving the greasy mixture on his head throughout the climb, to the horror of Sherpas and Swiss alike. Lambert, although unable to communicate verbally with the Sherpas and porters, had a warm nature and developed an obvious rapport with my grandfather that transcended talk: the two came to understand each other perfectly well.

When the expedition reached Namche on 13 April, after a fifteen-day march, there was a great celebration, since it was the first time most of the Darjeeling Sherpas had been home for many years—eighteen in Tenzing's case. His elderly mother, Kinzom, having learned of the expedition's approach from runners, walked four hours from Thamey with his three sisters to meet him, and cousins, uncles, and many old friends joined the reunion. Soon the expedition continued on to Everest, with one of my grandfather's sisters, Sona Dolma, joining as a porter as far as base camp. After stopping at the famed Tengboche monastery to obtain a blessing from the Head Lama, the team followed the route of the

Top Left: Namche Bazaar as seen on Shipton's 1951 British Reconnaissance Expedition. Bottom: Namche Bazaar in the 1990s. To this day no cars are allowed in this Sherpa village, and it remains an important waypoint on the route to Everest, with the Khumbu Glacier still 18 miles distant. Top Right: A lama of the Tengboche monastery.

A shrine at the Tengboche monastery.

1951 Reconnaissance Expedition, making good progress. Along the way, two Swiss scientists accompanying the expedition came across a line of strange footprints at around 16,000 feet. When they brought this news back to camp, Tenzing went wild with excitement, for he was an ardent yeti hunter. He led a small group to investigate, but the tracks could not be relocated.

Eventually they established the expedition base camp on the Khumbu Glacier at 16,570 feet, and began the difficult and frustrating work of finding a route through the massive frozen maze that is the Khumbu Icefall.

The icefall is a river of ice some hundreds of feet thick that spills from the floor of the Western Cwm down a steep slope more than two thousand feet long before swinging ninety degrees to the left and continuing a further eight miles over a more level bed of rock to its snout. To this day it remains the greatest barrier between base camp and the mountain and, in terms of fatalities, the most dangerous segment of the entire ascent from the Nepal side. Its thick, icy surface is a maze of crevasses and chasms towered over by ice pinnacles and blocks of twisted and broken ice the size of houses that are likely to topple at any moment, crushing unwary climbers below. The crevasses themselves are no more secure, appearing and disappearing in the smooth surface with alarming speed, often swallowing monstrous blocks of ice and, on occasion, the odd misplaced tent and piece of equipment. No human skill or foresight can prevent disaster once the icefall begins to move and crack, and transiting it resembles nothing so much as a game of Russian roulette.

Like Shipton's team the year before, the Swiss found the going painstakingly slow, but working in two teams, they eventually found a route. Tenzing, meanwhile, began to arrange the Sherpa loads for the carry-through. Finally ropes were fixed and the Sherpas began their tentative carry-up. The words of the great Ang Tharkay, sirdar on the 1951 Reconnaissance, rang in Tenzing's ears: "You'll never be able to carry a single load up that icefall." Indeed, the two had made a friendly wager on Tenzing's chances, but it was Ang Tharkay who would end up the poorer. On 7 May, Tenzing and his Sherpas brought the first load to Camp V, at the foot of the Lhotse Wall. Strong and experienced though they were, and despite having made *puja* (a religious observance) before the climb, the Sherpa climbers were afraid of the icefall, and with absolute justification. Tenzing later recalled that his Sherpas made their way up the established rope route in a constant state of fear, continually looking above to check for falling ice. But Tenzing climbed with them, usually in the lead, constantly reassuring them and building their confidence.

Above the icefall, the great obstacle that had cut short Shipton's reconnaissance in 1951 soon loomed before the team. It was the most frightening crevasse Tenzing had ever encountered—broad and bottomless, with sides of solid, smooth ice. Somehow they had to get across and into the Western Cwm, but how? Tenzing thought the chasm was impossible to cross and was sure the climb would be called off, but the Swiss had other ideas. The gallant and highly skilled Jean-Jacques Asper volunteered for the attempt. After a false start, he climbed precariously down into the crevasse onto a lower rim and then swung by means of attached ropes to the far side, somehow managing first to grip the wall, then to climb up and out. He crawled exhausted onto the far rim. Tenzing and the Sherpas were dumbfounded; none of them would have tried it, and Tenzing recounted the story of the defeat of the crevasse many times in the years to come. The Western Cwm was now reachable and, once ropes and bridges were set up, the way to the top of Everest was open.

A Sherpa crossing a crevasse in the Khumbu Icefall, Swiss Everest Expedition, autumn 1952. During the early expeditions ropes were fixed to bridge these ice chasms. Modern expeditions use aluminum ladders to span these ever-changing and harrowing crevasses. Note the ice ax on the far side of the Sherpa, as well as his snow-filled crampons.

As the climb progressed, Tenzing worked increasingly closely with Lambert. This was not prescribed by the team; the two men simply worked well together and trusted each other implicitly on the mountain. They were both strong—it was Lambert who first made the comment that Tenzing had three lungs, such was his strength at high altitude—and both were determined that the expedition succeed. Both hoped to be included in the summit team, but this was in the hands of Wyss-Dunant and Dittert.

Tenzing, for the first time, felt that he was a full-fledged member of an Everest climbing team, even if unofficially. For the first time there was a real chance he might be able to make a summit bid on Everest, and that meant everything to him. With Lambert he knew he could make the top, given the chance. Lambert felt the same way, and the two shared everything from then on: a tent, food, gear, and their dream.

The next obstacle was the Geneva Spur, which the team would have to climb before descending to the South Col. At this juncture the success of the Sherpas in ferrying loads was crucial, for without the tents and provisions the climbing team could have gone no farther. The icefall had been difficult enough, but now the Sherpas must climb the Lhotse Face with full loads. Below the spur, at 25,260 feet, two Sherpas, Mingma Dorje and Ang Norbu, turned back, afraid of frostbite. The wind was howling, the sun was beginning to set, and even Tenzing could not prevent them from retreating. They were his friends and they were brave climbers, but he realized they had reached their personal limits. They faced not just tangible hazards—extreme as these were—but the even greater fear of the unknown. Each step they took carried them farther beyond previous human limits.

Tenzing and the other Sherpas—Pasang Phutar, Da Namgyal, and Phu Tharkay—assumed as much of the abandoned loads as they could add to their own, leaving the remainder behind to bring up later. Again, at this juncture, Tenzing's abilities proved pivotal to the success of the climb. Had the remaining Sherpas not been induced to carry on in these abominable conditions, the Swiss climbers would also have been forced to retreat. Acutely aware of this, Tenzing was as determined as the Swiss to continue; only he could cajole the Sherpas onward. In this way they all battled on, but could not make the South Col by 7 P.M. and were forced to bivouac just below the spur. It was unimaginably cold and the

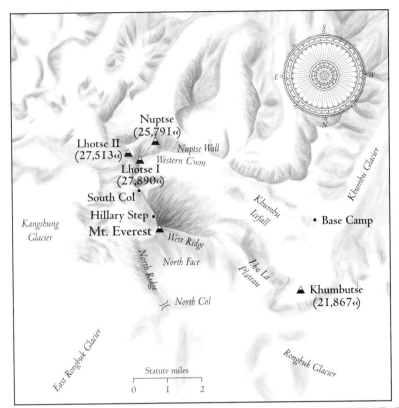

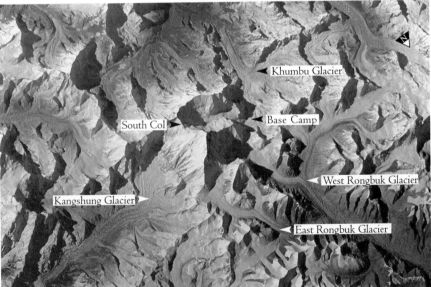

Mount Everest (center), November 1994. This southeast-looking satellite photo shows the Khumbu Glacier—the route attempted by the Swiss in 1952—as well as the Rongbuk valley of eastern Tibet, where the East and West Rongbuk glaciers meet before sweeping westward onto the high, wild Tibetan Plateau.

wind worsened. With great difficulty they all managed to erect their tents and crawl inside to spend a nightmarish evening in this exposed, hazardous perch.

Despite these conditions my grandfather, staying in the Sherpas' tent to keep them company, managed to cook some soup. The Swiss were incredulous when, roped to keep himself from being blown off the face, he appeared at their tent with hot food and drink. As dawn broke they packed their tents and prepared again to head for the Col. Tenzing's three remaining Sherpas were again reluctant to go on, being ill and exhausted from the carry of the previous day coupled with little or no sleep in the freezing conditions. Leaving them to rest, Tenzing shouldered a double load and climbed with the Swiss on to the Geneva Spur and down onto the bleak wilderness that is the South Col. Then, with extraordinary endurance, strength, and determination, he went back down to the previous night's camp, shouldered another double load, and induced the three Sherpas to follow him back up to the South Col.

What other Sherpa or Western climber, I wonder, could have matched my grandfather's performance in these conditions? Where would this expedition, or indeed the British climb of the following year, have been without him? There were many who could have climbed the route, but without the loads and supplies laboriously hauled up by the Sherpas they could not have survived a night, and without Tenzing these Sherpas would never have hauled to the heights they did.

With Aubert and Flory, Tenzing and Lambert then began the historical first assault on the southeast summit ridge. Every footprint they left was without precedent. It was meant simply to be a reconnoitering, but Tenzing was carrying a small two-person tent and he and Lambert were feeling fit and strong. The chance was there to make a high camp and try for the summit the following day. Flory and Aubert, after sensitive consultation with Lambert, retreated, leaving the two friends to spend a bitterly cold night at 27,500 feet with the summit in their sights.

But with the new dawn, heavy clouds rolled in from the south over Nuptse. Tenzing and Lambert had to make a decision as to whether they would carry on upward or retreat. No words were exchanged; Lambert simply gave a characteristic upward jerk of his thumb and raised his eyebrows, and Tenzing nodded his agreement. But it was the wrong decision. The wind and cold finally stopped their campaign at 28,250 feet, the highest altitude ever reached by anyone at that time. The oxygen they carried could only be used at rest, with a manual pump. As a result they began to suffer dizziness and, sporadically, that deceptive feeling of well-being that occurs when high-altitude exertion begins to take its toll. Tenzing stopped and rested his head on his ice ax. He had never felt so weak before; even his "third lung" was giving out. He and Lambert dropped in the snow. They looked at each other, realizing that to go on would mean a possible summit but certain death. Both men loved life too much to give it up now. Without a word or gesture, they turned and climbed down, bitterly disappointed but at peace with the decision they had made together. Another attempt was made by five other Swiss climbers (Dittert, Roch, Asper, Hofstetter, Chevalley) and five Sherpas (including Mingma Dorje and Sarki) the next day (29 May 1952), but with even worse conditions they could not make it past the South Col. The spring 1952 attempt was over.

Even in the depths of disappointment there was consolation: the Swiss had booked Everest again for the autumn of that year, and an unbreakable bond had been forged between Tenzing and Lambert. Another benefit of this expedition was the scientific data from rock samples and deep ice specimens the two Swiss scientists who accompanied the team were able to collect, especially from the higher camps on Everest where no one had ventured before. This information was passed on to the British for any assistance it might provide to their attempt the following year.

One of the Sherpas was given the task of carrying down the valuable rock specimens that had been collected from the Western Cwm and South Col. Each specimen was labeled and cataloged and carefully packed to be sent to Switzerland for study. The Sherpa, however, thought it absurd to carry rocks down from Everest. Instead he dumped his load, climbed down to just above Base Camp, collected a new pile of rocks from the icefall, and dutifully handed these over to the Swiss. One can only imagine the horror of the Swiss scientists when they realized at Base Camp what had happened. New samples had to be obtained from the cwm, but the Sherpa was oblivious to all the fuss and lost no sleep over the matter.

The Swiss spent the summer planning the 1952 autumn attempt, and

Above: The Swiss Everest team, at their camp above Namche Bazaar, with Thamserku in background—1 December 1952. (L to R) Ernst Reiss, Jean Buzio, Gustave Gross, Dr. Gabriel Chevalley, Raymond Lambert, Arthur Spöhel, Tenzing Norgay, and Norman Dyhrenfurth. Below: Tenzing (smiling, in center) with the rest of the Sherpas on the autumn 1952 Swiss Expedition.

this time Tenzing was asked to join as a full climbing member as well as sirdar. He was deeply honored, and despite the fact that Ang Lhamu vehemently opposed the idea, he accepted. Ang Lhamu was a strong and capable woman, much loved by everyone who knew her. A Sherpani, she knew the duties and risks of high-altitude climbing. Married to a mountaineer, she accepted what this entailed. Tenzing, for his part, trusted her judgment and knew that when she raised an objection she had good reason. Two major expeditions in one year was asking a great deal from any mountaineer. Among the Swiss climbers, only Lambert matched Tenzing's determination to try again so soon. Tenzing and Ang Lhamu knew this second effort would be hard. Further, as she correctly pointed out, Everest had never been attempted in the autumn (post-monsoon) season before. No one knew what to expect. She voiced her opinion loudly and clearly, and everyone in Darjeeling knew she disapproved. My grandfather listened closely; he respected her opinions and accepted her concerns. But this was not only his job, it was his passion in life. She eventually capitulated, and he left again for Kathmandu with his band of Sherpas, grateful that his daughters and his home were in her capable hands.

The leader of the autumn expedition was Dr. Gabriel Chevalley, of the spring Everest team. Other members included Lambert, Ernst Reiss, Jean Buzio, Arthur Spöhel, Gustave Gross, and Swiss-American Norman Dyhrenfurth, son of the famed Swiss Himalayan explorer Gunter Dyhrenfurth. Tenzing's Sherpa team was a strong one, including veterans like Ang Dawa, Ajiba, Nima Norbu, and Mingma Dorje, as well as a newcomer, Tenzing's nephew Topgay. It was a huge expedition, numbering some four hundred porters, Sherpas, and sahibs.

The autumn attempt began problematically with Dyhrenfurth's late arrival due to visa delays, followed by a late monsoon that made the walk-in a mud bath for everyone and especially hard for the porters with their heavy loads. Illness followed illness—first Dr. Chevalley with a gastrointestinal bug, then a Sherpa, then a porter. Two Nepali porters died from exposure while crossing a high pass on the walk-in. By the time they reached Namche Bazaar at the end of September, however, the weather had cleared, everyone's health had improved, and they were able to move on to the now-familiar base camp without incident. Tenzing, however, felt uneasy. Perhaps it was the unfamiliarity of an autumn climb, or perhaps it was an inner foreboding as they climbed up the great icefall and into the Western Cwm. There in the "Valley of Silence," as the Swiss called it, the weather began to change its mood. The wind howled, the cold became intense, and Tenzing wondered how they would survive higher up if conditions were so bad in the protected valley. But they all had excellent cold-weather gear, which the Swiss had brought with them, and the teams forged on up the Lhotse Face.

There then occurred a tragic accident that deeply affected the Sherpas. A mass of loose ice dislodged from a slope above the climbing teams and shattered as it fell on those below, most of whom were able to bury their heads into the cliff face for protection. Mingma Dorje, however, an Everest veteran and much-loved Sherpa, looked up at precisely the wrong time and was hit full in the face by the ice. He fell limp on his ropes, his face covered in blood. It took several hours and a great deal of effort to get him down. Gabriel Chevalley then realized that not only had Mingma Dorje been hit in the face, but a sliver of ice had penetrated his body through his neck and had pierced his lung. Despite the doctor's determined efforts over the next few hours, Mingma Dorje died. Even worse, three Sherpas—Aila, Da Norbu, and Mingma Rita, who were roped together—had lost their footing and had tumbled seven hundred feet to the ice below. Mingma Rita suffered a broken collarbone and cracked ribs, Aila's face was so badly damaged he was unrecognizable, and Da Norbu somehow managed to escape with only bruises. The traverse of the Lhotse Face was costly.

Tenzing had not been with his Sherpas when these accidents occurred, but when news reached him he immediately hurried up the mountain to take care of his men, whom he knew would be devastated and afraid. The climb was halted as the Swiss and Sherpas came together to bury Mingma Dorje. Tenzing had the difficult task of digging the grave in the rock and ice of a lateral moraine beneath the massive southern face of Everest, and he erected a rock cairn above it. He led a short prayer in his own language, and openly wept with his colleagues over the loss of a dear friend.

Grief mixed with fear, and the Sherpas were thoroughly demoralized. Mingma Dorje had been a good climber; if the mountain could pick him off, seemingly at random, it could do the same to any one of them. They had lost their nerve, yet the climb could not go on without

Base Camp pitched near the foot of the Khumbu Icefall, with Lingtren (22,142 feet) in the background and the west shoulder of Everest at right. Swiss Everest Expedition, autumn 1952.

them. The Swiss, too, were deeply upset. Good men as well as true mountaineers, they valued the Sherpa team as much as Tenzing did. They felt it morally wrong to insist that the Sherpas again carry up such a dangerous route, and instead left it to Tenzing and the Sherpa team to decide whether or not to go on. Tenzing and his men talked far into the night, with Tenzing summoning every ounce of his persuasive powers to convince them to continue. He desperately wanted the Swiss to reach the summit of Everest, not only because of his deep affection for Lambert but because he had seen how hard they had tried and what hardships they had endured. They deserved the summit; they had worked too hard to fail. In the end, to the muted elation of the Swiss, the Sherpas agreed to carry on.

The Swiss were by then determined to fix a safer route up the Lhotse Face. Only after sustained effort by Lambert, Tenzing, and Reiss did they secure a route, and finally, at 5 P.M. on 19 November, they reached the Col. The view was breathtaking, but the wind and cold were unbearable. They immediately set about erecting the tents, but the wind became so violent that as fast as the tent pegs were hammered in they came out again. Only after a great struggle were the tents finally pitched, and the Sherpas and climbers collapsed inside.

In temperatures as low as -58 degrees Fahrenheit (-50 degrees Celsius) they spent an uncomfortable night. The food was frozen, but somehow, after an hour of boiling water on a kerosene stove, Tenzing produced some hot chocolate and carried it through the tempest to the Swiss tents. The wind and cold grew even worse through the night, and sleep would have brought certain death, so the men talked, shouted, and slapped each other to keep warm. The storm did not abate with the dawn, yet by late morning the team of Lambert, Tenzing, Reiss, and seven Sherpas—Ang Temba, Pemba Sundar, Ang Nyima, Ang Namgyal, Goundin, Pemba, and Topgay—began their seemingly impossible attempt on the summit ridge. At 26,680 feet, the wind and cold became so intense that all good sense told them it would be madness to carry on. They turned back dejectedly toward the Col, and as soon as they arrived there the Sherpas left to continue down to the lower camp, uncharacteristically abandoning an ailing colleague, Goundin, who was lying in the snow unable to move. Their will had failed, and all they could think of was getting down from that deadly place. Tenzing, Lambert, and Reiss roped Goundin in with them and carried him down to Camp VII on the Lhotse Face. The party continued their descent the next day, with Tenzing ensuring that no equipment was left behind. They had lost the battle with Everest. The British turn would come next.

* * *

Tenzing's reputation as a great mountaineer was firmly established. The Swiss could not speak highly enough of his contribution to their two expeditions. He had carried loads heavier than most and had performed many of the Sherpa tasks himself—cooking, setting up tents, and the many jobs associated with running an efficient camp. He had done almost twice as much climbing as anyone else, with his endless trips up and down the route, checking supplies, cajoling his Sherpa staff, and sharing their loads. His strength and endurance had become legendary. On one occasion he had started with a double load from a point between Camps IV and V at 8:30 A.M., descended five thousand vertical feet through treacherous terrain to Camp I, organized the Sherpas

Members of the Swiss team, autumn 1952, at Camp IV. (L to R) Tenzing Norgay, Raymond Lambert, Dr. Gabriel Chevalley, Arthur Spöhel, Ernst Reiss, and Gustave Gross.

camped there, giving them encouragement and support, and then, at first light, hurried back up to Camp IV in eight and a half hours.

Norman Dyhrenfurth spoke of Tenzing's personal contribution and dedication to his colleagues:

> I recall that on the Swiss expedition the night of 12 November at Camp IV, I had just come down from Camp V at 23,000 feet with a serious case of laryngitis and high fever. During the night my tent collapsed. Owing to my weakened condition I was unable to get out of the tent to fix the pegs and guy ropes. I tried to call for help from some of my Swiss friends in the neighboring tents but because of my laryngitis and the storm they could not hear me. As I lay there in the dark, holding onto the flapping tent and trying to keep it away from my face to avoid suffocation, I was really desperate, thinking that I would have to hold onto the tent like that for the rest of the long night.
>
> All of a sudden I heard the noise of a tent's zipper opening and Tenzing's voice just outside of my tent coming through the

Above: The greatest of friends, Raymond Lambert and Tenzing Norgay, autumn 1952. Below: A teak Buddha in the Lamberts' sitting room in Geneva is draped in the scarf Tenzing wore to the summit on the 1953 British Everest Expedition. He mailed it to Lambert immediately after the historic climb.

storm: "I arrange, sahib." How he did it I'll never know, since it usually takes two men, even in calm weather, to set up a tent, but he managed it despite the storm and soon everything was back to normal again. I could breathe again and the terrible feeling of suffocation and claustrophobia passed. I tried to shout my heartfelt thanks to Tenzing but managed only a whisper, lost in the noise of the wind. Tenzing said, "Okay, sahib" and returned to his tent. The next day I thanked him profusely for his heroic deed and his handsome face lit up in one of his big smiles.

Dyhrenfurth also recalled the small things that Tenzing noticed and which endeared him to his colleagues:

> On 1 November, when Tenzing and Lambert left Camp V to reconnoiter the route through the steep Lhotse Face toward Camp VII, there was a terrific storm. The two men made their preparations, drinking and eating their breakfast while standing up. Tenzing helped Lambert with his preparations, picked up Lambert's gloves when he dropped them and the wind threatened to carry them away, lifted the oxygen apparatus onto Lambert's back and himself shouldered a heavy rucksack (at least forty-five pounds, which is more than anybody else carried at that altitude). And yet as they moved up through the steep Lhotse Glacier, he moved with his usual ease and graceful stride, using no oxygen.

For all Tenzing's camaraderie with the Swiss and his great efforts to get them to the top of Everest, in the end they had failed. Tenzing wept when he and Lambert parted at the end of the expedition. Yet together they had achieved more than any other climber on Everest, and Lambert knew in his heart that Tenzing had greater things to come. He removed his red scarf from around his own neck and placed it, with a big bear hug, around Tenzing's. When they parted, my grandfather carried a part of Lambert with him.

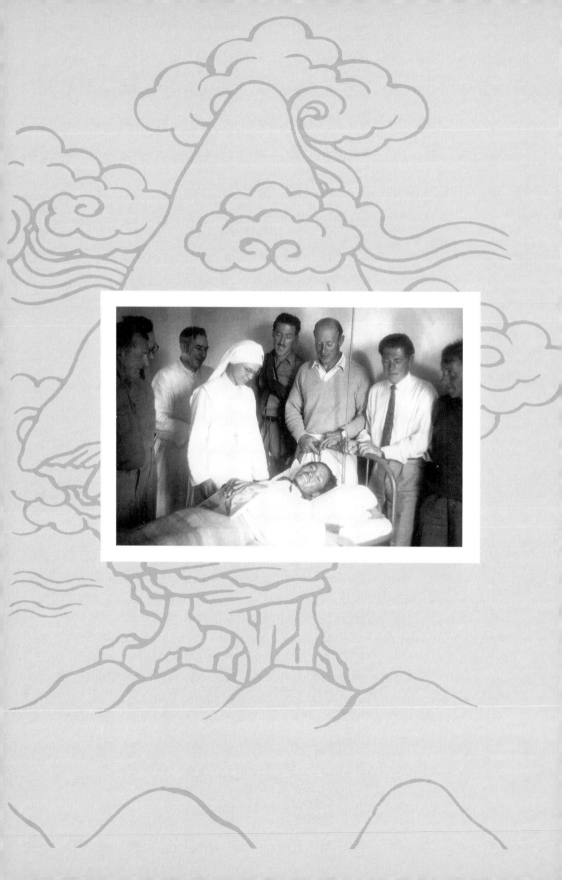

- CHAPTER 6 -
EVEREST
1953

T ENZING HAD BECOME ILL AND WEAK on the walk-out from Everest in late November 1952, and by the time he reached Kathmandu he was suffering from what appeared to be malaria. In Kathmandu there was a royal reception for the Swiss climbing team in recognition of their historic first attempts on Everest from Nepal, and the king awarded the Nepal Pratap Bardhak medal for highest achievement to Tenzing. During the reception, however, Tenzing's urgent need for medical treatment became apparent. The Swiss took him with them as far as Patna, India, and there he lay in a feverish stupor in a Holy Family Hospital bed for ten long days. Eventually, in the pleasant winter warmth of the northern Indian plains, he recovered suf-

A rare photo of an ill Tenzing Norgay in the hospital in Patna, India, after the autumn 1952 Swiss Everest Expedition. (L to R) Jean Buzio, Dr. Gabriel Chevalley, Father Niesen, an unidentified nurse, Ernst Reiss, Raymond Lambert, Gustave Gross, Arthur Spöhel.

ficiently to make the long journey back to Darjeeling and the comfort and care of his Toong Soong home.

Two Everest expeditions in the dual role of sirdar and climber had sapped every ounce of his strength. He had lost over fifteen pounds, and he desperately needed time to recuperate. Ang Lhamu and the girls fussed endlessly over him, for they had never seen him so gaunt and lethargic, and Ang Lhamu began to lay down the law about his climbing plans for 1953.

Waiting for him at home had been a letter from Major Charles Wylie of the Himalayan Committee in London, which his daughters—both of whom read and wrote English and Nepali—dutifully read to him. The letter asked Tenzing to join the British attempt on Everest in spring 1953, again as sirdar and climber. Having climbed higher than any person had ever climbed before, Tenzing would be a great asset to any team. Lambert had foreseen this possibility, but Tenzing had told his friend that he did not wish to dare the mountain again so soon or with anyone but the Swiss. The two men had spoken and dreamed of stepping onto the summit together, and Tenzing was willing to forgo his chance of being first to wait for Lambert when the Swiss tried again in 1956. "You couldn't think of going to Everest without him, or him without us," Lambert recalled in a 1997 BBC interview.

But as fiercely loyal as Tenzing was to Lambert, Lambert was just as selflessly ambitious for Tenzing. He finally convinced Tenzing that he should take the chance when it came. There was a good possibility the British would succeed. Did Tenzing want to be sitting in Darjeeling while his mountain was climbed without him?

"Take the chance," Lambert had said. "It doesn't matter who it is with."

Trusting Lambert's judgment, Tenzing had decided that, if asked, he would probably accept. Convalescing in Toong Soong, he listened dutifully to Ang Lhamu's proscriptions, for he was too weak—and too grateful for her ministrations—to argue. But in his heart, he knew what he wanted to do.

In January 1953 he took Major Wylie's letter to Jill Henderson of the Himalayan Club and accepted the offer of a place on the team.

Ang Lhamu was livid. "What about me and the children? What will happen to us if you die?" she asked him. She knew her husband was a strong and responsible climber, but his recent ill health and the prospect of a third Everest attempt in just over a year haunted her. They argued, shouted, agreed, and argued again. Finally she admitted defeat. There was no arguing with Tenzing where Everest was concerned; he had to go.

Ang Lhamu wasn't the only person in Darjeeling concerned about the families of Sherpas left behind when their loved ones worked high in the mountains. Ravi Mitra, who would become known as Ravi Babu (*Babu* is a Hindi term of respect and endearment) to Tenzing and others who were close to him, was a well-educated Bengali who ran a small Nepali newspaper, *Saathi* (meaning "friend" in Nepali), in Darjeeling. Mitra had taken a keen interest in the Sherpas and their Himalayan expeditions, and in late 1952 he went to Tenzing's tiny house in Toong Soong to interview him about the Swiss climbs. Mitra later recalled being put immediately at ease by that famous smile. He was singularly impressed by Tenzing's bearing:

> He was quite different from other coolies. He deliberately sought to learn the best of the ways of the Westerners. For instance he was the only coolie I had ever seen who used a hand-kerchief to wipe his nose! He also used to take particular care with his appearance—always neat, even his shoes.

For his part, Tenzing trusted Mitra, who soon became protective of his new friend. My grandfather was a skilled mountaineer and a wise and respected sirdar, but in the ways of the world at large he was naive. Mitra saw that he needed guidance and support and took it upon himself to provide these things. Tenzing had consulted Mitra before accepting the British offer for 1953, and Mitra, as had Lambert, advised him to take the chance. Mitra vowed to take care of Tenzing's family in the event of his death or injury, thereby easing for Tenzing one of the great burdens any climber carries to a mountain.

Mitra's keen personal interest in the Sherpas, however, earned resentment from some Himalayan Club members, in particular because rights to the Everest stories were owned by the powerful national Indian newspaper, the *Statesman*. In fact the rights violation was more perceived than actual, since Mitra published only the Sherpas' stories, putting the money he was paid when he sold reprint rights to a large newspaper or magazine into a special fund for the Sherpas' families. Though modest, the fund gained him strong support from the Sherpas. Mitra was a tea planter and man of independent means; his newspaper was purely for his own interest, and his fundraising came from a genuine desire to help the Sherpas.

On 1 March 1953 Tenzing left for Everest with a Sherpa team of twenty that included two of his nephews: Topgay, age sixteen, who had been with him on both Swiss attempts and had climbed above the South Col, and Nawang Gombu, seventeen, who would later make the first American ascent of Everest with Jim Whittaker in 1963 and would become the first man to climb Everest twice. They were the youngest members of the Sherpa climbing team, and rather in awe of the task they were about to undertake. Topgay had seen what the great mountain could serve up in the Swiss expeditions and was concerned about his safety. On one of the Swiss climbs he had been roped to another Sherpa ferrying loads up the Khumbu Icefall when a large block of ice, the size of a small hut, hurtled down and killed his comrade. With every load he would carry up the icefall in 1953, he later recalled "looking up rather than ahead."

Tenzing received a special farewell from Darjeeling, since everyone knew that this time, having come so close in 1952, he might just make the summit. A palpable excitement filled his small house and mingled with the gnawing fear his family always felt when he headed out for a big peak. Nima and Pem Pem, my mother, teenagers at the time, remember the house crowded with well-wishers. Copious amounts of tea were served, and innumerable *kadas* (white ceremonial blessing scarves) were placed respectfully around Tenzing's neck. Wanting him to carry something of hers, Nima ceremoniously handed him a small red-and-blue pencil from her school satchel. Mitra, ever confident, presented him with a small flag of newly independent India. Tenzing's parting was uncharacteristically emotional; there was something in his mien, perhaps due to his recent ill health or perhaps because he felt that this time he would do it or die. Many tears followed him out the door, but at his small altar the yak butter lamps that would burn constantly throughout his climb glowed brightly in the traditional Buddhist blessing, as they did in family homes throughout Darjeeling and the

Khumbu. Tenzing's team would follow the customary route to Kathmandu: south to the plains of northern India, west by train to Raxaul, then north to Nepal.

The following day Mitra convened a meeting of the Himalayan Club (whose members by then included Indians) at the old Hotel Pliver (later renamed Glenary's Restaurant) in Darjeeling. He hoped to convince all the members to sign a circular that he would then print and send to mountaineering clubs and publications worldwide, the goal of which was to raise funds for the families of mountaineering and expedition Sherpas. As it happened, however, one of Mitra's articles on Tenzing had been reprinted that day in Bombay's *Saturday News*. In it, Mitra repeated Lambert's joke that "Tenzing Sherpa must have three lungs." A few of the club members, thinking the sentiment a bit silly, questioned Mitra about his motives for writing stories about Sherpas, seemingly indignant that he was paid for them. Mitra replied that any monies he received went directly into the Sherpa fund, and he steered the meeting to the subject of the circular. The discussion did not go well. Many club members were unwilling to sign the document, declaring the initiative unnecessary. Mitra tried to explain that Tenzing would be a hero of India if he reached the summit of Everest, but this argument met with table-slapping mirth and retorts such as, "What? A coolie conquer Everest?" Ignoring the skepticism, Mitra battled on, and throughout the expedition he continued to raise funds for the Sherpas.

This apparent lack of faith in Tenzing was not shared by those best in a position to judge, the organizers of the climb. From the beginning, Colonel John Hunt, the expedition leader, considered Tenzing a full climbing member, as much in contention for a place on the summit team as any other climber. In order not to overload cornices, outstrip oxygen supplies and provisions, or otherwise tempt fate, only two strong climbers would be in the summit team, and it was well known to all the British team members that Hunt was keen to include a Sherpa. He had a strong sense of indebtedness to these mountain people who had contributed so much to previous British attempts on Everest and indeed to all Himalayan exploration.

Hunt's approbation was not immediately returned by Tenzing and the Sherpas, however. My grandfather, along with many on the British

Tenzing Norgay at the start of the 1953 British Expedition.

The start of the march at the staging area at Bhadgaon, eight miles east of Kathmandu. Moving eight tons of equipment and provisions was a monumental task. March 1953.

team, was at first disappointed that Eric Shipton, the legendary Himalayan climber and explorer to whom Everest had in so many ways "belonged" for years, was not to lead the team. To the Sherpas, "Shipton Sahib" was a true man of the mountains and a tough yet considerate expedition leader. Many knew him personally from previous expeditions, and all at least knew *of* him. They trusted him. The last-minute appointment of Hunt by the Himalayan Joint Committee of the Royal Geographical Society and the Alpine Club, which chose the leadership for all British expeditions to the Himalaya, worried them, as it did the British team. The committee had sound reasons for their choice, however, though they handled it badly. Shipton was a member of the "OBOE club," as the old climbers termed it: On the Back Of an Envelope (a play on OBE, Order of the British Empire). If an expedition couldn't be planned on the back of an envelope, it was too big for Shipton's taste. He preferred to move fast and light, and his yearning was less for summits than for new and unknown horizons, characteristics that made him one of the world's great explorers. Hunt, on the other hand, was a military man and a brilliant organizer. In the end, he was the man for the job, but neither the Sherpas nor the British climbers knew that right away.

In Kathmandu, despite the friendliness and respect in his welcome from Hunt, Tenzing did not sense the same warmth from these Englishmen that he had felt with his Swiss companions. That Tenzing and his Sherpa team were assigned a bathroom-less garage at the British Embassy as accommodation their first night in Kathmandu did little to endear the British climbers to them, though in truth the quarters were allocated before the British arrived, with the embassy staff simply behaving in a manner typical of a colonial power in those days. The Sherpas felt they were being treated as "coolies," a designation their mountaineering accomplishments should have left behind years ago, and they protested by using the road in front of the garage as a latrine. The incident launched expedition relations to a bad start.

The following day, however, they were transported by truck to the staging area a few miles east of Kathmandu, and there Tenzing was struck by the efficiency and scale of the British expedition with its eight tons of equipment and provisions. He could see at once that this attempt had a strong chance of success, and again he felt his dream draw nearer. There was to be no Lambert, no Shipton, but he had been granted another opportunity.

In Kathmandu, Tenzing and his Darjeeling Sherpas met the whole British team, including the two New Zealanders, Edmund Hillary, age thirty-three, and George Lowe, age twenty-eight. Tenzing was struck by Hillary's great height, but everyone was too busy for lengthy cordialities, and the pair who would soon make history together were to have little contact until the real climbing began. On this expedition, unlike previous ones, Tenzing was to have an invaluable ally and supporter in his duties as sirdar. Major Charles Wylie, age thirty-two, a quiet, modest, but superbly capable organizer and Himalayan climber, was the commanding officer of a Gurkha regiment and spoke fluent Nepali. He understood the Nepali mind—no mean feat in itself—and handled the coolies and Sherpas with kindness and tact. Tenzing's Sherpa climbing team and the Nepali and Sherpa coolies all warmed to him instantly, and this relationship contributed greatly to the expedition's ultimate success. In Wylie they found a sahib who could meet them on their own terms and in their own language. Strained relations and misunderstandings between foreign climbers and Sherpas had been the source of considerable stress for the sirdars of many previous expeditions. Wylie relieved much of that stress for Tenzing. He could, for example, share the burden of negotiating, which up to that point had rested so heavily on Tenzing. In 1953 there were the usual disputes with Sherpas and porters—ownership of equipment, wages, load weights, and so on—but this time they were quickly overcome, letting the expedition get on with the business at hand, climbing Everest. Tenzing was to remain close friends with Wylie for the rest of his life; to this day Wylie is known fondly as Uncle Wylie to Tenzing's children and grandchildren, myself among them.

At last the massive team began to move out of Kathmandu. There were eleven men including Tenzing in the climbing team, three British support staff, and some forty Sherpas for work above Base Camp, sixteen of whom would be expected to carry as high as the South Col, at 8,000

It took 350 porters and Sherpas—each carrying loads over sixty pounds—to transport the 1953 Expedition gear from the staging area east of Kathmandu to Everest Base Camp.

meters the highest stocked camp. To carry the tons of provisions to Tengboche there were 350 Nepali and Sherpa coolies, each with a load of sixty pounds (the climbers and high-altitude Sherpas carried about fifty pounds each). Indeed, so unwieldy was the amassed expedition that Hunt sent it forward in two groups separated by twenty-four hours. The first set out on 10 March with 150 porters under Tenzing's direction, and the second group, with 200 porters under Major Wylie's direction, followed a day later. For seventeen-year-old Nawang Gombu, it was hugely exciting to be part of this vast caravan as it wove its way through the Himalayan foothills toward the high peaks. This was his first expedition. He thought little of the mountain itself or its summit, he simply reveled in the fun and local adulation the Sherpas received for being a part of the Everest team. Michael Ward, the expedition doctor, age twenty-seven, later remembered Gombu as the only Sherpa he had ever met who asked a sahib to "walk a bit more slowly."

Tenzing's mother again journeyed from Thamey to meet her son in

Above: Tenzing and his mother, Kinzom, at Tengboche monastery. Below: As sirdar on the 1953 British Expedition, Tenzing played an important role in smoothing the relations between the high-altitude Sherpas and the sahibs. Here Tenzing and Hunt pay the Sherpas.

Namche Bazaar, where the expedition arrived 25 March to a thunderous welcome. She was more concerned for his welfare this time than she had been the previous year. They had not met again as he passed through Namche on his way back to Kathmandu that year, but she had heard of his exhaustion and fever. To her relief, she found him looking fit and well. "Don't fret, *amala*," he told her. "This time we may get to the top, and then I won't have to go back anymore." Giving her blessing, she headed home to Thamey to spin her prayer wheel, sending its prayers to the higher spirits, and await the outcome of his climb.

The expedition marched on to the Tengboche monastery, where they stayed several days setting up a preliminary base camp, reorganizing loads and stores, and sorting out the last of the disputes between the high-altitude Sherpas and the sahibs. The normal practice in those days was to distribute personal climbing gear, clothing, and equipment to the Sherpas at the beginning of an expedition, and the Sherpas had expected this custom to be observed. John Hunt, however, had other ideas. On this expedition the gear was not given out until they reached Tengboche—the idea being to keep it in top condition for the mountain—and even then only for the duration of the expedition. Only those Sherpas who worked hard and proved their worth would be allowed to keep their gear after the climb. This new wrinkle was deemed totally unacceptable by the Sherpas, a wound to their pride and a sign of bad faith. Their resentment may have been somewhat exacerbated by two Sherpas, Pasang Phutar and Ang Dawa, who, it was alleged, were active members of the young Marxist Party in Darjeeling and had been encouraged by political colleagues to "cause trouble" on this "imperialist" British expedition. There is no evidence to substantiate such claims, but the party was indeed gaining strength at that time among the workers of Darjeeling and West Bengal. After an investigation involving Hunt, Tenzing, and Wylie, the two agitators were paid off and sent back to India. Tenzing and Wylie, the chief peace brokers, were profoundly relieved to get on with the business of climbing Everest.

Tenzing requested a formal blessing from the Head Lama of Tengboche monastery, a ritual that has since become an Everest tradition. Once offered to respect the Sherpas and their Buddhist beliefs, it is now seen as an essential part of any climber's mental and spiritual preparation. After the blessing, they climbed some smaller peaks for practice and acclimation before setting up Base Camp and commencing the assault. Tenzing and Hunt first climbed together on nearby Chukhung Peak, and Hunt wrote in his 1953 book, *The Ascent of Everest*, that Tenzing "showed me not only what a capable mountaineer he is but also that he was, even at that time, fitter than the rest of us." Tenzing was then thirty-nine; of the other climbers, only Alfred Gregory, thirty-nine, and Hunt himself, forty-two, were as old.

As time passed, Hunt came to understand Tenzing's humility and his great passion for climbing:

> All through our work of stock-piling he had necessarily undertaken the least exciting tasks of all, leading the Low Level Ferries, organizing ration and firewood parties, sending and receiving mail runners at Base; maintaining order there and helping to keep all his men cheerful. These things he had done well and willingly, for it was in his nature to do so. But I knew that his heart was set on getting higher, and higher still. Always he was happiest when climbing.

But Hillary seemed to comprehend Tenzing's mindset even more astutely than Hunt. In his 1999 book, *The View from the Summit*, Hillary wrote:

> The same afternoon a big party arrived with the first major lift up the icefall and everything seemed to have gone well. It was Tenzing's first trip above base camp for the year and I didn't think he seemed very happy. With the Swiss he had been one of the lead climbers but John Hunt had felt that at this stage his influence and experience would be more valuable organising the other Sherpas and their loads up the icefall. I had considerable respect for Tenzing's reputation but it never entered my mind that we needed his help in tackling the difficult ice problems which I accepted we were quite capable of dealing with ourselves. No wonder Tenzing always had a warmer affection for the Swiss than he ever did for us.

Later, in the Western Cwm, Hillary climbed with Tenzing. As he wrote in *High Adventure* (1957), despite the horrendous conditions and enervating heat—which reaches 113 degrees Fahrenheit (45 degrees Celsius) when full sun is absorbed and reradiated by the steep rock walls surrounding the cwm on three sides—he found Tenzing easily his match:

> This was the first time I had climbed with Tenzing or indeed, ever seen him climbing, and I was very interested to watch him in action. Although not perhaps technically outstanding in ice-craft, he was very strong and determined and an excellent acclimatizer. Best of all, as far as I was concerned, he was prepared to go fast and hard.

Hillary's regard for Tenzing's mountain prowess increased a hundredfold with an event that could have ended Hillary's Everest quest forever. On their way down the icefall just after 4 P.M. one afternoon, Hillary and Tenzing stopped in at Camp II, where George Lowe was holding down the fort. Feeling fit and spry, Hillary casually bet Lowe that he and Tenzing could get down to Base Camp in time for the 5 P.M. call-out on the radio. Lowe laughed off the notion, saying "That'll be the day," but Ed took up the challenge with Tenzing hot on his heels. They literally ran down the ice, leaping crevasses as they reached them without checking the stability of the other side. One such crevasse was Hillary's undoing, for the far lip gave way under his weight and he fell, in a flurry of ice, straight into the void. He managed to get his crampons into the wall on one side and his back wedged against the wall on the other before the rope went taut as Tenzing, above him, dug in his ice ax and wrapped his rope around it in an excellent belay. By the time Hillary struggled up and out of the massive crack, he was sure that he and this Sherpa would make an invincible team, and he resolved to convince Hunt that they should be the summit pair.

As it happened, Hunt named Charles Evans and Tom Bourdillon to the first summit bid and Tenzing and Hillary to the second. Standing on the South Col with Hunt and Hillary, watching for Evans and Bourdillon's return, Tenzing became decidedly morose, for he began to believe that these two would seize the prize that he had coveted so long. Hillary understood and shared Tenzing's feelings, and later admitted to a sense of guilt about his relief when the first pair did not succeed.

Right: The technical problems presented by the icefall were many, including crevasses that changed hourly. Here a Sherpa puts on crampons before heading across the icefall. Below: Sherpas carrying loads across the icefall.

Left: Sherpa crossing a crevasse above Camp II, in the icefall. Then as now, crampons, metal ladder rungs, and heavy loads made these crossings a tricky balancing act. Below: Hillary (standing) assists Tenzing across a crevasse near Camp III, just above the icefall.

EVEREST SUMMIT SOUTH SUMMIT
9
LHOTSE
SOUTH COL
8
GENEVA SPUR
7
6
WESTERN CWM
5
4
ICE FALL
3
2
BASE KHUMBU GLACIER
NUPTSE

1. *Tenzing's tent at Base Camp, with the icefall and Lingtren as backdrop.*
2. *Crossing the lower part of the Western Cwm to Camp IV.*
3. *Party at the foot of the Lhotse Face starting up toward Camp VI.*
4. *Hillary and Tenzing on the shelf at the top of the Lhotse Glacier. The flags intended for the summit are wrapped around Tenzing's ice ax handle.*

Mount Everest from the southwest. The Khumbu Valley and Glacier are lower right; the foot of the ice-fall is at the point where the Khumbu Glacier bends sharply to the right; the Western Cwm, partly hidden by cloud, runs up to the steep wall known as the Lhotse Face. Above that Lhotse is on the right; the gap between Lhotse and Everest is the South Col.

Above: Bourdillon and Evans, the two climbers Hunt selected for the first summit attempt. Right: Hillary and Tenzing.

Top: The British climbers and the high-altitude Sherpa team at advance base camp (Camp IV) on 31 May 1953. Above: The South Col carry party with Noyce and Wylie.

Much has been said of Hillary and Tenzing's relationship. They were somewhat of an odd couple, with the six-foot, three-inch Hillary towering over the five-foot, eight-inch Tenzing, neither speaking much of the other's language. In an article for *Time* magazine, Jan Morris, who (as James Morris, prior to a sex change operation) covered the climb for the London *Times*, a major expedition sponsor, wrote of them:

> They made an oddly assorted pair. Hillary was tall, lanky, big-boned and long-faced, and he moved with an incongruous grace, rather like a giraffe. He habitually wore on his head a home-made cap with a cotton flap behind, as seen in old movies of the French Foreign Legion. Tenzing was by comparison a Himalayan fashion model: small, neat, rather delicate, brown as a berry, with the confident movements of a cat. Hillary grinned; Tenzing smiled. Hillary guffawed; Tenzing chuckled. Neither of them seemed particularly perturbed by anything; on the other hand, neither went in for unnecessary bravado—Hillary and Tenzing were two cheerful, courageous fellows doing what they liked doing, and did best.

The close emotional bond that existed between Tenzing and Lambert—a bond that comes only rarely to any of us, and only as the result of extraordinary luck—was absent between Hillary and Tenzing, at least to the same degree. But that bond is not an essential prerequisite to a successful personal or climbing partnership. The two men respected each other, they trusted each other on the mountain, and they climbed as one. A climber can ask nothing more of the partner on the other end of the rope.

On 29 May, Tenzing and Hillary stirred at 3:30 A.M. in their bivouac tent high above the South Col, having barely slept. At 6:30 A.M., after three hours of slow and labored preparations, they resumed the push they had begun the day before, and reached the South Summit at 9 A.M. To that point they could be seen from the South Col by George Lowe and Wilfred Noyce, but once past the South Summit they were hidden from view, so that no one saw them reach the true summit at 11:30 A.M. At that moment in time, a moment too perfect to last, the two men stood above and apart from the rest of the world, wrapped together in

Hillary checks Tenzing's oxygen set at Camp IV. Designed by climbing team member Tom Bourdillon and his father, the oxygen system was mounted at the top of a metal backpack frame and when fully charged added thirty pounds to the climber's load.

a private triumph. Three days later James Morris would send the news in a coded radio message to the *Times*, which would break the story on the morning of 2 June, the day of young Queen Elizabeth's coronation. War-weary England, brooding over the erosion of its empire, would seize the British expedition's success as a Coronation Day sign of renewed promise. Nepal, India, and Tibet would each claim Tenzing for their own. Hillary and Tenzing would have to descend into the clamor of this human tide. But for a few moments in the late forenoon of 29 May, high in a clear, blue day with a gentle five-knot breeze, none of that existed.

Only after the summit was reached and the two became "world property" did their relationship, their ambitions, and their characters come under sometimes painful scrutiny—a development abhorred by both, as indeed by all true mountaineers. The summit itself was the culprit in this destructive process, for it was on this that the entire world seemed to focus. Few mentioned the tireless efforts of the other members of the British team and the anonymous band of Sherpas who toiled up and down the mountain week after week, setting the stage for the final summit bid. No one asked about John Hunt's burden of responsibility in ensuring that the last-ditch British attempt did not fail, as so many had before it. Not a word was spoken about the families of all those involved, who endured months of loneliness and worry knowing their Sherpa, British, and Nepali husbands, brothers, and sometimes, wives and daughters were toiling in often life-threatening conditions. To those who were there, the summit was the end of a million steps, thousands of loads carried, hundreds of helping hands and small, heroic gestures on high, oxygen-starved slopes swept bare of comfort and human voice by bitter cold and all-conquering wind. To the world's media, only the summit counted, as if that moment in time existed free of any context or support. But it is always so. My grandfather would later say in *Tiger of the Snows*, "No less than a mountain itself, the press can raise a man high and drop him down low. That was one of the lessons I was to learn painfully from the climbing of Everest."

Who reached the top first? It's a question that has echoed around the world ever since 29 May 1953, a question that attacked Tenzing and Hillary's great partnership like a corrosive acid—a question that, as John Hunt put it, "climbers would never think to ask." Yet the world asked

Hillary and Tenzing about to leave the South Col to establish Camp IX below the south summit.

and, when told, would not accept the answer. To the climber of any peak, let alone an 8,850-meter Himalayan giant, the matter of two or three paces ahead or behind is so irrelevant as merely to ridicule the asker. To John Hunt it simply did not occur; it was the team that had succeeded, and he could view their achievement no other way. To Tenzing and Hillary it meant nothing at all; not a word on the subject was mentioned when they brought the news of their success back to the group waiting on the South Col and later to Camps VII, VI, V, and IV in succession. The question never crossed the minds of the Sherpa climbing team; to them, the mountain had been climbed by Au Tenzing (Uncle Tenzing) and Hillary Sahib. Had the question been asked in those first days after the ascent, Tenzing and Hillary would have answered with their characteristic candor that Hillary stepped up first and Tenzing followed a couple of paces behind. Less than two years

Edmund Hillary's photo of Tenzing Norgay on the summit of Mount Everest, 11:30 A.M., 29 May 1953. Tenzing's ice ax is adorned with the flags of the United Nations, Britain, Nepal, and India. After this photo was taken Tenzing dug a small hole in the snow into which he placed various small gifts—bits of chocolate, cookies, and a pencil—a Buddhist offering to the gods of the mountains.

later, in *Tiger of the Snows*, Tenzing said as much, even though Hunt, in his official account, *The Ascent of Everest*, and Hillary, in *High Adventure*, both wrote that Hillary and Tenzing simply "stepped up" to the summit. Hillary and Tenzing mutually vowed never to discuss the matter publicly, and Tenzing held true to this agreement. Only in 1993, at the fortieth Everest Anniversary celebrations in Britain, did Hillary, his tolerance and patience sorely tested, state finally and publicly that he had stepped on the top first.

Strangely, this admission disappointed many Sherpas who felt that their hero, Tenzing, had been in some way betrayed. Their disappointment, they say, is not that Tenzing did not technically reach the summit first, but rather that Hillary had in the end broken a gentleman's agreement not to discuss the matter publicly. Privately, Tenzing confided to his family that what he had said in his autobiography was quite simply the truth, despite politically motivated objections that his account had been mistranslated, perhaps deliberately. No climbers climb a steep slope side by side. It is impossible. So it was with this pair of mountaineers. Tenzing was a step or two behind Hillary.

On top of the world, Tenzing experienced joy and emotion he could never have imagined. Hillary in fact expressed surprise that Tenzing was even more excited than he was. Like all Sherpas he was not given to great displays of affection, but in *Tiger of the Snows* he wrote that he could not content himself with a mere handshake with the rather reserved Hillary:

> I waved my arms in the air and then threw them around Hillary, and we thumped each other on the back until, even with the oxygen, we were almost breathless.

There is no doubt that in their own ways both men were profoundly satisfied and proud of their achievement. The ever-practical Hillary set about gathering photographic evidence of their successful summit, first having Tenzing pose on the snowy dome—the size of a large sitting room—that is the summit, his ice ax held aloft, the flags of the United Nations, Britain, Nepal, and India fluttering in the icy winds. That there is no photo of Hillary on the summit is further testimony that the issue of who summited first meant nothing to either man. Tenzing had not carried his camera with him, and the mountaineering component

Hillary and Tenzing return to Camp IV.

Tenzing and Hillary drinking tea on the Western Cwm after their historic summit, 30 May 1953.

of Hillary's mind overpowered any sense of ego he may have felt, for his only concern was with photographing the view from the summit—not himself standing on it.

For Tenzing, Everest's summit was not a religious experience, though he felt "a great closeness to God." His desire to climb Chomolungma was born of his own love of climbing and personal affection for this mountain:

> At that great moment for which I had waited all my life my mountain did not seem to me a lifeless thing of rock and ice, but warm and friendly and living. She was a mother hen, and the other mountains were chicks under her wings. I too, I felt, had only to spread my own wings to cover and shelter the brood that I loved.

Tenzing thought of all the great climbers who, for thirty-three years, had struggled and failed to stand where he and his companion now stood. He thought of the climbers below, without whose help they could not have summited. And he thought of Lambert: "He was so near, so real to me, that he did not seem to be in my thoughts at all, but actually standing there beside me. Any moment now I would turn and see his big bear face grinning at me. I would hear his voice saying, 'Ça va bien, Tenzing. Ça va bien!' "

Tenzing was a traditional Sherpa and Tibetan Buddhist by faith, so he dutifully paid homage to the deity of the mountain by burying in the snow of the summit cone some sweets and Nima's small blue-and-red pencil. The goddess Jomo Myolangsangma was well satisfied.

The pair then began the long descent to warmth and safety, as the anxious climbers below counted every second of their climb. George Lowe was the first to spot them as they neared the South Col, just before sundown. He rushed up, throwing his arms around them. They had made it! Wilfred Noyce was right behind him, and together they plied the exhausted pair with hot lemon juice and tea before escorting them back to their South Col camp. Noyce and Hunt had agreed on a special signal to enable Hunt and the others at the advance base camp (Camp IV) to know whether or not Tenzing and Hillary had been successful. Either above or just below the South Col, Noyce would set out sleeping bags in prearranged positions; one bag would mean they had failed to reach the summit, two bags placed side by side would mean only the South Summit had been reached, and two bags placed in a T would signal the ultimate success.

Noyce fulfilled his duty, but the mist obscured his signal from the base camp. The whole procedure was a mystery to poor Pasang Phutar (not to be confused with the Pasang Phutar who had been sent back from Tengboche). Hunt, in *The Ascent of Everest*, wrote:

> Wilfred had set out again with a very puzzled Pasang Phutar to the top of the Geneva Spur carrying two sleeping bags. What could this eccentric sahib be doing at this hour of the day, starting off so soon after getting to the Col, apparently determined to sleep out? The mystery deepened for him when, on arriving at the slope which seemed to Wilfred most likely to be seen from below, he arranged the sleeping bags in the form of a 'T' and proceeded to lie down on one of them—the wind was strong

and this was essential to prevent the bags from being blown away—bidding the astonished Sherpa to do likewise. Surely, thought Pasang, this was carrying hardihood too far? So they were not even to get inside the bags? Thus they remained, shivering, for ten long minutes as the sun went down behind Pumori, until Wilfred decided they had done their best to pass the great news down to us.

After much excited talk, Tenzing and Hillary fell into exhausted sleep. The following morning they headed down the mountain, tired but euphoric. At each camp the great news was received with joy and relief: at Camp VII, by Charles Wylie and his Sherpas; at Camp VI, by cameraman Tom Stobart; at Camp V by more Sherpas, including Dawa Thondup and Gombu. The main part of the team, including John Hunt, was assembled in Camp IV, and as the descending party approached, Lowe, who could contain his excitement no longer, held his arm aloft with the thumbs-up signal and his ice ax pointing to the summit. The Camp IV climbers walked and then ran (as fast as one can at that altitude!) to meet them, and there was much hugging and back slapping all round. Among the Sherpas, only Tenzing appreciated what this summit meant to the sahibs, and only because it meant as much to him. He had no inkling what lay ahead for him when the news broke to the world. Later he would joke to his family that, had he known what was to come in the weeks to follow, he would have stayed on the mountain forever.

A little apart stood a row of Sherpas, perplexed but grinning broadly. How could the ascent of this mountain—any mountain—make a man like Colonel Sahib (as they referred to John Hunt) cry? Yet their happiness for their colleagues' success was transparent. Tenzing eventually walked over to share that success with them. They had worked so hard. He knew they had overcome their fears and exhaustion for him and for Major Wylie. They were in awe of Tenzing, and their faces beamed as he shook their hands. They could not have known it on that day, but what Tenzing had just achieved would change their lives forever. It would make them a household name throughout the world and would bring opportunities for them and their descendants that they could never have imagined. Yet, while the British savored every syllable of Ed Hillary's recount of the final ascent, Tenzing and the Sherpas

Above: Hillary greeting Sherpas after the ascent, Camp IV. Below: Tenzing at Camp IV, surrounded by Sherpas.

got on with the task of packing up the camps for the withdrawal from the mountain.

Tenzing's first task was to hire extra porters for the carry-out. He managed to mix business with pleasure by heading directly to his home village of Thamey to recruit the hundred or so load-carriers they would need. With his neck swathed in *kadas* presented by Sherpa well-wishers along the Khumbu trails, he finally met his mother, who asked him about the climb and what he had seen on the summit. (Sherpas are often curious about the summits of their sacred peaks, believing that deities, demons, or other mythical beings, such as the yeti, may abide there, and Tenzing's mother was particularly inclined to believe in such legends.) He then joined in a huge celebration of success with his family and friends ("breaking training," as he put it in his autobiography) before returning to join the expedition at Tengboche. These were happy days, in fact the happiest Tenzing would experience from his success on Everest. He had been freed from his addiction to Everest and could think ahead to other things in life—other mountains to climb, and other expedition work. He gave no thought to protocol or politics, and apart from a short note to his wife and daughters (which he asked a friend to write) telling of his summit success, he had no intention of announcing his triumph to anyone at all. That was the business of the sahibs. His job was to organize porters and get the expedition back to Kathmandu, and he and the rest of the team immersed themselves in this task.

As the expedition walked the high trails of the Himalayan hills toward Kathmandu, messages of congratulation arrived by wireless and runner at various points. Yet the expedition still remained largely a self-contained unit, indulging in laughter, joking, and tomfoolery as they went. Hillary had been told that he had been knighted by Her Majesty Queen Elizabeth II but refused to believe it, telling Lowe that he would now have to buy a new pair of overalls. Tenzing kept his porters and Sherpas at work, but enjoyed the sweet aura of success reflecting from family and friends met along the way. A great sense of relief and euphoria swept through the team, Sherpa and sahib alike, and in fact the Sherpa ranks sometimes seemed to fall apart in the excitement of it all. John Hunt later recalled a humorous incident on the walk-out, after a rather exuberant night of Sherpa celebrations in Namche Bazaar. The following morning three sahibs—Gregory, Bourdillon, and Hunt—waited impatiently for their Sherpa team to surface, and eventually gave up and headed off with only Dawa Thondup, who seemed able to cope with any amount of alcohol. Hunt sent a message back to Charles Wylie, who was at Tengboche with the main party, to send a Sherpa to them urgently. Charles Wylie chose Pemba, a quiet and reliable man, and in order to speed his progress arranged a pony for him. Pemba left carrying a message to Hunt, but the following day, as Wylie's party approached Namche, they came across Pemba sitting on a grassy knoll above the trail, nursing a sprained ankle and in a very befuddled state. Nearby was another Sherpa, out cold, lying across the trail, but there was no sign of the pony. Sitting up, swathed in fumes of alcohol, Pemba handed Wylie his own message. "It's very important, sahib," he announced.

The main party met another obstacle, this time in Namche, in the form of an irate Sherpa mother. One of the Sherpa climbers, Da Tenzing, had headed off to other regions of the Khumbu with Charles Evans, but Da Tenzing's son, Mingma, had decided that he would stick with the team and head back to see the big, wide world in Kathmandu. His mortified mother faced her son's "abductors" as they were leaving Namche. "You have taken my husband, now you would snatch my son away from me, too," she wailed. Mingma was duly retained in Namche. Back at base camp, another Sherpa mother had arrived with a large basket of eggs ready to bargain back her son from the covetous sahibs. She ended up keeping both her son and the eggs.

It took the expedition ten days to make it to the outer rim of the Kathmandu Valley, and during this period Wylie took Tenzing under his wing and began, with great sensitivity and wisdom, to prepare him for what he knew was in store for all of them, particularly Tenzing and Hillary. Tenzing could not grasp the seriousness of what Wylie was saying, but listened dutifully and tried to imagine the scenarios Wylie described. He was illiterate, a man from the high mountains who knew only the duties of a sirdar and climber. He was an innocent in the ways of life outside the Himalaya and ill-equipped emotionally and experientially to cope with the world into which he was about to be thrust. Wylie and the rest of the British team were only too aware of what was about to befall them, although even they could never have predicted the depth of the scrutiny to which they would be subjected by the world media.

Those days before his arrival in Kathmandu could never be taken away from Tenzing: the final climb up the perilous summit ridge, the elation of finding that there was no more "up" and that they had indeed reached the top of the world, the raw excitement of their descent into the excited embrace of those who had worked so hard with them to reach the shared goal, mountaineering's greatest prize. Those were halcyon days such as no other mountaineer is ever likely to experience. Jan Morris would later call the first summit of Everest "the last innocent adventure."

CHAPTER 7

TENZING
AFTER EVEREST

I REMEMBER A TALL FELLOW arriving at the door of our house in Toong Soong. He was named Natmal and Ravi Babu had sent him. It was 2 June and Mummy and Nima and I were at home. Natmal said, 'Mrs Tenzing, I have good news for you. Tenzing has climbed Everest!'

Even after almost fifty years, Pem Pem, Tenzing's eldest daughter and my mother, still recalls this moment with great clarity. Ravi Mitra heard of the British team's success over All-India Radio and rejoiced to learn that my grandfather had been one of the summit pair. He immediately sent word to the family and set about preparing for the media circus he knew would descend on Darjeeling and this soon-to-be-world-famous Sherpa.

Hillary, Tenzing, and Ang Lhamu looking strained and confused as they enter Kathmandu to a rapturous reception, June 1953.

"We were all so happy," Pem Pem recalls. "Mummy had been very worried and now, with this great news, we knew things would be good for us."

The tiny house in Toong Soong was deluged with excited visitors: family, Sherpa friends, media, and local dignitaries. The kitchen buzzed with a gaggle of Sherpanis who arrived to help Ang Lhamu cope with the duties of hostess. Tea poured forth in great quantities. After all the years of strain and hardship in the Himalaya, and after seven arduous Everest expeditions, Chomolungma had finally given back some of what she had taken away. A mountaineer's life is hard on everyone, but especially on those at home, who for weeks or months at a time must shoulder the daily tasks and responsibilities of the absent husband, father, son, or brother; who can only wait and worry, powerless to help the loved one or even to know when help is needed; and who, if the climber does not return, must find the strength to carry on without him. Ang Lhamu and her daughters had lived in constant fear of Tenzing not returning. They knew he was a capable and experienced mountaineer, but skill and experience count for nothing when an avalanche a kilometer wide sweeps down a mountain. Tenzing climbed knowing that whatever fate befell him, his daughters would be loved and cared for. For the lifting of this otherwise incalculable burden, he knew he owed Ang Lhamu his undying gratitude; his success on Everest was as much hers as his.

Ang Lhamu's boundless joy was a source of great satisfaction to the entire Sherpa community of Darjeeling. Often, when friends and neighbors were out of work, she and Tenzing had drawn from their modest savings to buy food, pay medical bills, and offer loans that might or might not ever be paid back. Whenever a climbing death plunged Toong Soong into mourning, Ang Lhamu would comfort the stricken wife and family. In a community built on mutual compassion, she was unusually compassionate, and her neighbors loved her in return. Beaming as she welcomed guests and retold the story of hearing the news, she laughed and giggled and sang and poured tea. Those who knew her well could see in her round, kind face that a great burden had been lifted. Her girls would finally have the life they deserved, and Tenzing could at last be released from the quest that had consumed him.

Ang Lhamu was eager to travel to Kathmandu to receive her husband in person, yet by June 4 she still had not heard from him. At Ten-

Tenzing and Ang Lhamu at Rosenlaui, Switzerland, 1953.

zing's request, Charles Wylie had sent a message by wireless from Tengboche to Darjeeling asking Ang Lhamu and the girls to come to Kathmandu, but the message hadn't reached them, and Ang Lhamu remained
tentative until Ravi Mitra stepped in, insisting that they go. To cover
their travel expenses, he gave Ang Lhamu 100 rupees he had earned by
selling photographs of Tenzing in Darjeeling and convinced Jill Henderson of the Himalayan Club to contribute another 400 rupees. In
their simple *bakus* (traditional Sherpa dress for women) and with minimal baggage, they embarked on the long journey to Kathmandu. It was
the girls' first trip away from home since the long, sad journey out of
Chitral on the back of a horse after their birth mother's death more than
eight years earlier. Ang Lhamu had lived and worked in England for a
short time, but the trip she now embarked on in such haste would take
her farther and for a longer time than any journey she had made before.

Meanwhile, on the walk-out from Everest, life for Tenzing had
become vastly more complicated than it had ever seemed before. At the
small village of Dhaulaghat, two days' march from Kathmandu, an agi-

tated band of Nepali journalists and political activists confronted the returning expedition. Ignoring Hunt, Hillary, and the rest of the team, they targeted Tenzing, yanking him aside to bombard him with questions and urge him to sign prepared statements regarding his nationality and the details of the summit climb. They had no real interest in Everest or mountaineering, or even Tenzing himself. Driven by political opportunism, they sought merely to use Tenzing for nationalist propaganda. They wanted, in short, to tell the world that a Nepali had been the first person in history to summit Everest. My grandfather was apolitical, but he was also illiterate, confused, and terrified by their aggressive attitude. Wylie, who was trying his best to shield Tenzing from a particularly tenacious questioner, lost his characteristic cool and tweaked the Nepali's cap—a singularly offensive gesture, as he well knew. A shocked hush fell on the crowd, and the man withdrew in disgust, but still the Nepalis pressed forward. Finally, in a desperate bid to free himself from his tormentors, Tenzing signed a document they had been waving in his face, having no idea what it said. In fact, it claimed that Tenzing had reached the summit of Everest before Hillary. To their credit, however, most informed Nepalis never accepted the statement as authentic. They could see that Tenzing was a "coolie," an illiterate man of the hills—not a self-promoting glory-seeker. For their part, Hunt and the British team realized immediately that Tenzing could not have known what he was signing. They had worked side by side with him for months; they had risked life and limb with him on the mountain. They knew him well enough to know that he was not a self-aggrandizing man.

At Banepa, on the edge of the great Kathmandu Valley, Ang Lhamu, Pem Pem, and Nima had an emotional reunion with their "Papa," dissolving all the strain of recent days. My mother remembers seeing a very tall man come up behind her father, "The tallest man I had ever seen, I think."

It was, of course, "Uncle Hillary." Then Wylie spoke to them in beautiful Nepali, and the girls were amazed to meet "a sahib who speaks our language so well." (Sherpas of that day spoke both Sherpa and Nepali; though illiterate, Tenzing also spoke Hindi.) The family reunion was brief, however. Soon Tenzing was hauled away, cajoled to change quickly into Nepali attire, had a Nepali flag pressed into his hand, and was hoisted into a jeep for the drive into Kathmandu. Along with Hunt and Hillary, he was swept along on a wave of hysteria and adulation that no one could have anticipated. It was, in fact, a curious reaction from the people of this remote Himalayan kingdom, who, despite having the highest mountains on earth in their realm, knew virtually nothing about mountaineering. The quest for Everest that had so consumed Western sahibs since the beginning of the twentieth century had eluded the Nepalese. Mountain climbing had no place in their culture, and the attraction of such a dangerous and fiscally unrewarding pursuit did not even register in the national psyche.

As the procession moved closer to Kathmandu it began to pass under broad banners stretched across the roads on bamboo scaffolding. The banners depicted the victorious Sherpa Tenzing atop Everest, hauling an apparently near-comatose Hillary up the final ridge. Initially all the climbers were amused, but the fervor with which the crowds were shouting "Tenzing Zindabad! Tenzing Zindabad!" ("Long Live Tenzing!"), made everyone decidedly uncomfortable about the way the climb was being interpreted. Even my mother, Pem Pem, then a fourteen-year-old with no experience of politics or expeditions, was acutely embarrassed that Hillary and the rest of the team, Sherpa and British, were ignored by the Nepalis. Ang Lhamu and the girls, alarmed at the frightened, hunted look on Tenzing's face, were beginning to wonder whether this experience was going to be a good one after all.

Yet many of the Sherpa climbers were swept up in the unprecedented excitement and the romance of heroism, although they would not have expressed it thus. Nawang Gombu was initially shell-shocked by the team's reception at Banepa, but as the adulation and feting of his uncle increased, and he began to see just what the expedition had achieved and how much it meant to the world at large, he found himself wanting to emulate Tenzing's great achievement. For the first time in his life, he passionately wanted to climb Everest. Not all Sherpas reacted in this way, but in some the seed of ambition was sown, and the future would deliver up, in the words of Indian Prime Minister Sri Jawaharlal Nehru, "a thousand Tenzings."

As the entourage reached the center of Kathmandu the party transferred to the King's royal carriage. With the seated Hunt and Hillary drowning in marigolds, my mother and her sister perched above them at the back of the heavily garlanded coach, and my grandfather standing, almost frozen with fear, at the front of the carriage with hands clasped in the traditional "Namaste" greeting, they made their way to the Royal Palace for a reception with King Tribhuvana.

Hunt later wrote in *The Ascent of Everest*:

> There was the Nepalese Court, attired to do us honor, seated along the walls to witness the ceremony of Investiture of decorations by His Majesty to certain members of the expedition. There were the members of the expedition, at the end of their three weeks journey from the distant mountain, bedraggled, unshaven, dirty, dressed in filthy clothes, shorts, gym shoes and the like. [Dr. Griffith] Pugh, standing I was glad to notice, somewhat in the background, was still wearing pajamas, the same pair of pajamas which he had worn throughout both the march-out and the return journey.

There, too, the adventurers heard for the first time a song hastily written about Tenzing and his great achievement for Nepal. Called "Hamro Tenzing Sherpa" ("Our Tenzing Sherpa"), it was sung throughout the Khumbu valleys in June 1953 and is still heard in the mountains today.

> Our Tenzing Sherpa climbed the Himalayan peak,
> Sound the tambourine with pride,
> Dance peacock in gentle grace
> For Tenzing Sherpa who shines above all
> And the entire world will applaud.
> Tenzing, the warm heart of the cold Himalayan peak
> Tenzing, the gem of the world
> Tenzing, from the vast Himalaya
> He must have quenched his thirst by the source of Sun Khosi†
> Must have guided Hillary through the confusing trails
> Tenzing hoisted the national flag
> On the tallest tower of the world

† A major river of Nepal.

Danphe†† must have spread its wings and danced
Gauri Shankar††† must have graced the event with smiles
With no water for them to quench the thirst
Still the heavens' head was the goal quest
Blessed be you brave and mighty incarnate
Born of mortal to live an immortal life

The king awarded Tenzing the Nepal Tara (Star of Nepal), the highest honor of the kingdom, and gave Hunt and Hillary lesser awards. But Hunt and Hillary's stars ascended shortly after when word arrived that both were to be knighted by Queen Elizabeth II, who also bestowed upon Tenzing the lesser honor of a George Medal. But much as the expeditioners appreciated these awards at the time, that appreciation deepened later in life, after the flush of Everest success had settled into quiet satisfaction. In June 1953, the greatest prize of all, the summit of Everest, had already been granted.

The days following his arrival in Kathmandu were traumatic and exhausting for my grandfather, as constant harassment from the local media took its toll. That members of the British team, especially Hillary, were ignored by the Nepalis became an increasing source of embarrassment and shame to Tenzing. At one function his taking of the stage brought the audience to its feet with deafening cheers and cries of "Tenzing! Tenzing!" After Tenzing's brief speech, Ed Hillary was introduced as the "second man to climb Everest," and then, as he approached the microphone, was met with pin-drop silence. My grandfather was mortified but could think of nothing to do or say. The master sirdar who, on the mountain, could always cajole, reassure, and reason with his men, found himself helpless, tongue-tied and overmatched, his sweet triumph turning bitter.

Elements of the British media picked up the controversy, finding plenty to write about. The King of Nepal had offered Tenzing and his family use of the royal jet for their visit to Calcutta where a large reception had been arranged in Tenzing's honor. John Hunt, Joy Hunt, Ed Hillary, and Alfred Gregory were also to attend. Tenzing could hardly

†† A pheasant, the national bird of Nepal.
††† A major Himalayan peak west of Everest.

refuse the king's generous offer, though he felt awkward about his British friends not being invited to take the flight with him. Hunt, Hillary, and Gregory were to fly by commercial airline, arriving in Calcutta five and a half hours after Tenzing. Though the three Britons didn't mention it, the British press pounced on the "slight." A press clipping from Charles Wylie's archives—under the byline of Sydney Smith but with the newspaper unidentified—is typical:

TENSING FLIES BY ROYAL PLANE; BRITONS LAG BEHIND HIM FOR HOURS

A royal Nepalese plane will fly "Tiger" Tensing and his family to Calcutta . . . and get them to the celebrations five and a half hours ahead of Colonel Hunt and Edmund Hillary.

So the carefully engineered campaign to split the conquerors of Everest reaches a new high. Colonel Hunt and the rest of his party are going on the regular commercial flight with a five-hour wait in Patna. This is the clearest snub yet and makes it perfectly plain that for the Nepalese Tensing is considered the personal conqueror of Everest.

SECOND PLACE

Since the whole expedition arrived in Kathmandu last weekend its leader Colonel Hunt and Hillary, who reached the top with Tensing, have taken second place. The other members have been almost ignored.

At the glittering Government reception last night Prime Minister Koirala called Tensing forward first and presented him with a wad of banknotes worth 500 Pounds and an elaborate kukri (heavy battle knife). Colonel Hunt and Hillary received a kukri, good tourist standard worth about 5 Pounds each, while the men of the party were given gilded brass Nepali boxes 4 in by 6 in which sell in New Delhi for about 22 Pounds and 6 Shillings.

Sydney Smith's information wasn't wrong—just slanted in such a way that it compromised even more the good relations that had existed between Tenzing, his Sherpas, and the British team.

Film footage and photographs from the time show only too clearly the acute stress experienced by all concerned. When Tenzing started receiving death threats, apparently from Nepali nationalists who were angry that he would not claim the first ascent of Everest for himself and Nepal, the accumulating pressure overwhelmed him. One evening with his family and friends, my grandfather broke down. Exhausted and confused, he had had enough. Gombu recalls that Tenzing had refused large amounts of money to make a false statement about the summit. That night he said he must leave it all in the hands of "our leader," and in fact Colonel Hunt soon came to his aid.

Hunt called a meeting of those concerned on 22 June at the office of Nepali Prime Minister Koirala, where a decision was made to counter the damaging stories and attempt to restore some sense and calm by issuing a formal statement concerning the summit. The statement read:

> On May 29th Tenzing Sherpa and I left our high camp on Mount Everest for our attempt on the summit.
>
> As we climbed upwards to the south summit first one and then the other would take a turn at leading.
>
> We crossed over the south summit and moved along the summit ridge. We reached the summit almost together.
>
> We embraced each other, overjoyed at our success; then I took photographs of Tenzing holding aloft the flags of Great Britain, Nepal, the United Nations and India.

It was signed by Hillary and countersigned by Tenzing.

The tactic seemed to quell the media fire somewhat, and Tenzing was able to get on with the business of planning his immediate future, which included traveling to India and then to England and Europe.

In Calcutta he met Ravi Mitra, whom he had asked to join him there. Tenzing gave Mitra his red scarf, the gift from Lambert, asking him to send it at once to Switzerland. Lambert had been with Tenzing throughout the climb—in spirit and in his love for the mountain and his Sherpa friend—and Tenzing wanted to close the circle by sending the scarf back home.

After another round of receptions, public gatherings, and awards, the party moved on to Delhi, the Indian capital, where they met the most overwhelming reception of all.

Tens of thousands of people were waiting at the airport, and as my grandfather emerged from the plane the crowd erupted into a frenzied chorus of "Tenzing! Tenzing!" In *The View from the Summit*, Hillary wrote of the occasion, "I have never seen a greater look of terror than in Tenzing's eyes."

As the team descended the steps the crowd surged forward, and Tenzing was swept away in its midst. Ang Lhamu, with a firm grip on Nima's hand, managed to stay with her husband, but my poor mother Pem Pem lost hold of her father's hand and disappeared into the tide of people. Terrified, she cried out for her frantic parents. Finally their hosts managed to hold the crowd at bay long enough to find the tiny Sherpani.

That evening Prime Minister Sri Jawaharlal Nehru hosted a gala reception at his residence, Rashtrapati Bhavan. Learning ahead of time that Tenzing had no formal attire to wear to receptions in India and those that would follow in Europe, Nehru gave Tenzing a number of articles of fine clothing from his own dressing-room closet. To Ang Lhamu he presented a pocketbook and raincoat, and, in a particularly touching gesture, he gave Tenzing two small pieces of jewelry that had belonged to his father, Motilal Nehru.

Nehru was to become one of my grandfather's greatest supporters. In part his motives were political: Tenzing was a resident of India and India had only recently, in August 1947, gained independence from Britain, so there was a great deal to gain from promoting Tenzing as a national hero. An astute politician, Nehru could not have failed to see the power of this image for his new nation. But he would also demonstrate time and again his genuine fondness for Tenzing and concern for his welfare. Nehru was a Kashmiri Brahmin, in spirit at least a man of the mountains, and he adored adventure and the pioneering world of early Himalayan mountaineering. Tenzing's climbing exploits fascinated him, and in the years to come he would make it his business to see that this Sherpa climber was treated with the respect he deserved.

Tenzing was committed to fly with the British climbers from India to London at the invitation of the expedition's sponsors. Ang Lhamu and the girls had not been invited, but Ang Lhamu had other ideas.

Her husband was tired and bewildered, and she had no intention of allowing him to go without the support of his family. She had let him go to the mountain against her better judgment, but this time she stood firm—either they all went or Tenzing stayed at home. In the end she won, and Tenzing and his family accompanied Hunt, Hillary, and some of the other team members to London. It was a long flight, but Pem Pem and Nima were entertained by Hillary, who teased them mercilessly and to their great amusement. En route they stopped at Zurich, and Tenzing was overwhelmed to see his Swiss friends amassed at the airport to meet him. Lambert, wearing his red scarf, gave Tenzing a great bear hug and congratulated them all on their success. Later Tenzing recalled the look in Lambert's eyes on that day; he knew his friend's thoughts were on what might have been had the weather on Everest been more kind in 1952, even as he joined in the joyful spirit of the occasion. Also at the airport was Annelies Sutter, who had become such a good friend of Tenzing during their 1947 Garhwal expedition and was to remain so until his death.

Approaching London, John Hunt asked Tenzing if he minded letting Hunt leave the plane first with his ice ax, Union Jack attached, held aloft. Tenzing, of course, did not mind at all, and was in fact delighted that the British team members might at last receive the respect they deserved. To him it seemed a welcome opportunity to recover a little anonymity, but Tenzing, Ang Lhamu, Pem Pem, and Nima became an instant attraction to the British press and public. After all, it was not every day that Sherpas in their traditional dress arrived at London's airport. Though Tenzing was attired in Nehru's formal wear, Ang Lhamu and the girls still wore the *bakus* they had donned on leaving Darjeeling for Kathmandu. A shopping spree was soon arranged for them by their hosts at the Indian Services Club.

London was a strange and wondrous experience for Ang Lhamu and the girls, and with much of the attention shifted to the British climbers, Tenzing found it more manageable and far less stressful than those first frenzied days in Kathmandu and Delhi. Hunt and Wylie were there to guide him through the huge and foreign city, and he was particularly delighted to meet his old climbing friends, especially Eric Shipton.

Pem Pem and Nima would later recall those few days in England with wonder: the receptions, the media sessions, the photo shoots, and above all the gala affairs arranged by Buckingham Palace to honor the team. The girls' most memorable experience was meeting Her Majesty Queen Elizabeth II, whose English greetings Wylie happily translated for them. When the queen asked Ang Lhamu what she did on the day she received the great news of her husband's success, Ang Lhamu replied that she went to the market to buy something special for him. The queen asked what that was, and Ang Lhamu replied that she had bought a large can of condensed milk. The queen smiled and commended her on such a sensible selection.

The queen also took the girls on a short tour of Buckingham Palace. They were overcome by Prince Charles and Princess Anne's playroom, and gazed in wonder at a child-sized motorcar the royal youngsters had been given. My mother, who had studied some English history at school, was fascinated by Henry VIII and asked the queen for a look at his portrait, which was duly located. Then, to the queen's great amusement, she asked to see portraits of all eight wives.

The garden parties, dinners, and grand receptions were fairy-tale experiences for Tenzing and his family, but so far removed from their experience as not to seem real. Though they attended and participated under the guidance of Hunt and Wylie, they had little idea what was actually going on. When they attended the knighthood ceremonies for Hunt and Hillary, Ang Lhamu and the girls gasped in horror as the queen raised the royal sword above the bowed heads of the two men, certain the men were about to be killed. Yet they soon began to grasp and savor the extraordinary circumstances in which they found themselves. My mother remembers how she and her sister perched atop the staircase above the grand ballroom in Gloucester House, where their parents were attending a magnificent formal reception in honor of the expedition. Secreted behind palms and balustrades, they saw the most fabulous array of ball gowns, fine jewelry and elegant people, and among them the dark, handsome face of their father and the familiar, rotund figure of their mother. They were especially fascinated and amused by the sight of all the ladies wearing elbow-length gloves, something they had never seen or heard of before.

From London, Tenzing and his family returned to Switzerland for two weeks at the invitation of the Swiss Foundation for Alpine Research, of which Ernst Feuz, one of Tenzing's climbing colleagues

Maria Feuz greets Tenzing at Zurich airport, July 1953.

from Garhwal, was secretary. Ernst and his wife, Maria, planned their
entire stay in Switzerland, and soon the cool, mountain air and the company of old friends rejuvenated them. They visited Rosenlaui, where a
local alpine guide, Arnold Glatthard, had established Switzerland's first
School for Alpine Guides in 1940. There Tenzing climbed some fine
peaks, including the Jungfrau, on which he joined his old friend Lambert, the two making a summit together at last. On the day before

Above: Tenzing Norgay's family in Switzerland, 1953. (L to R) Nima, Tenzing, Ang Lhamu, Pem Pem. Below: Swiss Alpine guide Arnold Glatthard and Tenzing, Rosenlaui, 1953.

Tenzing and Lambert, Murën, Switzerland, 1954. This photo shows Lambert's heavily modified footwear.

Tenzing in his element, climbing Jungfrau, Switzerland.

Tenzing and Lambert climbing together again, Swiss Alps, 1954.

Tenzing and his family departed for India, the Feuzes hosted a reception for them at the Swiss Foundation in Zurich. There they were joined by Dr. B. C. Roy, Chief Minister for West Bengal, who was in Zurich for treatment of an eye problem. Tenzing, Roy, Carl Weber (president of the Swiss Foundation), and Ernst Feuz had a long discussion about the establishment of a climbing school in Darjeeling, an idea that had originally been advanced by Ravi Mitra and to which Roy was receptive. The Swiss were eager to help and suggested Arnold Glatthard as the ideal candidate to plan and program the school with Tenzing and the Indian and West Bengal governments. The plan they roughed out was for Glatthard to go to Darjeeling in October to select a site for the school and a mountain area suitable for novice climbing, then for Tenzing to return to Switzerland in the summer of 1954 to train with Glatthard for three months as a climbing instructor. After that, six top climbing Sherpas—Ang Tharkay, Gyalzen Mikchen, Da Namgyal, Ang Temba, Nawang Gombu, and Topgay—would follow to begin their training under Tenzing and Glatthard as staff for the school.

My grandfather and his family left Zurich for home full of optimism and plans for the wonderful future that lay ahead. In India, Nehru assured him that his position of director of field training at the school was a "job for life," and Tenzing trusted Nehru implicitly in this, as he would in all things. In the autumn of 1954, Panditji officially opened the Himalayan Mountaineering Institute (HMI), which is still in operation and turning out first-class mountaineers.

Throughout the rest of 1953 and into 1954, Tenzing traveled the length and breadth of India. In Madras he received a tumultuous welcome and was embarrassed that he could not thank the crowds in Tamil, the regional tongue. Through Mitra he found someone to teach him a phrase of thanks in Tamil, then won over a crowd of fifty thousand people with his effort. The man of the mountains was doing his best to become a modern public figure. It had to be daunting, climbing an Everest of worldly sophistication while trying not to lose sight of base camp, and realizing as he climbed that he was carrying the weight of Sherpa aspirations on his back.

He was acutely aware of the public responsibilities his new fame thrust upon him. On a visit to Delhi with Mitra in 1954, Tenzing was again a guest of Nehru at Rashtrapati Bhavan. One morning Nehru's

The opening of the Himalayan Mountaineering Institute, Darjeeling, 1954. Back row (L to R): Pem Pem, Rajiv Ghandi, Indira Ghandi, Sonam Doma, Ang Lhamu, Sri Jawaharlal Nehru, Tenzing, Sona Doma (Tenzing's sister), Thakchey (Tenzing's sister). Front row (L to R): Nawang Gombu, Sanjay Gandhi, Nima, Topgay.

secretary asked him, "What are you planning to do today, Mr. Tenzing? If you are free you may like to borrow Indira Gandhi's car, as she is not using it. You could drive to Agra and see the Taj Mahal." Mitra was keen to accept, but Tenzing declined the offer at once, explaining that he had seen coming and going from Panditji's house many people who were obviously working hard, and he did not want Panditji to think he had come to Delhi for idle pleasure. Later, when Ang Lhamu and Mitra tried to drag him to a nearby cinema to watch Hindi movies, Tenzing again refused, saying that while he was at the prime minister's house he must always be available for visitors. Ang Lhamu, a devoted Hindi film buff, went without him.

There would be other occasions for Tenzing and his family to sit at the prime minister's breakfast table, taking tea and toast. Tenzing's dignity, humility, and devotion to duty probably cemented his friendship with Nehru—a friendship as complicated as it was improbable. Tenzing was in awe of Nehru, yet regarded him more as a staunch ally

Tenzing, photographed in a Darjeeling studio with various medals.

than a powerful one. He knew little of Indian politics but was stead-fastly determined not to offend the prime minister or to misuse their friendship.

Ravi Mitra still recalls a time in 1954 when Tenzing and Ang Lhamu visited Delhi en route from the Punjab region of northwest India. Ten-zing had not informed Nehru of his flight arrangements, but Panditji learned of his arrival time and sent a car to the airport to collect the pair and bring them as guests to Rashtrapati Bhavan. It was high summer, and the heat of the Delhi plains left Tenzing prone on his bed in an upstairs bedroom. As Ang Lhamu desperately tried to ease his distress with wet towels, Nehru and his daughter Indira paused at the door. Seeing that the bed was in a corner far from the *punkah* (fan), Nehru beckoned Indira to help, and the two pulled the bed with Tenzing on it across the room and into the cooling air, then brought him iced water and cold packs until he was resting comfortably again. Nehru could have summoned servants to perform such tasks, but he seemed to want to "father" Tenzing, and Tenzing came to think of him almost as a father. He took Nehru's advice in all things to heart, and followed it to the letter.

Tenzing received some money as gifts from various state govern-ments and organizations during formal visits in the months after Ever-est, but it was not enough to pay for a new, larger home in Darjeeling, which his family needed. While wanting to help, Nehru felt that Ten-zing's pride would be wounded if the Indian government bought him a house outright. Instead, Nehru wrote a letter to Mr. Roy, the Chief Minister of West Bengal, asking him to help Tenzing raise funds. The newspaper campaign that Roy mounted elicited a strong response, and eventually Tenzing was able to purchase a fine home in Darjeeling with views to the breathtakingly beautiful Kanchenjunga. He named the house *Ghang-La*, after the sacred monastery of his birthplace in Tibet, and Panditji and his family—including Indira, Rajiv, and Sanjay Gandhi—attended the house blessing.

In Darjeeling, as the Tenzing family settled into their new home, Ang Lhamu was in her element. She filled the house with gifts and mementos they had accumulated since Tenzing's Everest triumph, turn-ing the large, angular building into a warm and welcoming home in which she, Tenzing, the girls, and an increasing assortment of relatives

Above: Ghang-La, the Tenzing family home in Darjeeling (taken in 2000). Right: A proud Tenzing standing with his family at Ghang-La, 1955.

could begin their new life. Tenzing was happy. The bewilderment of those heady first few months passed, and gradually he grew more comfortable with the position he now realized he held in his community and the world at large. As James Ramsey Ullman, who helped Tenzing write his autobiography *Tiger of the Snows*, noted in the book's introduction:

> His new home in Darjeeling hums with life. Presiding over it is his wife Ang Lhamu, a round and animated lady with a shrewd eye and a girlish giggle. Completing the cast are two daughters, two nieces, an assortment of sisters, cousins, brothers-in-law and cousins of brothers-in-law plus a variety of semi-identified visitors (and cousins of visitors) who wander in and out at will. Dogs are everywhere. Scrapbooks, souvenirs and photographs clutter the tables and walls. From upstairs, as likely as not, where a lama brother-in-law is in charge of the Buddhist prayer room comes the sound of chanting and a tinkling bell. And downstairs, whatever the time of day, it is a safe bet that tea is being served. In the centre of it all is Tenzing himself—busy, cordial, perhaps a little confused as to just what is going on; talking, it often seems, in several languages simultaneously. His dark eyes glow. His teeth are strong and white. You are very conscious of his teeth because he smiles so much.

An endless stream of strangers came to meet Tenzing: foreign journalists, political dignitaries, autograph seekers, and, on some occasions, local poor who in all innocence believed him to be a deity. When the latter prostrated themselves before him, his great embarrassment was a source of considerable mirth to his family. Even the enigmatic stars of Hindi films were guests in their home (generally at Ang Lhamu's invitation!), and crowds would gather outside Ghang-La to catch a glimpse of stars such as Shashi Kapoor, a heartthrob of the Indian silver screen, Jeevan, and Dilip Kumar. Tenzing welcomed them all, always giving of his time, and Ang Lhamu always prepared home-cooked food. No one was ever turned away from Ghang-La.

The publication of *Tiger of the Snows* in 1955 fulfilled part of Tenzing's contract with United Press, signed the moment he arrived in Kathmandu at the start of the 1953 expedition, in which he agreed to a series of interview-articles as the expedition unfolded. The copyright on all the photographs, articles, and books from the British team members belonged by prior agreement to the Royal Geographical Society, but Tenzing was not a part of that arrangement and was not bound by its restrictions. Tenzing earned only a modest amount from sales of his book, but it gave the world a chance to know him as a man, and not the "conquering" Everest hero.

Tenzing still loved to climb and had lost none of his strength and skill. Dorjee Lhatoo, a family member and later an instructor at HMI, remembers him at the age of forty-eight climbing with far greater ease and strength than most of his young Sherpa students. By the mid-1950s, however, his commitments at HMI and abroad prevented him from joining large-scale expeditions. He was content to climb in Sikkim and sometimes in Nepal, and his occasional trips to Switzerland and Britain provided opportunities to join old friends for some challenging fun on less technical European peaks such as Mt. Blanc and Jungfrau. And, of course, there were his forays into the hills around Thamey in search of the elusive yeti!

In the winter of 1954–55, Grandfather took my mother and Nima back to Thamey to visit their family. They left Darjeeling on foot on Christmas Eve and made the long trek up the vast Arun Valley from southern Nepal, over the passes of the middle foothills and into the Khumbu. The girls were made to carry their own packs, for Tenzing was determined that his two young daughters not forget their Sherpa roots. After a day of complaining and laboring, however, the girls were finally relieved of their loads, Tenzing taking Pem Pem's and another Tenzing, the eldest son of the great Ang Tharkay, taking Nima's. From that moment, Tenzing knew their lives would be different from his. My mother did inherit her father's passion for the mountains, however, and in 1959, at the age of twenty, she seized the chance to join the International Women's Expedition to Cho Oyu. (The expedition ended after two European climbers and Sherpa Ang Norbu were killed in an avalanche at Camp IV and Sherpa Tsewang was lost at Camp III.)

After his Everest success Tenzing was approached by many relatives, both close and distant, for help and support. He could not turn them away, for he too had been born into poverty and insecurity, and it was his duty to help when he could. He and Ang Lhamu were forever feeding, housing, and sorting out the problems of a variety of family members, some of whom had questionable claims on family links but were welcomed all the same. Tenzing also felt a responsibility to make the lives of Sherpa climbers a little more secure, so in 1954 he helped establish the Sherpa Climbers' Association in Darjeeling (now known as the Sherpa Buddhist Association). Its roles were to keep a complete record of all Sherpa climbers, ensure that all their children were offered a free basic mountaineering course at the Himalayan Mountaineering Institute, and provide a convenient way for foreign climbers to contact Sherpas for expedition work. In the latter respect it would in a way replace the Himalayan Club, even as Kathmandu was replacing Darjeeling as the primary staging point for eastern Himalayan expeditions.

When not traveling abroad, Tenzing was absorbed in his work at HMI. The mid- and late-1950s led him into an existence beyond his dreams: a secure job that paid a Sherpa born to poverty comparatively well, a fine home to which he returned almost every evening, and a life at which he excelled in his beloved mountains. His daughters were educated at Loreto Convent, one of Darjeeling's premier schools for girls. In 1959, Pem Pem married a Tibetan from an aristocratic family. Nima married a Filipino graphic designer and moved abroad, and both daughters settled happily with their own families. Tenzing had been honored by the world and, more important to him, by his own people, and could walk the cobbled roads and broad promenades of Darjeeling in his knickers, argyle socks, and tweed hat as if he were royalty. He had come a long, long way from his harsh beginnings in remote Tibet. Acclaim and notoriety did not seem to go to his head; despite the personal influence he wielded at HMI and in Darjeeling generally, he kept his feet firmly planted on the ground.

Dorjee Lhatoo recalls an incident from this time that reveals a man at once proud and yielding. Lhatoo and Tenzing had a rather serious disagreement over certain family matters and did not speak to each other for some time. Such was their animosity that neither man would work at HMI when the other was there. Eventually it became obvious that someone would have to swallow his pride and offer an olive branch, and it fell on the younger of the two to make the first move. Reluctantly, and only under the determined prompting of Tenzing's nephew, Nawang Gombu, Lhatoo walked to Ghang-La to offer a *kada* as a token of his "surrender" and apology. When one disputant places this white silk Buddhist scarf around the neck of the other, all is forgiven and forgotten. It is a beautiful custom, for as hard as forgiving can be, forgetting is even harder. Lhatoo made it to the door and Tenzing met him there, standing expectantly with head slightly bowed to receive the *kada* in Lhatoo's hands. But Lhatoo's pride and stubbornness still held him back from making the final submissive gesture. In the end Tenzing sighed heavily, took the *kada* from Lhatoo, placed it about his own neck, and gave Lhatoo a cursory hug of acceptance. The matter was over; both sides were appeased.

Tenzing was content in all matters but one. He adored his girls, but since the death of his son, Nima Dorje, in 1939, he had longed for another son to carry on his lineage. His marriage to Ang Lhamu had brought him happiness, support, and the peace and security of a long-standing friendship, but it did not bring children, and in particular it did not bring a son. With his daughters at home to occupy him the longing was muted, but as they grew to adulthood, married, and moved out of the house with families of their own, it became ever more intense. The taking of a second wife while the first is still living is uncommon but not unknown in Sherpa culture, and not unusual in many surrounding Eastern cultures. In the early 1960s, while Tenzing was working at the HMI training camp in Dzongri, in Western Sikkim, he met a young Sherpani from Chanakpa, a small village just above Thamey Teng in the Khumbu, whose family had employed him in their fields during his youth. Her name was Daku, and she, like so many other Sherpas from Nepal, was working as field staff for the training camp. She was pretty, strong, and vivacious, and soon a passionate relationship developed between her and the much older Tenzing. Eventually Tenzing decided to bring her into his home in Darjeeling.

Though deeply saddened, Ang Lhamu knew how desperately her husband wanted a son. She knew also that her health was failing—she had begun a long battle with lung cancer—and she knew that with his two daughters married and beginning their own families, Tenzing would need a wife and companion to care for him and his home. Thus, with Ang Lhamu's selfless forbearance, Daku settled into Ghang-La and increasingly assumed the role of mistress of the house, with all its associated tasks and responsibilities.

On 10 December 1962, Daku gave birth to their first son, Norbu.

(L to R) Pem Pem, Tenzing, Daku, and son Norbu, Darjeeling.

Tenzing doted on Norbu and was deeply in love with Daku, who was now managing his affairs with energy and zest. Ang Lhamu, meanwhile, battled her illness at home, with support from her girls and family in Darjeeling, as long as she could, with frequent hospital stays. But at midnight, 30 November 1964, just two hours after my mother had given birth to me, Ang Lhamu passed away. Her death was a terrible loss to the family and to all who had known her. Her laughter, her joy, and her seemingly endless compassion are still fondly remembered in Darjeeling.

Above: The children of Tenzing and Daku (L to R): Norbu, Jamling, Deki, and Dhamey (1973). Below: Tenzing instructing students at HMI. This photo was taken toward the end of his climbing career.

She was a tower of strength during both good times and bad in her husband's life, and she maintained the equilibrium of our family when it could so easily have been lost in the heady days and years after Everest.

Tenzing and Daku went on to have three more children: a second son, Jamling, in 1965; a daughter, Deki, in 1966; and a third son, Dhamey, in 1969. Tenzing continued at the Himalayan Mountaineering Institute as director of field training until 1976 when, four years past the Indian government mandatory retirement age of fifty-eight, he was told he must take his leave. He was devastated. He had had his disagreements with HMI, mainly over his meager salary, which had increased little from when he was first appointed over two decades earlier, but he had always assumed his position was, as Nehru had promised, for life. Everest had brought him many advantages, but substantial disposable income was not one of them. Without his post and with only a small lump sum retirement benefit, he was without income and had a young family to support.

He tried to convince the director of HMI to retain him, reminding him of Nehru's promise of a lifelong job. But Nehru had died in 1964, and there was nothing in writing to confirm their verbal agreement. In accepting the Indian government's enticements to remain in India—citizenship, a new home, and lifetime employment—Tenzing had trusted that whatever Nehru agreed to was unconditional. He had turned down offers from the Nepalis, the Swiss, the Americans, and others over the years to cast his lot with India, and now it seemed that his loyalty was not to be repaid. He was not alone in his indignation. Many in India supported him, and there was widespread public condemnation of this strict, unyielding interpretation of India's civil service regulations. Surely Tenzing was an exception, they argued. Eventually the authorities capitulated and Tenzing was retained by HMI as an advisor, a post currently held by Tenzing's nephew, Nawang Gombu. Tenzing's salary remained low, but his future was at least financially secure.

The episode, however, extinguished his enthusiasm for HMI and his job. His heart was no longer in his work, and since his advisory duties did not require him to attend HMI every day, he became more and more removed. This twilight end to a wonderful career caused him deep sadness that bordered at times on depression. He had been sidelined by an institution he had helped to build. He had always worked, always been busy and full of energy and enthusiasm, and now found time weighing heavy on his hands. Advancing years were slowing him, but he still had a lot to offer and desperately needed useful work to rekindle his inner flame. He needed a renewed purpose.

In 1977, Lars Eric Lindblad, a successful tour operator, came to Darjeeling intent on adding a Himalayan trek to his portfolio of tours. Meeting Tenzing, Lindblad asked him how much money he earned. When Tenzing told him, Lindblad replied, "I can help you make that in one day!" So it was that Lindblad helped Tenzing establish a trekking and touring company in Darjeeling and use himself as the promotional centerpiece for his tours. It was lucrative and agreeable work for Tenzing, and he found in it the new spark that he had been seeking.

With Daku's support and hard work, he handled the trek and tour groups that Lindblad sent to him and occasionally accompanied Lindblad's "mainstream" tours, mostly cruises, as tour leader. On one occasion they even journeyed to Antarctica. My grandfather's friends and family in Darjeeling saw a change in him overnight. He was busy, he was mixing once more with Westerners, which he thoroughly enjoyed, and he was building a future for his young children. He was also finally able to build some wealth. Lindblad was a master marketer and Tenzing was a travel promoter's dream, yet Lindblad's involvement in Tenzing's life went well beyond mere business. This generous man later took Tenzing's children under his wing and arranged for their ongoing education and future in the United States. He opened up a new world for Tenzing and his family.

All who knew my grandfather wish that the story of this great man could have had a happy ending, but this was not to be the case. Despite his new business, prosperity, and purpose, Tenzing grew increasingly disillusioned and depressed in later life. I have often tried to understand how this could have happened to a man who by hard work, intelligence, and the nurturing of a dream had elevated himself from the life of a feudal vassal to that of an explorer, mountaineer, much-traveled public figure, businessman, and revered figurehead to his people—and this in one lifetime. It has been said that he drank too much in his later years, but those who knew him well, in Darjeeling and abroad, feel that this was simply a symptom of a deeper malaise. Perhaps he had grown too old for touring, and the long layovers between trips, alone in foreign

Hillary and Tenzing reunited at HMI.

Tenzing, Hillary, and George Lowe, Lhasa, Tibet, 1981.

cities, were depressing and isolating. In 1981 he was in Lhasa, having completed a tour, with a one-month wait for the next group. Sir Edmund Hillary and George Lowe also happened to be there, and as good luck would have it they met and spent an evening together. Lowe later recalled that Tenzing looked unwell and unhappy, and when pressed, opened up to his old comrade Hillary. He still carried the pain of his forced retirement from HMI and seemed unable to purge this resentment and anger. He was lonely in Lhasa. He was sixty-seven, knew no one, and would rather have been at home. Both Hillary and Lowe did their best to reassure him that he had good friends who were always with him in spirit, if not in person.

Lord Hunt would also recall meeting Tenzing by chance in China when both were there on business, Hunt with a delegation and Tenzing with a tour group. Hunt had always had great affection for Tenzing, and Tenzing a deep fondness for his old leader. They were delighted to see each other and managed to spend some time together. Again Tenzing poured out his heart. He talked of his loneliness and his inability to find a middle line through life. He wanted, indeed needed, his touring business, yet it wore him down physically and spiritually. At home, life with Daku was increasingly sad. Tenzing intimated that their age difference had become an issue. He was possessive of Daku and could not accept that she wanted a life of her own, one that now often excluded him. Hunt could only listen, and in an interview with the BBC in 1997, he recalled this meeting with Tenzing with sadness.

In 1985 Tenzing's health began to fail, and he was hospitalized in Delhi with what appeared to be pneumonia. While there he was visited regularly by Hillary, who was then stationed in the hot and dusty Indian capital as New Zealand High Commissioner to India. Tenzing's English was good by then, and the two old climbing companions developed a deeper friendship than they had ever had before, conversing and reminiscing with an ease that had been impossible thirty-two years earlier. Hillary was a fine confidant, and the two talked of the old days of Everest and their post-1953 experiences. Tenzing of course knew of Hillary's work in Solu Khumbu through the Himalayan Trust, and like the world at large was in awe of what the trust had achieved for Sherpa communities. Tenzing expressed his regret at not having done more for his own people, but Hillary told him that the example he had set would

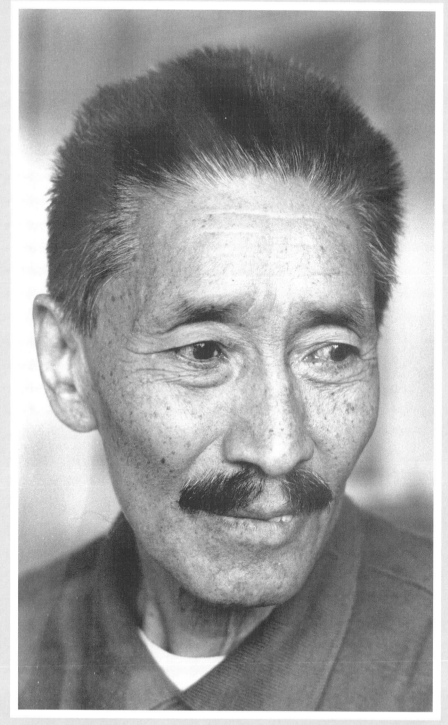

Tenzing in Switzerland, November 1985, six months before his death.

inspire Sherpas for generations to come. He had been a wonderful sirdar, a fine mountaineer, and a good father and husband. He had always worked hard: on expeditions, at HMI, and in his travel business. He had much to be proud of. Hillary's words and the cementing of their old friendship were a great comfort to Tenzing. There was a symmetry in the reappearance at his nadir—sick, lonely, and deeply depressed in a hospital bed far from home—of the man who had stood beside him at his zenith. It closed a circle, and Tenzing would carry the warmth of that chance renewal until his death a year later.

In November 1985 he made one last journey to Switzerland. The Lamberts and Annelies Sutter were taken aback at the sight of him; he was gaunt, and his eyes had lost their distinctive sparkle. Even his famous smile had faded, and this worried them most of all. They had known this man for more than thirty years, and in that time had never seen him looking so lost and alone. Maria Feuz, another dear friend, arranged for him to have a complete medical checkup, but nothing untoward was found. His troubles, it seemed, were in his mind and heart.

At the Lamberts' home in Geneva, Tenzing had long discussions with Annette about his unhappiness and loneliness. On tour he was with strangers, and when he was home his children were all away in the United States and Daku was rarely around. He yearned for the days when Ghang-La was abuzz with friends and family and when his life had fullness and purpose. Much as Raymond and Annette loved Tenzing, there was little they could do to help him except allow him to vent. They urged him to make peace with himself and his world as it now was. He was too old to make drastic changes and had earned the right to rest on his laurels.

After bidding farewell to the Lamberts, Tenzing stayed in Zurich one last time with Annelies Sutter. Sutter recalls feeling that Tenzing knew his end was near, and she believes, like others, that he would have lived longer had he been happier. When they parted at the Zurich airport he hugged her warmly, seemingly reluctant to let go, as if aware this would be their last meeting.

Back in Darjeeling he resumed his daily routine: early morning walks to visit my mother, Pem Pem, in our home in Toong Soong, strolls to Chowrasta to meet old friends and watch the world go by, and evenings at home at Ghang-La. He was abidingly interested in the progress of his four youngest children and would relay their achievements to all he met. His greatest joy was their visits home from the United States, visits that helped sustain him in his final years. His two eldest daughters were, of course, always there for him, although Nima had settled abroad and was able to visit him only occasionally. He came to rely heavily on my mother. She worked at St. Paul's Anglican School for Boys as matron of the Primary Wing, but would spend her Tuesdays off with him at Ghang-La, where they would chat, drink tea, and reminisce. Nights alone in his home were hard, and he would call Pem Pem on the phone, distraught, at any hour, and she would have to go and calm his fears and soothe his distress.

One Sunday they spent excitedly planning a trip to the grave of Dawa Phuti, Tenzing's first wife and the mother of Pem Pem and Nima. Tenzing had long wanted to take Pem Pem back to visit the grave in Chitral, and they planned the trip for later in the spring.

Daku arrived back in Darjeeling the following Tuesday afternoon. Then on Friday morning, 9 May 1986, at 4 A.M., my mother received an urgent summons from Ghang-La: her father was gravely ill and near death. She rushed up the hill but was greeted at the gate by Tenzing's doctor with the news that my grandfather had just passed away. She was shattered. Death had seemed far away for the man who was planning a journey, and Pem Pem was not prepared. No one was.

The cremation took place at HMI in full Sherpa tradition, with Norbu, Tenzing's eldest son, presiding. Sir Edmund Hillary was the only foreigner present, for it was a time of great political tension in Darjeeling, with demands for Gorkhaland (a separate Nepali state within India) in full swing and an absolute curfew in effect. Hillary had to use all his influence as "Hillary Sahib" and New Zealand High Commissioner to force a way through the police barriers and up the hill roads from the Indian plains. Tenzing's final journey was undertaken amidst family and friends in the shadows of his beloved Himalaya.

Time heals and redeems, and the Tenzing we remember is the man atop his Chomolungma, the man who battled Everest's wildest weather with Lambert, the father who doted on his children, the instructor who taught so many young Sherpas to climb, the man with the famous smile that dazzled the world.

Now he is gone. Yet in the hearts and minds of all who love Everest and her great history, Tenzing Norgay Sherpa lives on. His life celebrated his people and his beloved mountains, and he personified the power of mind and spirit. He knew what it was like to savor life's greatest pleasures: family, good friends, and the sheer joy of having a dream, then living it.

Though he didn't know it at the time, Tenzing's pure and innocent achievement on Everest recharted the future of his Sherpa people. Perhaps it was simply fate that placed him on that successful summit team, or perhaps it was his own quiet determination and calm resolve to climb the mountain on his record seventh attempt. With this one extraordinary achievement he took his people from a life of isolation and obscurity to international renown and acclaim—a leap of decades, even generations, in one day. It may be that the leap was too great and weighed too heavily on this man of the mountains, and in his final years the strain of holding the feat together in his mind overcame him. Or perhaps the road was simply too long and the burden too heavy for one who, in a shy and private corner of his heart, still craved the simple life of a yak herder. He may have blamed himself for not doing more for his people, but we do not judge him as harshly as he judged himself. As Dorjee Lhatoo has said, "How could Tenzing do more for others? He did not do enough for himself." The illiterate man of the mountains was never meant to be a promoter or politician or administrator. He could, however, be an inspiration, and indeed he was one.

Hillary was right. Tenzing had much to be proud of. He still stands as a symbol of the Sherpas—a man of dignity and grace whose legacy is a remarkable people adapting their rich traditions and culture to the modern world.

CHAPTER 8

MY QUEST
FOR EVEREST

•

ERY EARLY IN THE MORNING my grandfather—*Gaga*—used to come down to my family's house in Toong Soong in Darjeeling and call out for us all to get up out of bed and come and take tea with him. As a boy, I liked being with this old man in his knickers and tweed cap. He was full of energy and everyone seemed to know him. But my hero was Tenzing, the great Sherpa of Everest. I had heard much of Everest in my early years, and it was always a magical word for me. My mother says that from the time I could walk and run I would try to climb anything that even faintly resembled a mountain peak, then stand on top with my arm held aloft, declaring myself to be Tenzing of Everest. Given my heritage, then irrelevant to me, this must have amused my relatives, including the old man himself. Not until my teen years did I realize that my gaga, who took us for our

Tenzing Norgay with a young Tashi Tenzing, Darjeeling, 1965.

morning walks and sat in our tiny kitchen drinking tea, was in fact the great Tenzing himself!

Throughout my childhood and youth I came to see that in many ways we were very much a like: full of energy, always restless in the confines of a town or house, and happiest and most fulfilled when in the high mountains. Above all there was between us the bond of Everest. Even after he had climbed to its summit, the mountain continued to fascinate him, as it has me. I remember clearly how his expression changed when he spoke, not of the politics or even of his Everest summit, but of the mountain itself. In his voice you could feel the wind of the South Col and sense the fear of the perilous Khumbu Icefall. His face beamed when he spoke of the great Sherpas—Ang Tharkay, Da Namgyal, Dawa Tenzing. I dreamed of following in the footsteps of these legends. In art class at St. Paul's Anglican School for Boys, my classmates painted flowers, lakes, and animals; I painted Everest.

My dream of Everest did not cause concern or fear in my family. The mountain is one of us, and we all know and love her well. Indeed, both my parents were climbers: my mother was a member of the 1959 International Women's Expedition to 8,153-meter Cho Oyu, led by Madame Kogan of France, and my father had climbed many Himalayan peaks, including Nanda Devi. Mountaineering was a known quantity to them, and they accepted its risks. Moreover, I was a strong athlete at school and college and a keen participant in my mountaineering courses at the Himalayan Mountaineering Institute (HMI) in Darjeeling. When I completed the instructor's course at HMI, my final evaluation read, "Tashi is in a class of his own." This praise from world-class instructors was gratifying, but mountaineering was second nature to me, and I loved it: there would be no other way for me. My passion, my destiny, were the mountains.

As soon as I graduated with an arts degree from the University of Delhi in 1987, I headed for Nepal to work as a trekking (hiking) and mountaineering guide. In this way I could earn a living, be in the mountains, and have the opportunity to climb when time permitted. I loved the life, but every trek to Everest fueled my desire to climb to the top. I would like to say that I waited patiently for my time to attempt the summit, but the wait seemed interminable and I grew more determined and restless with each passing year.

Team members of the 1959 International Women's Expedition to Cho Oyu. Nina and Pem Pem are standing in the back row, fifth and seventh from the left, respectively.

In Nepal I met an Australian, Judy Pyne, who was also working as a trekking guide. She was unlike other Western women I had met. Because her passion for the Himalaya was deep and sincere, she learned as much as she could about my culture and understood my relationship with the mountains. My climbing did not alarm or frighten her: most of her friends were guides or climbers, and she understood the mountaineering world.

We had much more in common than I could ever have imagined—a passion for the mountains and Himalayan culture, but also a deep sense of family and the importance of a solid and long-lasting home base. I had seen many relationships between my people and Westerners dissolve as quickly as they had been born, but with Judy I felt that it would be different. She accepted—in fact admired—our ways. Although not a Buddhist, she empathized with our beliefs and attitudes toward life, duty, reincarnation, and family roles and values. She, more than I, had bridged the cultural gap between our traditions, and I learned a great deal from her. My mother—as the groom's mother a crucial player in the selection of a wife—was happy with my choice and, despite some reservations about the problems Judy and I might face, gave the union her blessing. Judy's parents had long accepted that the Himalaya had found a permanent home in her heart, and that acceptance led naturally to their acceptance of our marriage plans.

A change in Nepalese regulations regarding foreigners living and working there meant that, after a decade in Nepal, Judy had to leave the country. She decided to return to Australia, where she was able to work as the manager of Nepalese trekking programs for a large adventure travel company, which still kept her closely involved in Himalayan trekking and mountaineering. After working as a guide in Nepal for three years, I was faced with the choice of staying on in Nepal alone or following Judy to Australia. Though leaving Nepal was a wrench—it was the home of my heart and I had always been happiest in its mountains—I knew also that Judy would help me follow my dream and that life abroad would hold many wonderful new experiences and opportunities for me. We settled in Sydney, marrying the following year on a day ordained by my family lama in Darjeeling for its auspiciousness.

A year later our first child was born, a son named by our lamas, in the traditional Sherpa custom, Pasang Gyalpo, meaning "Friday-born king." He is a gentle child with a deeply ingrained empathy for all creatures on earth, particularly creatures of the ocean. When he was very young many Sherpa people said that they felt sure he was a very high Buddhist reincarnation since his heart was full of compassion and without malice. At the age of five he was asked to formally receive His Holiness The Dalai Lama when he arrived in Sydney in 1996 to perform a *Kalachakra* ceremony, which brings blessing and spiritual good fortune, for all Australians. This gesture meant a great deal to my people and in particular to my family, because His Holiness had been a dear friend of my grandfather and had visited the family home in Darjeeling. Now he was being welcomed to our new home by Tenzing's great-grandson. Such events hold great significance in our Sherpa culture, and I was very proud.

✸

The fortieth anniversary of my grandfather's 1953 ascent of Everest with the British would be in 1993, which seemed the perfect time for my own attempt on Everest. Now an Australian citizen, I decided to climb as an Australian to advance the fledgling group of Australian Everest climbers. The funds needed to field an expedition, however, are great; the Everest peak royalty alone was then $10,000 U.S. Then there were the many other expenses; airfares, transportation, oxygen, cargo, insurance, porters, food, equipment. How could I raise so much money? Judy was completely supportive—she knew too well what Everest meant to me—so we decided to aim for a 1993 pre-monsoon expedition, commencing planning in 1991.

Our first task, which held great significance for me, was to ask Lord Hunt, leader of the 1953 British team, to be the patron—a nominal but respectful designation—of my expedition in the name of my grandfather. I received a prompt and warm letter of assent, expressing his honor and absolute delight. Another gesture of support from England came just as we were due to depart Australia for Nepal, a letter from Her Majesty Queen Elizabeth II, wishing me a safe and successful expedition. The spirit of 1953 was truly with me on this anniversary Everest attempt.

Fund-raising for climbing expeditions is a daunting task, especially in a country like Australia where mountaineering is not a high-profile sport, as it is in Switzerland, Germany, and Britain. The hundreds of letters we sent seemed to fall on deaf ears, and the entire plan looked doomed until the evening a fax came through from Paul Stuber, who had known my grandfather and whose company, Rolex, had sponsored Tenzing throughout his climbing career. Rolex's generous contribution jump-started our fund-raising and, more importantly, gave us the hope to continue.

Soon other sponsors queued up. Thai Airways International offered to sponsor our airfares, and Mountain Designs kicked in equipment. Clarks, an Australian sink manufacturer, promised to help on the condition that I take one of their stainless steel sinks with me to Everest! If they were prepared to support me, then I was ready to do the same for them, so we struck an agreement and the sink was duly packed and shipped.

All of this was wonderful, of course, but I still needed to raise the remaining two thirds of the expedition funds, basically what was needed to cover land costs in Nepal. At last, in January 1993, Phillipa Saxton and

Tashi Tenzing enjoys an easy climb in Nepal.

Mike Ferris—a Sydney couple who had attended one of the many slide shows I gave to raise awareness of and funding for my climb—stepped forward to help us raise money. They phoned almost every company in the country, always with an angle and an idea that might appeal to corporate Australia. Cadbury's offered up chocolate, Uncle Toby's supplied muesli bars and snacks, and Motorola provided radiophones—all gratefully accepted, but we were still without the urgently needed cash. Then at the eleventh hour Phillipa, inspired, convinced Lipton's Teas to support this son of Darjeeling—and so the expedition would finally become a reality! After our team had left for Nepal, Hyundai Australia also came forward with a cash bonus.

This expedition would not be on the scale of the 1953 attempt, but the $80,000 U.S. we raised would cover basic costs and fees. Our bare-bones budget meant that we had to forgo hiring Sherpa porters and purchasing insurance for team members. Normally an expedition would have four to five climbers, three to four climbing Sherpas (nearly one for each climber), and about twenty Sherpa porters to carry loads in to Base Camp. We would ultimately have seven climbers and five Base Camp staff (three were kitchen staff), but no porter support. This meant the team would carry their own loads, including up the icefall and to the high camps. The additional carrying trips would tax the climbing strength of the team, but it wasn't possible to raise additional funds in the short time left. I felt the forty-year mark was significant, so it was now or possibly never.

The structure of my team represented a unique role reversal in a number of ways, for not only would Western climbers be the ones ferrying loads up and down the mountain but, to the best of my knowledge, it would be the first—and still only—international Everest team led by an ethnic Sherpa.

The first person to join me on the team was my paternal uncle Lobsang Tshering Bhutia, the only son of Tenzing's sister Thakchey and Lhakpa Tshering. Lobsang, then forty, was a veteran Himalayan climber and senior instructor at the Himalayan Mountaineering Institute. This would be his second expedition to Everest, having been a member of the 1984 Indian team. He shared my dream to climb Everest, and I had always thought that when the time came for me to mount an expedition, Lobsang would join me: we would climb and summit together. I think he felt a little protective of me, as I was only twenty-eight and he was such an experienced mountaineer. A soft-spoken man with a gentle face and perfectly groomed hair that was parted down the center and never out of place, he reminded me of a hero in a 1920s silent film. Loved by all who knew him in Darjeeling and throughout the entire mountaineering community in India and Nepal, he carried himself with dignity and maturity. Apart from being an absolute gentleman, he was a strong and determined climber, and there were many on the mountain that year, especially from the Indo-Nepalese Women's Expedition, whom he had trained at the HMI and who held him in esteem. He was never without a place to "dine out" at Base Camp, such was his popularity.

Four members of my grandfather's family had climbed Everest by 1993—Tenzing Norgay, Nawang Gombu (Tenzing's nephew), Dorjee Lhatoo (husband of Doma, Tenzing's niece), and Nima Norbu (brother of Daku, Tenzing's third wife). Whenever one of us attempts the mountain, we are inevitably asked if we feel we must follow a tradition established by my grandfather. Lobsang and I discussed this question on occasion. Yes, we were Tenzings and we had grown up under Everest's shadow, so to speak, yet neither of us felt that our attraction to her had its root in Gaga. In the same way that old Tenzing had no precedent for his *personal* passion for the mountain, neither did Lobsang nor I. We loved climbing, any climbing, any mountain. Yet Everest was always the one we dreamed of and the one we valued most in climbing terms. Everest, too, had played a prominent role in the lives and destiny of my family.

For Lobsang and me, the real essence of our devotion to this quest was the sacrifice, the inestimable effort and the passion with which so many before, both Sherpa and Westerner, had tried to "conquer" her; men such as Shipton, Ang Tharkay, Mallory, Irvine, Ang Nima, Lambert and, so many times, my grandfather. We felt we climbed for all of them, but we also climbed for ourselves, for when the flame of Everest burns inside you there is nothing that will quell it until the summit is reached; whether one person knows you have climbed it or a million pay homage to your success does not matter. In your heart you know you have made it; you know your dream has come true.

My climbing team was a large one, in retrospect too large for the funds at our disposal, but the members as they came together seemed fated to form a team. Two Macedonian climbers, Alex Aleksov and

Lobsang Tshering Bhutia performing the traditional puja at Base Camp before his 1993 attempt on Everest.

Dimitar Todorovski, requested places in order to climb high above the South Col to try to retrieve the body of a friend and colleague who had died on the mountain after reaching the summit in 1990. I could not refuse them. Andrew Locke, a Sydney climber whom I did not know well but who seemed to be prepared to make a strong contribution to the team as load-carrier, requested a place. Granted. Then from Brisbane came Michael Groom, an experienced Himalayan climber. I had heard great things about him in Australian climbing circles. He had twice attempted Everest and had planned to field his own team for 1993, but this had fallen through. I called him a week before we left Sydney to ask him to join. I knew his determination to summit would match mine and Lobsang's. At the eleventh hour came David Hume, a Sydney computer programmer who had little climbing experience but who was so desperate to try he won the last place. Our all-important Base Camp manager was Mike Wood from Mountain Designs in Perth, who would manage the kitchen staff and our liaison officer. Judy and I had known Mike from our Nepal guiding days. He was an old Himalaya hand, an

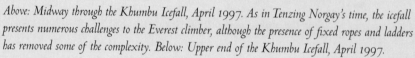

Above: Midway through the Khumbu Icefall, April 1997. As in Tenzing Norgay's time, the icefall presents numerous challenges to the Everest climber, although the presence of fixed ropes and ladders has removed some of the complexity. Below: Upper end of the Khumbu Icefall, April 1997.

experienced mountain guide and whitewater kayaker, with wonderful rapport with the Sherpas and Nepalis. He was also a superb organizer and a good man to have around when the going got tough—and the going would indeed get tough.

Raising the spirits of everyone at Base Camp was our Clarks stainless steel sink. As agreed, we established it at Base Camp, where it did wonders for the morale of our cook and two Sherpa kitchen staffers for the next two months or so of the expedition. It stands today in a small tea shop in Lobuche village, a day's walk down from Base Camp. The total lack of plumbing there does nothing to detract from its prestige.

Among the eighteen pre-monsoon expeditions on the Nepalese side of Everest that year was the Indo-Nepalese Women's Expedition, whose deputy leader was Rita Gombu Marwah, eldest daughter of Nawang Gombu and my second cousin, several times removed. She was a strong climber and had attempted Everest herself in 1984, but on this 1993 expedition her role was as deputy leader and expedition coordinator with perhaps a chance to get to the South Col. Lobsang and I were very fond of Rita, and we three were delighted to be on the mountain at the same time. Rita had a well-equipped, well-staffed expedition, and she knew I was working with a skeleton crew. As she watched us haul our loads up and down the icefall and on to Camps III and IV, she resolved to help. Some of our heaviest loads of oxygen, prepared one afternoon for the carry-up early the next morning, would miraculously disappear overnight, and we would find them safe and sound at the appropriate high camp, having been carried up by Rita's Sherpas on her instruction. She and I didn't speak about this, but I was deeply grateful.

In the old days of mountaineering, Everest was booked by one team each season, and that team set up its own route through the treacherous Khumbu Icefall, fixing its own ropes higher up the mountain. Those days are long gone, and in recent years a system has developed by which each expedition contributes financially to setting up the icefall route for the season (pre- or post-monsoon). One team opts to set up ropes and ladders from Base Camp to Camp I, and the other teams using the route pay that team a fee; in 1993, it was $1,500 U.S. Although the new system is more practical, it is not the way I would prefer to attempt Everest. But that is only one of many things that have changed in Everest climbing since my grandfather's days.

In his autobiography, *Sheer Will*, Mike Groom accurately describes the Khumbu Icefall as "a giant mousetrap ready to snap shut at any time on an unsuspecting climber." A safe route through the Khumbu Icefall is essential before loads can be carried through to establish the higher camps. As soon as the route was open on 1 April 1993, our team started the carry to Camp I, which is just beyond the top of the icefall at 6,000 meters. The work was exhausting: ferrying heavy loads of 65 to 80 pounds (30 to 35 kilos) for five to six hours at an altitude of over 5,000 meters is extremely draining work, so we were concerned about the inevitable toll this would take on our reserves of strength for the summit bid. But we were all strong, and before we left Australia we knew this is what we would be facing. Each of us believed nothing would stop us from reaching the summit if conditions were right.

We spent the following four to five weeks carrying, camping at the higher camps, and then returning to Base Camp to replenish our energy. Camp II is in the center of the great Western Cwm, below the west shoulder of Everest at 6,200 meters. Camp III is on the massive Lhotse Face at 7,300 meters, and Camp IV—the last camp and the one from which summit attempts are made—is on the South Col (the saddle between Everest and Lhotse) at 7,900 meters. During these relays I kept my eyes and ears sharp for a sign of the *chowkidar*, or ghost caretaker of Camp III. We Sherpas believe in ghosts, and I had long heard stories of one at this camp who would walk around the tents at night keeping watch over the sleeping climbers. It is supposed to be the spirit of all lost climbers on Everest, and I had hoped to encounter its presence. Lobsang had heard its boots and crampons crunching in the snow beyond the tent walls on his previous attempt on the mountain, as had Mike Groom. To my regret, I neither heard nor felt a thing.

The members of the eighteen teams became good friends at Base Camp and looked out for each other on the mountain. On any mountain, and certainly on Everest, one's climbing companions are easily the most important element of success. During the long weeks of preparation at the camps, you come to trust your comrades and rely on them for support, both physical and mental, forging bonds that could literally mean life or death. However, the pressure of long, strained weeks huddled in close quarters in uncomfortable, dangerous, and frustrating circumstances can allow personal idiosyncrasies, rivalries, and even small irritations to break these all-important bonds. If this mutual support network is compromised, it is difficult for the team to function well. The summit can then become an individual pursuit, which is always a dangerous way to play the Everest game.

That year, there was a Nepalese Sherpa team whose goal was to put the first Nepali woman on the summit of Everest, Pasang Lhamu Sherpa. A strong woman, she had attempted Everest three times before, but she had seemed nervous and more than a little reluctant at Base Camp when we had spoken of her coming climb. While the rest of the teams were planning to attempt the summit the first week of May, Pasang Lhamu and her five climbing Sherpas left Camp IV on the South Col for the summit on 22 April, more than a week earlier. Later that day, word spread through the camps that, after reaching the summit, the team's oxygen had run out, stranding and plunging them into a semicomatose state on the south summit of Everest, just a hundred meters below the main summit. During the night of 23 April, three of the five Sherpas made it down to the South Col, but two, Pemba Nuru and Sonam Tshering, remained with Pasang Lhamu. By some miracle Pemba Nuru was able to descend to Camp IV the following morning after a night exposed near the summit. Pasang Lhamu and Sonam Tshering perished.

In achieving her dream—becoming the first Nepali woman atop Chomolungma—Pasang Lhamu paid the ultimate price. Her death worried me because I knew I wanted to succeed on Everest as much as Pasang did, and I didn't know if I would push the limits, as she had done. Climbing is as much a journey into your own mind as it is a physical one up a mountain, and you do not know how much it all means until you are faced with such choices. I was soon to find out where I would draw my own line.

We waited in the camps for May to come, and then we waited for good weather. At last, word came that a twenty-four-hour window of good weather would open on 10 May. This was it; this was our time. All the teams began to make their way up to the high camps to prepare for the ascent. During the climb I began experiencing problems with my snow goggles: the body heat generated by exertion kept fogging

Looking down on the Western Cwm.

Climbing the Lhotse Face, heading from Camp III to Camp IV, 9 May 1993.

them, so I had to keep removing them to wipe them. This compounded problems I had been having the day before in the Western Cwm, and consequently I suffered minor snow blindness, a temporary but painful condition that generally heals itself in a day or so with rest. Such a problem at this stage of the climb made me concerned that my vision might deteriorate higher on the summit ridge. Not knowing what else to do, I decided to see if rest improved the situation.

By the afternoon of 9 May, Mike Groom, Lobsang, and I were settled into our tents at Camp IV on the South Col and preparing for the day we had anticipated so long—summit day. Andrew, Alex, and David had decided to spend another night at Camp III before making their summit bids; Dimitar, suffering from altitude sickness, remained at Camp III. Mike then made the courageous decision to attempt the summit without the use of bottled oxygen. Climbing at altitude is the ultimate test of humanity against the mountain, and many climbers consider climbing without bottled oxygen a "pure" attempt on a summit—pitting themselves and their trained, acclimatized bodies against the peak, the weather, and the altitude. It is an arduous and dangerous quest, because at such altitudes, above 5,000 and especially over 8,000 meters, the body screams for oxygen and begins to degrade quickly without it. One must move quickly and in the optimum weather window to ensure a safe ascent and, more importantly, descent. Oxygen deprivation quickly causes highly dangerous and ultimately fatal symptoms such as hypoxia and cerebral and pulmonary edema—the rapid filling of the brain and/or lungs with fluid. Lobsang, who had become very close to Mike over the course of the expedition, worried about this decision but respected Mike's judgment and supported his bid.

Of the total 294 climbers from eighteen teams to attempt Everest from the Nepal side that spring, 51—including New Zealand climbing legends Rob Hall and Gary Ball—would attempt the summit on 10 May—if they made it, the day would break the record for number of summiters, a scenario that worried all of us greatly. There would be no established order: whoever was ready first would begin their ascent, and the others would fall in behind. There is just one route up the summit ridge of Everest from the south, one pencil-narrow and precarious path. The timing and rhythm of your climbing pace is of utmost importance at these altitudes, and to have to alter and constantly adjust this pace to suit a stream of other climbers that ebbs and flows can mean the difference between success and failure.

On the early evening of 9 May, Mike, Lobsang, and I were tense and strained as we squeezed into one tent amidst oxygen bottles, day packs, and cumbersome climbing boots. Mike worried that our tiny stove, on which I was melting snow for drinks, was dangerously close to the oxygen bottles and declared that if the bottles went up we would all be blown to the summit of Everest. My immediate response brought the tent down: "Yes, but would it count as an oxygenless ascent?" Our laughter eased the pressure, and we tried to get some rest.

Mike left that night at 11 P.M. for the summit under a clear sky and full moon. Slower off the mark, Lobsang and I left two hours later, the last in the long queue of fifty-one that laboriously snaked its way up the southeast ridge toward the summit. The speed at which this column was moving troubled Lobsang and me because it was virtually impossible to pass other climbers on the narrow path, and we knew that every second consumed precious oxygen and energy. At around 8,200 meters we came across Gary Ball from the New Zealand team, who was clearly having problems. Coughing up blood and looking weak,

Lobsang took this photo from the South Summit of Everest, looking up to climbers on the Hillary Step, 10 May 1993.

he had decided to head back down to the Col. At that point Lobsang suggested we increase our oxygen flow rate from one liter a minute to two. Although I was having difficulty, too, I would have preferred to conserve our supplies, given the crowd and the distance ahead. Finally, I agreed to do as Lobsang requested, and I turned up his valve.

"Are you OK?" he asked, ready to turn up my valve, as well.

"I'm fine," I replied through my oxygen mask. "You carry on." At that he looked happy and set off at a strong, faster pace to catch the queue now thirty meters ahead of us.

In fact, I was not fine. The snow blindness that had begun to bother me the day before was settling in with a vengeance at this crucial stage: the pain worsened and my vision blurred. I struggled on for another hundred meters, then slumped in the snow, where I sat for over an hour, trying to work out what to do. I had worked long and hard to get this far, and I still had enough strength, eyesight, and determination to get to the summit. Everest was my dream, my life's burning ambition, but mountaineers know that getting to the top is only half the climb: in what state would I be making the crucial descent? On the other hand, I was unable to foresee a future in which I would be able to raise another expedition. Would I let the dream end here, so close to my goal? But what meaning did that goal hold if I lost my life? I had a wife and son at home. I had a family to whom I was far more important than Everest. I thought of my mother. What would she tell me to do? *Descend, descend, descend.*

There was no choice. I turned and headed, alone, down to Camp IV.

There I went immediately toward the New Zealand tents, where Gary Ball was resting. He administered medication for my eyes, which by then felt as if red-hot needles were being driven into them. I returned to my own tent and lay down to rest and await the return of my team. Instead, one of the women from the Korean team came by to ask if I wanted to go down with her to Camp II. I knew my eyes would heal better at a lower altitude, so I agreed to join her. Gary Ball was also ready to descend, and the three of us headed down together. As we passed through Camp II, Gary received a radio message that a record forty climbers, including Mike Groom and Lobsang from my team, had reached the summit by around 1:30 P.M. and were on their way back to Camp IV on the Col. I was overjoyed. Even though I had had to turn back from the summit, my teammates had succeeded. I imagined the euphoria on Mike and Lobsang's faces, and I looked forward to reaching the summit vicariously through their recounting.

At Camp II I took shelter in one of the Indian tents with Nima Norbu, the younger brother of Daku, my grandfather's third wife. A fine climber, he took good care of me that day, seeing that my eye medication was administered regularly and passing along the roll call of climbers returning to the Col from the summit. By late afternoon, however, the weather had deteriorated. The wind was howling over the summit and the cold was worsening by the minute. Mike Groom had reached Camp IV safely and was resting in his tent. I assumed Lobsang was also back at the Col; he had summited easily and was the most experienced climber on the mountain that season. By about 9 P.M. all but two of the fifty-one climbers that day were accounted for; only Lobsang and a British climber, Harry Taylor, who had climbed without oxygen, were missing. Concerned, I radioed various colleagues to try to locate Lobsang in one of the tents. The weather was by now so foul that the climbers returning from the top were taking shelter in any tent that could fit them in.

Finally, at 11 P.M., I received a radio message through Base Camp that Lobsang had been located in another team's tent. It had been a tough day for me, for the other climbers of my team in Camps II and IV, and for Mike Wood at Base Camp, who was endeavoring to keep track of everyone and keep us informed about events as time went on.

The three remaining team members, Alex, Andrew, and David, were in their tents in Camp IV on the South Col preparing for their own attempt on 11 May, and Lobsang was presumably asleep in a friendly tent somewhere nearby. Yet I could not sleep. A terrible sense of foreboding unsettled me. At dawn I radioed David at Camp IV.

There was no sign of Lobsang; it was now established that he was not in any of the tents. In the nightmarish conditions and confusion of the previous night, messages and confirmations had been vague, and those who thought Lobsang had returned were, in fact, mistaken. In my heart I knew the truth, but I clung to a small ray of hope throughout the day. The wind raged and visibility was zero, which meant that no one on the Col could leave their tents to search for Lobsang, much less attempt the summit. On the morning of 12 May, Alex shouldered his oxygen supply and, despite the blizzard conditions, set out to look for Lobsang. I felt helpless at Camp II, but my vision was still compromised and I knew that my participation in the search would only add to the chaos at Camp IV.

Alex's original search for one comrade had sadly turned into a search for another. After hours of scouring the slopes above, he found Lobsang's body just two hundred meters above Camp IV at the bottom of a gully. He was curled up in the fetal position, his face unrecognizable and near his hand an open Swiss army knife. His smashed wristwatch read 2:55 P.M. Alex surmised that Lobsang had fallen from somewhere below the south summit, apparently briefly surviving the fall.

I could not accept the loss; I could not even begin to think of how it had happened or what had caused the fall. I had never felt so lost and distraught in my life, before or since. It came to me that Lobsang was the only member of my family to lose his life on Everest. He had reached his summit, yes, but this price was far too high. My heart no longer in the effort, I did not want to continue my climb—for me the expedition was over. Andrew, Alex, and David returned to Base Camp, and from there Andrew and David headed for Kathmandu and home to Australia.

Although all human cultures have their own ritual ways of dealing with death, the mountain imposes its own culture. Getting oneself down the Lhotse Face, over crevasses, and through the icefall to Base Camp is dangerous in itself, but doing it with an unwieldy, 180-pound body bag increases both the danger and difficulty exponentially. Then there is the question of the wishes of the family: a tradition has grown up around high-altitude fatalities that leaves the choice to the family as to whether the body should remain undisturbed, be "buried" as feasible, or be retrieved. Because of the danger and expense of repatriating the dead, many Westerners decide to leave their dead on the mountain. But this is anathema to Sherpas, for whom Buddhist last rites are of utmost importance because they facilitate the transition to our next reincarnation. In the Buddhist tradition, corpses not buried or cremated properly also dishonor the mountain deities.

In Buddhist as in other traditions, respectful handling of the body prior to cremation is carefully prescribed. The body is stripped, washed, and anointed with sacred oils. It is then wrapped in a clean cloth and placed on a newly constructed pyre of juniper and local wood. A mixture of yak butter and kerosene is poured over the body, and the pyre is lit by the senior male of the family. The pyre remains lit until the entire body is consumed. The ashes are then carefully gathered and placed in a *chorten* (a large rock cairn memorial) built high on a ridge or near a monastery or sacred place.

Lobsang was a devout Buddhist, and his family, when informed of his death, requested that his body be carried down for cremation in accordance with our Buddhist ritual tradition. This became my first and only priority.

Rita and the members of the Indo-Nepali Women's team were also bereft. Although everyone had been aware of the risks, the loss was nevertheless difficult to accept: no one could believe it; no one *would* believe it. We helped each other in the next dark days and were strengthened by the members of our own team who chose to stay to see Lobsang's journey through to its end. They all had compelling reasons to leave: Mike Wood had a wife and children and a business at home; Mike Groom was newly married and had just climbed Everest (the first Queenslander to do so); and Alex and Dimitar had not been able to retrieve the body of their own dear friend, yet had helped us immeasurably by finding Lobsang. I treasure these people to this day and will never forget their support during that time.

I stayed on at Camp II while a team of Sherpas sent by Rita and her colleagues went to the South Col a few days after Lobsang's body was discovered to begin the slow and dangerous task of bringing it down. It was a strange time for me, in limbo between Base Camp and the South Col. Rita's Sherpas, fresh and capable, could easily handle the job without additional help or guidance. In short, although my eyes were by then completely healed, there was nothing for me to do, yet I could not bring myself to leave for Base Camp. I wanted to wait for Lobsang and descend with him.

During those days at Camp II, a strange accident occurred that haunts me still. As I stood on the glacier looking up toward the Col, I heard a wild and almost tortured scream descending from high above. Looking up, I saw a member of the Korean team flying through the air, arms and legs spread-eagled, his dive accompanied by the clink and clank of tin mugs and other gear falling from his pack onto the rocks below. He hit the ground about two hundred meters from me and slid a few meters before being swallowed in terrible silence by a huge, gaping crevasse. I stood dumbstruck: he had jumped from the southwest ridge. When I later learned that he had been one of his team not to achieve the summit, I wondered at the sense of failure and shame that prompted such a dramatic suicide. I had never questioned this mountaineering path so many of us had chosen, but on that dark day I pondered what climbing mountains, and especially this mountain, really meant to me. It was a sad and confusing time.

I inhabited a strange, twilight purgatory for several days in Camp II.

Only one other incident, at once alarming and humorous, remains clear in my memories from this time. One afternoon as I lay alone in my tent waiting for Lobsang, I overheard a heated discussion on the radio between some foreign climbers in a nearby tent, their Base Camp, and their Sherpas on the South Col. Two of the foreign team were caught in a blizzard on the summit ridge above the Col and were radioing down to their Sherpas on the Col, pleading with them to climb up and give assistance. The Sherpas, in shaky English, were steadfastly refusing, and the foreign climbers in my camp were trying to cajole them, obviously fearing the worst for their comrades. Language barriers were aggravating the situation, so I climbed out of my tent to offer my help. I felt I had to do whatever I could to avoid additional deaths on Everest that year. The foreign climbers welcomed my intervention, and I took the radio and spoke to the South Col Sherpas: "I am the grandson of Tenzing Sherpa," I stated in Nepali, "and I have been listening to this problem. Tell me why you will not go and help these two men." Because Sherpas very rarely deny help on a mountain, I knew there was more to the story than I had overheard. In Nepali they could tell me honestly. They said the climbers had been very rude—a serious offense in Sherpa culture—and inconsiderate of the Sherpas' safety on the Col. I could understand why they were upset, but it was unlikely the two foreigners would survive unless the Sherpas went back up and brought them down. "I understand why you are angry," I told them sincerely. "But we are Sherpas, and we have never willingly let anyone die on a mountain. It is not our way. We have a great tradition, especially on Everest, and to not help would bring such shame on our people." I had spoken from the heart, but they stood firm in their resolve to stay put. I tried one last plea: "If this is how you feel, what can I do? But remember: one day this life will come to an end, and you'll be reincarnated—probably as a *Western climber*." That did it. That scenario was all too much, and they quickly agreed to head out. The foreign climbers were found and brought safely down, and we Sherpas have a great laugh when the story is told now.

In all it was ten days before Lobsang's frozen body finally rested at Base Camp, draped in the flags of Australia, India, and Macedonia, the three nationalities of my team members. Some members of our extended family—some of whom had been on the mountain—had already gathered to help with and participate in the cremation rites. The lamas of the Pangboche monastery, the oldest and most revered monastery in the Khumbu, did *pujas* (prayers) the entire night, and the next day we carried the body down to their monastery grounds for cremation. As the senior male family member present, it fell on me to light the pyre. The Head Lama presided—a great honor for Lobsang and the Tenzing family. None of us will forget the grief that enveloped us during this time, but I was consoled by the knowledge that our careful attendance to Buddhist ritual would release Lobsang to his next life.

I sent the other team and extended family members home—they had done all they could—but I stayed on several days until the pyre was completely extinguished. We built a *chorten* above Pangboche for some of Lobsang's ashes, but the rest I took with me to Kathmandu and then on to Darjeeling, Lobsang's home. Though the 600-mile journey was not difficult, emotionally it was the hardest I have ever made. I did not know what I would say to Lobsang's immediate family, or how even to begin to explain a death that remained incomprehensible. But we in the Tenzing family, if not mountaineers ourselves, have at least lived in the climbing world all our lives; we understand that tragic accidents occur, and I hoped that from that common knowledge we would reach a common acceptance. The journey to Darjeeling was a journey home for me as well—home to my mother and family and a solace I needed badly. I was little more than a hollow shell of the Sherpa I had been when I began the climb of Everest.

Arriving in Darjeeling, I spent the night in my parents' home, and in the morning my mother walked with me as I carried Lobsang's ashes to his home a few miles away. There, grief had sparked anger, and I was met by recriminations that I could only endure. I understood how they felt, but how could they possibly imagine that I had deserted or failed Lobsang? Would I deliberately leave him in dire straits on the mountain? Never. I left feeling numb and dazed, and I talked with my parents long into the night. As climbers who had faced death in the mountains before, they knew the risks and dangers and they knew how close Lobsang and I had been. After several days of discussions my mother and I decided to do what we could for Lobsang's household: his wife, son, and aging parents.

Although load-carrying Sherpas can get life insurance, adequate life insurance has traditionally been difficult, almost impossible, for climbers to procure because climbing is a maximum-risk activity and its fatality rate is so high. In common with all our team members, Lobsang had not been insured. Sherpa mountaineers go to Everest knowing that should they not return there will be little for those left behind, save what the goodwill of family and friends may provide. I sold my small house near Sydney, and my mother surrendered her retirement fund. Hyundai made a generous donation, and Australian friends gave what they could. We were able to purchase for the family a comfortable house in a respectable part of Darjeeling, near HMI. Ever loyal and generous Mike Wood, our Base Camp manager, also offered to support Lobsang's son, Tenzing, throughout his school years.

Having done what we could, I went home to Australia feeling lost, disillusioned, and profoundly depressed. I became a stranger to those who knew me, a man they could not recognize.

Yet even in those dark days I felt that my Everest dream was not over. My mother had given me a small statue of the Buddha, blessed by our lamas and wrapped in a sacred saffron-colored cloth, that I had carried with me on my climb. As I carefully returned it to my altar in our rented home in Sydney, I felt a faint flicker of hope that my quest was not yet over. Perhaps, still, the day would come when the statue would be placed where it should be—on top of the world.

It is said that time heals all wounds, and after many months I began to regain my old energy and love for life. I was able to make peace with what had happened and set my mind and heart on rebuilding a life with my family. To that end, Judy and I established the Himalayan Travel Centre in October 1993. In December 1994 Dechen Lhamu was born, fulfilling our long-time hope for a daughter. Her arrival took away a great deal of the pain of 1993, and life was sweet again. With this child we chose the name rather than ask the lamas, for I had always known what I would call a daughter if I were fortunate enough to have one: Dechen, which means "joy and happiness" in Tibetan; Judy chose Lhamu in honor of my grandmother, Tenzing's much-loved second wife.

Tashi, Pasang, and Judy Tenzing at Sydney airport, relieved and happy to be reunited after Tashi's tragic 1993 Everest Expedition.

Dechen has grown into an energetic and charismatic child, full of energy like her father and great-grandfather.

By now I was happy and contented, and we were slowly rebuilding our lives. All through this period, however, the flame that burned inside me for my mountain, though dimmed, was never extinguished. In 1996 it began to rekindle strongly, and I told Judy I wanted to try for Everest again. The pain on her face was unmistakable, but she replied that she had known all along this time would come and she was prepared to endure it one more time.

This time, however, I knew I had to join a good team and give myself every chance of summiting. No more exhausting carrying up and down from Base Camp to Col, which had sapped all our energies in 1993. I wanted the best backup and support I could find, so in late 1996 I contacted Guy Cotter of Adventure Consultants in New Zealand and asked to join his Everest 1997 attempt. Guy had been part of the Everest nightmare of 1996 (recounted in Jon Krakauer's *Into Thin Air*, Lene Gammelgaard's *Climbing High*, and Anatoli Boukreev's *The Climb*), when Himalayan legends Rob Hall and Scott Fischer perished with six others in a storm that caught them all high on the mountain. Guy had picked up the reins of the company—Rob Hall and Gary Ball's dream—and revived it. Courageously he was going back to the mountain in the following spring as part of a "Dream Team" that included American mountaineer extraordinaire Ed Viesturs, who featured in the tragedy of 1996 while filming the IMAX movie *Everest* but found himself a helpless observer to his friend Rob Hall's sad end; Veikka Gustafsson, a Finn and Himalayan veteran who was attempting Everest for the third time, this ascent without bottled oxygen; and David Carter, an Indiana woodmiller who had attempted Everest once before but without success. We were joined by Peter Weeks, a South Australian. There were six of us: a small, experienced and well-equipped group who were determined to wipe the mountain clean of the bad press and gloomy reputation it had gained in the 1996 season.

Then, of course, there was the matter of money. Joining an existing team eased the financial burden, but climbing Everest is still a costly business, and as soon as I had secured a place on the team I began to look for supporters. Corporate Australia again seemed disinterested in mountaineering. The faithfully supportive Thai Airways covered my airfares and cargo transport, but I needed funds. After yet another long series of disappointments and setbacks I took a deep breath and once more contacted Rolex in Geneva, not hopeful they would come to my aid a second time. Within days I received a fax from Paul Stuber, who offered me an amount that, along with funds I borrowed, would cover my expenses. I was grateful for their show of faith in a man they had

Sir Edmund and Lady Jane Hillary visit the Tenzing family in Darjeeling before Tashi's successful 1997 attempt on Everest.

never met, based on the reputation of my family and their long association with my grandfather. Finally, I was surprised and delighted when the K2 Gear Shop in Brisbane and Patagonia in Sydney offered clothing and equipment. I believe in karma and fate, and deep inside I knew that this time Everest would allow me to realize my dream. I left for Nepal on 12 March 1997 in the highest of spirits.

I arranged to meet the team at Base Camp, as I had important business to attend to in Darjeeling. I needed to see my parents before the climb and, in what seemed an auspicious coincidence, I was scheduled to attend the unveiling of my grandfather's memorial statue at HMI. Present for the ceremony, Sir Edmund Hillary came to my family's house in Darjeeling to give me his blessing before I left for Everest. All in all it could not have been a more fitting prelude to my second Everest attempt.

Above: The "Dream Team" of Everest (L to R): sirdar Ang Tshering (standing), an unidentified cook, an unidentified helper, Guy Cotter (standing), Ed Viesturs (center, front), Tashi Tenzing (with champagne), Veikka Gustafsson (standing), David Carter (front, second from right), and Gyalzen Sherpa (far right). Below: Looking down on Everest Base Camp, 1997.

As planned, our climbing team all met at Base Camp in early April. Apart from Dave Carter and Peter Weeks I knew them all, and it was an easy transition into the team. We were all climbers, and Dave and Peter proved to be well prepared and great company. We also had the "Sherpa Dream Team" with us, four young and strong Sherpas who had gained vital experience with Rob Hall in their short climbing careers; Ang Dorje (who has now summited on Everest six times); Ang Tshering from Rolwaling who, at that point, had summited three times before and who would become a father for the first time during this expedition; Chultim from Khumjung, who had climbed Everest once before; and Gombu, another Rolwaling Sherpa who was an Everest veteran.

On my walk-in I met with all of my many relatives in the Khumbu, and they showered me with prayers and *kadas*, the white silk blessing scarves of Buddhist custom. My extended Sherpa family is very important to me, and the 1997 climb was as much for Lobsang and for them as it was for me. They had been through the loss of Lobsang with me in 1993 and had given me their unequivocal support, both emotionally and physically through that mournful time. They had helped me arrange the cremation and the pujas (prayers) at Pangboche monastery and helped me on the return to Kathmandu when I was alone and shattered. Now I passed again through their villages, finally receiving a blessing from the Head Lama of Tengboche monastery. Later, I would discover that throughout my climb every home in the Khumbu kept incense burning on the Buddhist shrines in their homes.

Base Camp brought back sad memories for all of us of previous losses and terrors. Yet this time it felt different. There was a clarity, a lightness that accompanied this season's expeditions, and we somehow felt that this time there would be no tragedy, and we would ease the pain of those earlier climbs.

That said, Chomolungma nevertheless reminded us of her power and ultimate control over our fate. After weeks of Sherpa porters routinely carrying loads and climbers going up and down between the camps to acclimatize, we were back at Base, ready for the summit attempt, when the goddess unleashed unbearable jet stream winds, making climbing impossible. Many of the higher camps that had been so laboriously set up were destroyed, literally ripped to shreds by the 125-mile-per-hour (200 kph) winds. By some miracle our tents at Camp II survived. We were thus grounded at Base Camp from 2 May until 18 May, ordinarily the tail end of the season. Waiting so long is demoralizing and depletes the strength one needs above Camp IV. On our last retreat from the blizzard conditions of Camp III, I called Judy in Sydney to tell her that we would try once more to get to the Col and if we were again turned back would abandon our attempt. The monsoon was approaching, it was late in May, and the process was grinding us down.

Judy had been afraid of my climbing Everest again, but this hint of surrender worried her more than her fear of the climb, for she knew what it meant to me. After our call she phoned Mike Groom in Brisbane, a good friend and an exceptional mountaineer who had faced this "wall" many, many times himself and who had been on our 1993 expedition, asking for his advice.

"Get on the phone," Mike told her in a calm and determined voice, "and tell him to get his ass moving and climb that mountain *now*." It was what she wanted to hear, and she relayed the message to me loud and clear. Meanwhile, my mother, who was following the expedition minute by minute from our family home in Darjeeling, had been to the family lamas, who had prayed and then told her that I must make my attempt on 23 May, the birthday of Lord Buddha. Not before and not a day later.

"Right," I said to myself when I got her message. "I'll just let the others know the date is fixed!"

On 20 May we moved up the mountain for one last push; the wind still howled across the summit but was calmer on the lower slopes of Everest. Taking a rest day in the Western Cwm, we thought 23 May was looking very shaky indeed, lamas' predictions notwithstanding.

During our rest, we discussed for hours the criteria for membership in the fictitious Everest Anonymous Club proposed by American climber and cinematographer David Breashears, who was on the U.S. team. It was an entertaining interlude for me, there in the company of some of the finest Himalayan climbers in history. Ed Hillary, of course, had automatic membership, as did Guy, who had summited in 1992. David Breashears was most certainly a member of the "club," having climbed Everest four times, and Veikka's 1993 ascent got him in, but the group thought Dave Carter and I were questionable candidates.

Tashi Tenzing at Camp IV, looking down on the Western Cwm.

I had tried and failed, as had Dave, but then I was a Tenzing, so that required special consideration! And so the hours dissolved in tension-easing banter.

On 22 May we all—both Western and Sherpa climbers—moved up to the South Col, optimistic about our chances of summiting since the wind had miraculously dropped suddenly to five knots. Our fearless leader, Guy Cotter, must have been even happier than the rest of us, for as we all lay resting in our tents that afternoon we heard a wild scream and emerged to see him running around the Col (at 8,000 meters) wearing only his mountain boots. The Sherpas' long-standing doubts about the sanity of Western mountaineers were hardly allayed by this incident. As night closed in the clouds blew away, exposing the most beautiful, calm, moonlit night I had ever experienced. I could feel my soul stir and my heart warm. Chomolungma had indeed saved her best until last for me.

At 9:30 P.M. we roused ourselves and began to pack for the summit. The most important item to be placed in my pack was the small statue of Buddha that my mother had given me in 1993 to place on the summit. In all the years of Everest climbing this had never been done, and it was most important to me that this symbol of the deeply held beliefs of all Sherpas and Tibetans be placed on top of the highest point on earth, the abode of the gods. On the very top of my pack I had attached a small, fluffy toy bilby, a highly endangered Australian marsupial. I carried it as a favor to my son and as a symbol of my heartfelt wish to conserve the wild places and creatures of our planet.

We left quietly at 11 P.M., before the other teams, to avoid the queue that had caused such havoc and delay in preceding years. We barely needed our headlamps, the brilliant white snow of the summit ridge was cloaked in full moonlight. It was extremely cold, -22 degrees Fahrenheit (-30 degrees Celsius), but the mountain was breathtakingly beautiful and, in contrast to 1993, I felt strong and happy and enjoyed every single step. This was how climbing Everest should be, how I knew it *would* be. I could not help but grin broadly under my oxygen mask as we made swift progress up the southeast ridge.

Our group made excellent time to the south summit, where we stopped for tea. This gave us a chance to take in the beauty and scale of the Himalaya. Words cannot do justice to how one feels in a place like this, gazing down in silence on Himalayan giants such as Makalu, Lhotse, and Kanchenjunga, watching Everest's great mass cast a morning shadow over the entire Khumbu region of Nepal. One cannot fathom a shadow so vast, such is the scale and dominance of this great mountain. We knew we had to move on but, at that moment, every one of us could have happily stayed on in that place.

The ridge between the south summit and the dreaded Hillary Step is one of the most dangerous and unforgiving sections of the ascent, the "sting in the tail" of Everest, as Guy Cotter put it. The ridge is just a meter wide and heavily corniced—one misplaced step on a weak section of ice and one will plummet down the Kangshung face to Tibet or down the southwest face to Camp II. There is no room for error, and we all climbed in silent concentration until we reached the Hillary Step a hundred meters on.

We knew what we would encounter here. Bruce Herrod, a British member of the 1996 South African post-monsoon expedition, had summited, but not until after 6 P.M., the last climber to reach the peak that year. It had been an exhausting and slow climb from the Col, and he had then faced a solitary descent in the dark, an unimaginably dangerous prospect. He had moved slowly down and made it as far as the Hillary Step, but while climbing down this narrow gully of rock his crampons had tangled in old climbing ropes and he was tipped backward, leaving him hanging upside down and unable to pull himself up. He had died in this manner, and his body had been left so, like other bodies on the mountain. Rob Hall's family had asked that Rob's body not be disturbed, so it remains where he died in 1996, just three feet below the south summit near a large boulder. In Bruce's case, his family had requested that Himalayan climbing legend Pete Athans, who was part of another summit team in 1997, cut Bruce free and commit his body to the southwest face of Everest. All the climbers that year were aware that Pete had agreed. Thus, David Breashears and I moved slowly past Bruce's frozen body and up the Hillary Step. Just behind our team were Pete Athans, Ed Viesturs, and Guy Cotter, who together retrieved Bruce's camera and personal belongings and then silently and respectfully released his body. With Bruce's body returned to the earth, everyone could climb safely on.

I can still see clearly in my mind that last snowy ridge to the summit. The summit is quite large—a snow cone—with a steep drop into Tibet beyond it. I had waited all my life for this moment, and it did not disappoint. I picked up my pace a little and caught up to David Breashears, who was the only climber ahead of me. He then offered a thoughtful gesture that will stay with me all my life: he stopped before the summit, waited until I stood next to him, then offered his hand for us to step up to the summit together. He had reached the summit the year before with my uncle Jamling and now stood atop Everest with the first member of the third generation of the Tenzing family to do so. He told me it was an honor for him, but the honor was as much mine, for he is a fine mountaineer who deeply loves these mountains and who climbs with great respect for them. David is certainly one of the Western climbers we Sherpas hold in high respect, as were my other Western colleagues on Everest that day.

It was now 6:50 A.M. We had made exceptionally good time from the South Col to the summit, just over eight hours, but this really meant very little in the context of the whole achievement. The joy of the climb and the safe return of all climbers are what counts. David and I had a

Tashi Tenzing on the summit of Everest, 23 May 1997.

Looking south-southwest from the summit of Everest, with the Nuptse ridge lower right and Taweche just behind it. Left of center is Ama Dablam, and beyond that Thamserku.

wonderful ten minutes to ourselves on top of the world before the rest of our team reached us. We spoke little, just taking in the wonder of that special place.

People often ask me what I thought and felt while standing on the summit. My first thoughts were of Lobsang: he was there with me at that moment, and I felt very close to him. I thought of my grandfather and how he must have felt on that spot forty-four years earlier when he and Hillary were the first to look down over the world from earth's highest point. Yet my overwhelming emotion was one of unparalleled appreciation for where I was and for the unbelievably beautiful scene before me. I wanted to stay there forever, feeling that euphoria and feasting my senses. I wept and laughed and prayed as I buried my small Buddha beneath the pure snow of the summit. My Sherpa colleagues were greatly moved by the placing of the statue; they felt it had kept them safe and that the mountain had now been duly honored. I also unfurled the traditional Buddhist prayer flags as well as the flags of Nepal, India, Australia, and even Bhutan—the first time the Bhutanese flag had flown on Everest. I felt deeply satisfied, and turned to head down.

The descent was considerably more hair-raising than the climb up: you *have* to look down, and the view is spectacularly daunting. I down-climbed with great caution and respect for these slopes that had seen the demise of many successful summiters, Lobsang among them, but I felt strong and not too tired and soon was back safely on the South Col. Base Camp patched through a call to Judy in Sydney, and I emitted an avalanche of garbled, adrenalin-fueled expressions of euphoria about my climb. Judy laughed at my unbridled joy. The feeling of pure relief was incomparable.

Back at Base Camp we packed up and our team set out for Kathmandu and home. I walked back slowly through the Khumbu on my way to the airstrip at Lukla village, visiting each Tenzing family home and lodge so I could share my happiness with those who had also shared my deep pain in 1993. It was a wonderful walk, *kadas* piled so high around my neck I could barely see!

My parents were waiting in the airport when I landed in Kathmandu. They were as relieved that I was safe as they were proud of my success. My mother presented me with a beautiful gold chain as a memento of my climb, and I wear it to this day. My friend from International Trekkers, Phintso Ongdi, and Chhunta Tuladhar from the Nirvana Garden Hotel, both held receptions for me over the next week as I met a stream of Nepali, Indian, and foreign media. Success on Everest is no longer a unique accomplishment, but the significance of a third generation of one family reaching the summit held an undeniable magic, and the world responded with great interest and enthusiasm.

There were celebrations at the Australian Embassy, with friends, and at various hotels and organizations, but of immeasurable significance to me and to my people was the presentation of a small silver statue of Buddha from the Nepal Buddhist Association in recognition of my placing a Buddha at the top of the world.

Exhausted and yet still in a euphoric state, I flew from Kathmandu home to Sydney. At the airport I was greeted by my family and a group of dear friends, all dressed in red T-shirts emblazoned with words commemorating my success. The dream had been realized.

Thuji chey Chomolungma—I am grateful, Chomolungma.

CHAPTER 9

OTHER TENZINGS
ON EVEREST

T O A SHERPA and a member of the Tenzing clan, the Himalaya and in particular Everest are an inextricable part of life. Although many in Tenzing's family have chosen not to climb, others have found the lure of the great peaks irresistible.

To the generation immediately following Tenzing Norgay, mountaineering offered a career in which to excel and a relatively secure future (save for the high risks of climbing, of course) within the bounds of the Himalayan Mountaineering Institute. Tenzing's nephews Nawang Gombu, Lobsang Tshering, and Dorjee Lhatoo (by marriage) all worked as instructors at HMI but were offered places on Himalayan expeditions, and all reached the summit of Everest. We in the next generation of Tenzing climbers are not professional mountaineers, climb-

Nawang Gombu receives help from an unidentified climber on his return to the South Col after his successful Everest ascent with Jim Whittaker and the American team, 1963.

ing simply for the love of it. Jamling Tenzing Norgay, Rita Gombu, and I all earn our livings in other fields, but the mountains have called to us, and we have responded. We carry on the Tenzing mountaineering tradition with passion, determination, and joy.

NAWANG GOMBU, 1936 –

Nawang Gombu is a man who speaks his mind. His outlook on life is clear and he is energetic and decisive, whether on a mountain or at home in Darjeeling working with his Sherpa community. He is bright, tough, and sharp-witted, and his worth as a mountaineer and climbing companion was quickly noted and appreciated by the leaders of the great expeditions of the 1950s and 1960s.

Born in Minzu in Tibet in 1936, Gombu is the son of Tenzing Norgay's elder sister, Lhamu Kipa, who had been a nun, and Lama Nawang La (younger brother of the local governor, the Dzongpen of Kharta), who had been a monk. The liaison between his parents was frowned upon in Tibet, not so much because both had been monastics, for such unions are not uncommon in the Himalaya, but rather because he was from an aristocratic family and she from a family of poor serfs who worked on the Dzongpen's land.

They decided it was best for them and their children to make a life outside of Tibet, so when Gombu was five years old and his baby sister Doma only a week old, they made the trek across the 5,716-meter Nangpa La into the Khumbu, where they settled around Thamey near members of the Tenzing family already settled there. Gombu spent his early years working the fields, tending yak, and listening to the stories of the great Sherpas who were working on expeditions to Chomolungma from the north side of the mountain in Tibet. He heard tales of Ang Tharkay, Anullu Sherpa, and his uncle Tenzing Norgay, who was beginning to make a name for himself among the sahibs and, hence, among the Sherpas of Darjeeling and Khumbu.

In traditional Sherpa and Tibetan families it is customary to send a son to a monastery to become a monk, for it is believed such devotion will bring significant spiritual bounty to the family, so in his early teens he was sent to study as a monk at the great Da Rongphu monastery. Gombu was meant to stay for at least five years, but he found conditions harsh and at times brutal, and punishments were liberally administered: for example, each mistake in religious readings was matched by a cut with a bamboo cane or worse. After a year of this, young Gombu resolved to return to his family in the Khumbu. A friend and fellow monk at Da Rongphu, Ang Tshering, was of like mind, and both boys saved scraps of food for weeks before finally making their move on a cold and icy Himalayan night. Clad only in their monks' robes, the teens stole from the gompa under cover of darkness, scaled the high fence around it, and made their way up and over the high, wild Nangpa La into the Khumbu. With Gombu's life as a monk over, his destiny lay on a very different path.

With the opening of Nepal to foreigners in 1950 and the gradual closing of Tibet after the Chinese invasion beginning in 1949, the focus of Everest mountaineering shifted to the high and remote valleys of the Khumbu. The Swiss Everest attempts of 1952 captivated Gombu. Since he felt that this new world held his future, his mother advised him to seek out his uncle, the great sirdar and climber Tenzing, who was to pass through Namche Bazaar on his return from the mountain in the autumn. Gombu took the chance and met his uncle with a request for work on his next expedition.

"You will have to work hard, Gombu," Tenzing declared sternly, and a deal was struck.

Gombu did not have to wait long, for the following spring the British team, with its long lines of Sherpas and porters, began to wend its way up through the Himalayan foothills and into the Khumbu en route to Everest. Tenzing kept his word, and the seventeen-year-old Gombu was duly outfitted and sent to Base Camp. Gombu still recalls his barely controlled excitement and anticipation; he had dreamed of this, and although he wasn't on the climbing team, he was part of this great expedition. This was enough for now. Yet his strength, initiative, and clear thinking on this and other expeditions quickly led to his becoming one of the most successful Sherpas ever and claiming some impressive firsts.

Gombu is not tall, just five feet, five inches, yet he is sturdily built and extremely strong. In addition, he possesses both a firm resolve to succeed on a mountain and a devilish sense of humor that amuses and endears him to all who work with him. While carrying oxygen bottles up into the Western Cwm on the 1953 British Expedition, he was teamed with John Hunt on one carry. Gombu noticed that he was loaded with two oxygen bottles to Hunt's one.

"Why aren't you carrying two, also?" Gombu playfully inquired of the expedition leader.

At camp Hunt relayed the comment in amusement to Tenzing, who shot a displeased look at his young nephew. John Hunt diffused the situation by laughing heartily and slapping Gombu on the back, telling Tenzing, somewhat prophetically, "Gombu will be a good climber one day."

The British expedition taught Gombu a great deal. He was struck by the lack of jealousy among team members and their absolute loyalty to their leader. He realized that individuals must make sacrifices in the interests of a team victory, and he saw what planning and teamwork could achieve under difficult conditions.

Gombu made a significant contribution to the 1953 ascent by twice carrying loads to the South Col, in so doing earning both the Tiger Medal of the Himalayan Club and the Queen's Coronation Medal. In addition he was selected as one of the first six Sherpas to be trained in Switzerland with Arnold Glatthard and Tenzing Norgay as instructors for the new HMI in Darjeeling. His future was assured. He moved from Thamey to Darjeeling and began a new life.

In 1954 Ang Tharkay was recruiting staff for a U.S. expedition, under the leadership of Dr. William Siri, to 8,470-meter Makalu. Gombu was recommended after his 1953 efforts, but Ang Tharkay undertook his own investigation before he accepted the young man of eighteen for a high and difficult peak like Makalu. Ang Tharkay asked his old friend Tenzing, whom he knew would give an honest appraisal irrespective of family bonds. "How is Gombu, Tenzing?" he asked. Tenzing replied simply, conveying all that Ang Tharkay needed to hear, "Gombu is good."

Apart from his work at HMI, Gombu joined several other Himalayan climbs. The U.S. attempt of Makalu in 1954 did not succeed due to horrendous weather conditions, but Gombu managed to reach almost 7,000 meters. In 1956 he joined an Indian expedition to Saser Kangri in the Karakoram. Failing to summit there, the Indian team turned their attention to Sakang, a virgin peak of over 7,500 meters on the Sakang Lungpa Glacier. This became Gombu's first summit. The following year took him, again with the Indians, to Nanda Devi East, where he came within two hundred meters of the summit after surviving a near-fatal avalanche and worsening weather.

In 1959 Gombu was invited to join the International Women's Expedition to 8,201-meter Cho Oyu. At one of the higher camps, two of the women and two Sherpas were killed in an avalanche, ending the effort. For Gombu the only satisfaction was witnessing the climbing of Tenzing's daughters, Pem Pem and Nima, whom Gombu had trained at HMI. They proved themselves true members of the Tenzing clan, and their father and cousin were pleased.

By 1960 Gombu was a highly renowned climber and instructor at HMI, and he was invited to join an Indian team making the first Indian attempt on Everest. Battling blizzards and heavy snowfall, the team forced their way to 8,600 meters but could go no farther without risking disaster on the descent. They withdrew, disappointed and dejected, and Gombu returned to Darjeeling with an even deeper resolve to make the summit one day.

Early in 1963 he received a letter from William Siri, then deputy leader of the first American Everest Expedition. Siri remembered Gombu from Makalu in 1954, but because so many Sherpas possess the same name, Siri could not be sure to which Gombu he was writing. "Are you the same Gombu who was with me in 1954 on Makalu and reached 23,000 feet?" queried Siri. Gombu replied with pride, "I am that Gombu, and I have since then been to Everest and climbed to just two hundred meters below the summit."

As he left Darjeeling to take part in the U.S. expedition, Gombu told Tenzing, "I will go where you have gone."

The 1963 American team was led by Norman G. Dyhrenfurth. Sponsored largely by the National Geographic Society, they would split into two teams, one attempting Everest by the Southeast Ridge (the route commonly attempted, and known in Everest circles as the "yak track") and the second team attempting the previously unclimbed and more difficult West Ridge, thus making the first traverse of the mountain. The expedition would also conduct scientific research. This ambitious program, heartily embraced by both teams, required outstanding leadership, which was masterfully provided by Dyhrenfurth. A rivalry developed between the West Ridge team and the Southeast Ridge group, resulting in fractious encounters that were resolved only with calm and

Above: Nawang Gombu, 1963. Below: Nawang Gombu meets President Kennedy, September 1963, during presentation of the National Geographic Society's Hubbard Medal.

highly democratic leadership. West Ridge team member Tom Hornbein would later comment, "Only an American expedition would attempt to vote itself to the top of Everest." The Sherpas on the expedition saw the sahibs holding "lots of meetings" and were amazed at how much talking now seemed to be involved in climbing Everest. In fact, some of the sahibs' discussions concerned the Sherpas themselves, for the usual frustrations and difficulties—salaries, load amount, allocated clothing and gear, food, etc.—demanded delicate handling. The older Sherpas were by now experienced expedition staff and knew how far sahibs could be pushed. Yet Dyhrenfurth, with Gombu's assistance, was generally able to placate the Sherpas and secure their ongoing commitment. Like Tenzing before him, Gombu had little patience with Sherpa procrastination and expedition politics and was persuasive when telling them so.

The team soon recognized Gombu's strength and climbing skills, which too were reminiscent of my grandfather's, and Gombu was named to the Southeast Ridge summit team. This caused some disquiet among the Khumbu Sherpas, who comprised the majority of the Sherpa team and who, since the opening of Nepal in 1950, had seen themselves as up-and-coming contenders for the lucrative climbing monopoly the Darjeeling Sherpas had once enjoyed. More experienced and sophisticated, the Darjeeling Sherpas still landed the plum roles on most expedition teams, and the 1963 American expedition was no exception. But Gombu handled the problem with tact and firmness, and continued working throughout his career to dismantle this feud.

Gombu's partner in that first summit attempt was six-foot, five-inch "Big" Jim Whittaker. With a whole foot difference in height, they made an even more curious duo than Tenzing and Hillary had, but like their predecessors, Gombu and Whittaker climbed smoothly and confidently as a team. At 11:30 A.M. on 1 May, the two approached the summit of Everest. Just before the summit, Big Jim stopped and gestured for Gombu to step up first.

"No, you go first," said Gombu, touched by the generous gesture.

"Come, let's go together," Big Jim replied, and they walked side by side up the last few feet to the summit. The Americans had made their first ascent of Everest with a generosity of spirit that has become part of expedition lore.

Exhausted and overwhelmed, Gombu at last fully understood what his uncle had felt on his return to the South Col ten years before.

This summit was just the first of many successes for this American expedition: they also climbed the West Ridge of Everest for the first time and made the first traverse of Everest. It was a record-breaker, part of the credit for which is due to that feisty and determined climber Tom Hornbein, whose refusal to abandon the West Ridge attempt carried the team into the annals of mountaineering history.

For Gombu it was a dream come true. Not only was he now installed in the record books of American and world mountaineering, but he had made lifelong friends. In his recollections of the climb, Dyhrenfurth cites one small example of Gombu's kindness and generosity as well as his great strength. Dyhrenfurth had had to shoulder an extra Sherpa load on a carry to the South Col and had nearly collapsed outside his tent on the windswept and barren wastes of the Col. Realizing Dyhrenfurth's distress and the exhaustion of the other team members, Gombu forsook the warmth and shelter of his tent to help Dyhrenfurth remove his ropes and crampons so he could enter his own tent to rest and recuperate. Gombu's solicitude and strength made a deep and lasting impression on Dyhrenfurth.

His friends and climbing colleagues invited Gombu to visit the United States in September 1963 to be presented to President John F. Kennedy and to receive the Hubbard Medal, awarded by the National Geographic Society for distinction in exploration, discovery, and research, among other awards. This young Sherpa had come a long way from his home in the wilds of eastern Tibet.

Gombu was again on Nanda Devi in 1964 with a team from the Indian Mountaineering Foundation (IMF) under Colonel Narinder Kumar. This time, on 20 June, Gombu, with his teammate Dawa Norbu, stepped up to the summit.

The following year the IMF invited him back to join a team attempting Everest under Captain Mohan Kohli. The expedition was successful, and Gombu became the first person to climb Everest twice. For this he was awarded numerous formal honors, including India's highest honor, the Padma Bhushan, and the Indian Mountaineering Foundation Gold Medal.

Gombu then returned to HMI in Darjeeling to find that he had been promoted to Deputy Director of Field Training under Tenzing. Between work and family obligations he continued to climb over the next decade. When he participated in the American North Face Expedition to Everest in 1982, even at forty-six he was one of the fittest members on the team. Gombu has since been invited to climb all over the world and has delighted in scaling the relatively smaller peaks of North America and Europe.

When Tenzing Norgay was forced to retire as Director of Field Training in 1976, Gombu assumed the position, which he held until his own retirement in 1999. He is now an adviser to HMI, just as Tenzing was after 1976.

His major work, however, is with the Sherpa Buddhist Association (formerly the Sherpa Climbers' Association), of which he has been president since 1999, in Darjeeling. Tenzing established this organization to help Sherpas permanently disabled by climbing accidents and the families of those Sherpas who do not return from the mountains. Today, with Sherpa climbers being recruited out of Nepal rather than Darjeeling, the association is primarily concerned with caring for the remaining old Sherpas and their families, comprising around 40 percent of the beneficiaries of the association's aid, and the poorer Sherpa families of Darjeeling, irrespective of whether or not they have mountaineering connections.

Gombu also continues his efforts to mend the long-standing rift between the Darjeeling and Nepal or Khumbu Sherpas. Professional jealousy and resentment between the two groups reached a crescendo during the 1970s, when Darjeeling Sherpas were denied permits to work in Nepal. Gombu and Tenzing aired the issue in a 1982 meeting of the United International Alpine Club, however, and were supported in their effort to rescind the ban by Sir Edmund Hillary and other prominent figures in the world mountaineering fraternity. Subsequently the situation improved markedly. In fact, the list of those who have reached the summit of Everest in recent years includes some prominent Darjeeling Sherpas, all Tenzing Norgay's descendants: Lobsang in 1993, Jamling in 1996, and myself in 1997. Gombu encourages any opportunity for interaction among groups of Sherpas in the eastern Himalaya and specifically encourages HMI to enlist the poorer Sherpas from the Makalu-Barun region of Nepal to work at HMI. There they gain the skills they need, and can use their native mountain skills and strengths to build a brighter, more secure future for themselves and their children.

Nawang Gombu now lives a quiet life in Darjeeling, although more often than not he is away at a conference or government meeting or visiting family and friends abroad. He is excellent company and still very much a headstrong man who will call a spade a spade. The love of the mountains still shines in his eyes, and he is highly regarded in the Sherpa homes of Darjeeling and the Khumbu. He is a credit to his profession and so honors the Sherpa people he most ably represents.

DORJEE LHATOO, 1941–

Dorjee Lhatoo's speech is soft and measured, giving the impression that he says nothing that he hasn't given a significant amount of thought. Unlike most Sherpas of his generation, he is literate, and the titles on his bookshelf reveal an interest in the world far beyond the Himalaya. His sophisticated manner and excellent command of English lead any newcomer to the world of Indian mountaineering to imagine that he is an academic or perhaps a learned man of leisure. Yet this man was, until his retirement in 1999, a professional mountaineer, one of the finest in the Himalaya and, for that matter, the world. Those who have watched him climb say he has one of the most fluid and impressive climbing styles around, strong and effortless with an endurance that belies his slight build.

Here, you imagine, is a man fortunate to have been able to climb for a living, to spend years as an instructor with frequent forays into the mountains to climb some of the greatest peaks in the Himalaya. Unfortunately for Lhatoo, his love of climbing was always compromised by the pressure of *having* to climb. The months away from family, the ever-present fear and danger, the cold and isolation of long expeditions and, above all else, the worry about his wife and children should ill befall him were a great burden. "Perhaps if I had climbed as an amateur I would have experienced the pure joy of the sport," he says.

Lhatoo still represents the reality of mountaineering for many Sherpa and Tibetan men. It is a financial necessity and not a career choice they would make given other circumstances. In Tenzing's genera-

Dorjee Lhatoo and wife Doma, Darjeeling, 1999.

tion, Sherpas told their sons; "I climb so you won't have to." Dorjee
Lhatoo's generation was on the cusp of change, but this statement is also
true of Lhatoo. Lhatoo, however, has a genuine passion for the mountains. When he speaks of the view from the summit of Nanda Devi or
days on previously unclimbed peaks in Bhutan, one senses the deep
personal satisfaction and joy he experiences. Whatever life he had chosen to lead, one senses that climbing clearly would have been an integral part of it.

Born in 1941 in the small village of Yatung near Phari in Tibet, Lhatoo was the eldest of five children. His father was caretaker of one of the
bungalows established and maintained for the use of expeditions and
other government officials from British India. This Yatung bungalow was
especially popular with Sherpa expedition staff since it was the only
Sherpa house in that district. Lhatoo remembers as a young lad meeting Tenzing when the latter was traveling with Professor Giuseppe Tucci.
Lhatoo was impressed by the Sherpa guide, who cut a dashing, roman-
tic figure in his riding breeches, stylish boots, and upturned collar, his
long hair falling into his eyes, and that flashing smile that could light
up a room. Lhatoo remembers that Tenzing "had a hearty laugh and

an easy manner that made him very popular with all who met him." Such encounters with outsiders were the only respite for Dorjee as a child in the harsh and demanding land of feudal Tibet.

One of his earliest Tibetan memories is of gangs of prisoners in shackles and rags, trudging from house to house begging for food. Some were missing hands that had been amputated as punishment, and many were ill. In comparison, Lhatoo's life was secure and happy, though not without great difficulties. His father died when he was just seven years old, and his mother, deciding to never remarry, trekked across the Himalaya with her children to resettle in Darjeeling in the late 1940s, where she had family to support her and her children. Lhatoo was enrolled in a Kuomintang (Chinese Nationalist) school in Darjeeling for two years until the 1960 fall of the Kuomintang in China spelled the end of school funding. That was the end of Lhatoo's only formal education: from that point his family needed him to help at home and to find local work when he could, though he continued his self-education by reading copiously. It fell upon Lhatoo as the eldest son to help his mother with family affairs, and the two returned to Tibet several times over the following years to try to sell their land and other assets there. This they ultimately did, although at less than their value. Still, the family was more fortunate than those who lost their land to the invading Chinese with no compensation of any kind. And the small amount of money resulting from the sale eased their new life in India.

Still in his teens, Lhatoo joined the Indian Army. The salary was meager, just sixty rupees a month, but it was regular work and he felt that the future was promising if he applied himself. But in 1962 his plans for a rising career in the army were routed when his mother arranged for him to marry Tenzing's niece, Sonam Doma. Though he had no objections to Doma herself, Lhatoo was terrified at the prospect of marriage. On his pitiful salary he could barely keep himself—how could he support a wife and children? Granted leave from his Lucknow-based regiment to go home for the wedding, he suffered dreadful panic on reaching Darjeeling and took flight back to Lucknow. His determined mother wrote to his commanding officer, and Lhatoo was duly ordered to go home and marry as his mother wished. Today Lhatoo laughs at the memory of his anxiety, for he and Doma have had a long and happy life together and are blessed with three successful sons.

It soon became obvious that Lhatoo's army life was not ideal for a family man, so he enrolled in two mountaineering courses at HMI. Recognizing Dorjee's exceptional skills as a climber, the principal of HMI, Colonel Jaiswal, offered him a teaching position upon his completion of the courses. Lhatoo accepted and in 1962 commenced his career as an HMI instructor.

He made his first Himalayan summit within a year, the 5,800-meter Frey's Peak in Sikkim. This was followed by several more summits on smaller peaks such as Palung, Rathong, and Koktang. Finding joy in the climb itself and not just in summiting, Lhatoo began to hone his technical climbing skills and swiftly became a formidable force on the most difficult routes in the Sikkim Himalaya.

He was asked to join a joint expedition of the armies of Bhutan and India to climb Chomolhari, a peak on the border of Bhutan and Tibet. The venture was financed by His Majesty King Jigme Dorji Wangchuk of Bhutan, who was keen to put a Bhutanese atop a Himalayan peak. The expedition met with opposition from a heretofore unconsidered quarter: the people of Bhutan, who believe the mountains to be the abode of the gods. To set foot on them would defile the peak and incur the wrath of the gods on the people beneath, they argued.

The king resolved the matter by ordering a special *puja* (religious ceremony) to be held, presided over by a senior Bhutanese lama. The lama duly presented the king with a sacred pot containing various amulets and precious items to be carried to the summit and offered to the goddess of Chomolhari, Tashi Tsheringma, the supreme member of the Five Sisters of Long Life, of which Chomolungma is a minor sibling. Designated the custodian of the pot, Dorjee Lhatoo ceremoniously placed it in his climbing rucksack at the start of the expedition. And with that, Lhatoo and Doma decided that their third child, shortly expected, would be named after this mountain whose deity he was to honor for the sake of all Bhutanese. When Lhatoo and his climbing partner Colonel Prem Chand reached the summit, they placed the sacred pot reverently in the snow. Lhatoo's son Lhari was so named in honor of the goddess of this sacred peak.

In the coming years this formidable climber achieved other Bhutanese summits: Khangri, and later the 7,500-meter Gangkhar Punsum South. On another occasion in Bhutan he made a solo, alpine-style climb of the 6,360-meter Jazela Khang, a virgin peak and one of his most pleasurable climbing experiences.

In 1975 Lhatoo took part in an Indo-French attempt on Nanda Devi East (in the Garhwal Himalaya in northern India), which previously had been climbed by only one non-European climber—Tenzing, who regarded this route as the hardest he had ever attempted. Yves Pollet Villard led the French and Balwant Sandhu the Indians. As one of the summit team, Lhatoo climbed with Villard and the legendary ice-climber Walter Cecchinel. Without being roped or using bottled oxygen, the three summited together, celebrating their astounding technical feat by dipping into a bottle of cognac. The down-climb must indeed have tested their mettle. Climbing with the world's best, Lhatoo had held his own, and his colleagues now recognized him as a world-class mountaineer.

Lhatoo joined an Indo-Japanese attempt at traversing Nanda Devi in 1976 from the main peak to the east peak. When two of the Japanese achieved the summit, the expedition goal was considered achieved and the team descended. Lhatoo returned to Darjeeling disappointed not to have had a summit opportunity. However, a partial compensation came in the form of an invitation later that same year to the International Mountaineer's Meet in Chamonix, France. The meet was a fascinating experience for a man with a thirst for knowledge and new experiences, and his climbs in the Alps following the conference proved to be an unexpected bonus. He scaled Mont Blanc and the Aigulle Vert and attempted Mont Modit, though without success. Climbing in the Alps appealed to Lhatoo because it offered him the ideal climbing scenario: challenging routes in beautiful mountains where the climber is responsible for himself or herself alone and where, at the end of a hard day's effort, one retires to comfort, good food, warmth, and a bottle of fine wine! Mountaineering purists would disagree, but Lhatoo was unapologetic.

With several smaller first ascents under his belt, Lhatoo returned to Nanda Devi in 1981 as part of a team of Indian men and women attempting the main peak, with the goal of getting the relatively inexperienced women to the summit. Dorjee Lhatoo always felt that Nanda Devi presented the greatest climbing challenges, and this attempt did not disappoint. Lhatoo led the summit team with the three female climbers, Rekha Sharma, Harshwanti Bisht, and Chandraprabha Aitwal, roped to the more experienced Rattan Singh, Sonam Paljor, and himself. Leaving their high camp at 4 A.M., they climbed without stopping until reaching the summit at 5:30 P.M., Lhatoo having fixed ropes all the way up the mountain, almost to the summit, to assist the women climbers. When the exhausted climbers started down after a brief rest at the summit, Lhatoo was struck with a case of what was probably retinal edema, altitude sickness of the eyes. He realized that, even with his vision blurred due to retinal internal bleeding, he was still the most capable person to lead the team, so he carried on, relying on his considerable skill and exceptional grit to get all six of them safely back. By the time they returned to camp, the team had been on their feet for twenty-three hours straight. This leadership and his continued achievements in mountaineering earned Lhatoo an unparalleled reputation in climbing circles in India and abroad. Promoted to Deputy Director of Field Training at HMI, he found the position demanding but still found time to accept selected expedition challenges when they arose.

Everest had never been high on Lhatoo's climbing wish list, but when he was invited to join the 1984 Indian Everest Expedition, he accepted, reaching the summit with Bachendri Pal, the first Indian woman to climb the peak. The views were breathtaking and conditions stable and relatively safe, and he was grateful for the opportunity to take part in this expedition, but Lhatoo didn't find Everest a great mountaineering challenge and candidly—but not very politicly—said so after the climb. By now a highly experienced and skilled technical climber, Lhatoo felt that, although Everest demanded stamina and physical strength, it was not a difficult task to reach the top, given good weather and snow-ice conditions. There are many who would agree.

Lhatoo continued to climb in the Himalaya and abroad. In 1986 the Himalayan Mountaineering Institute awarded him the first Tenzing Norgay Award for excellence in mountaineering, and in 1999 he retired from HMI. His children—three sons—have all pursued nonmountaineering careers, and for this he is grateful.

If the opportunity of pursuing another career had presented itself, would Lhatoo have taken it?

"Yes, certainly," he says without hesitation. Then, after a pause and a wry smile, "Well, probably not." I have the distinct impression that little could have kept this man away from the mountains, and it was no coincidence that Lhatoo is arguably the best technical climber India has ever produced.

LOBSANG TSHERING BHUTIA, 1953–1993

Lobsang Tshering was forty years of age and one of the most experienced climbers in his party when on 10 May 1993 he climbed the final ridge of Everest and placed the Indian and HMI flags on the summit of Chomolungma. He was a fine climber, strong and dependable, and a much admired and trusted teacher. He was also an integral member of many expeditions throughout the Himalaya. His summits included Jomsong (7,330 meters, Sikkim, India), Kabru Dome (6,580 meters, Sikkim), Saser Kangri in the Karakoram (7,580 meters, Pakistan), as well as Kamet (7,500 meters, Sikkim) and numerous other peaks in Sikkim.

In 1984 he reached the 8,000-meter South Col on the Indian Everest Expedition with ease, but he did not have a place on one of the summit teams, a great disappointment to him. In 1991 he did climb to the top of Kanchenjunga, so that when the call to Everest came two years later he was ready.

Sadly, Lobsang lost his life on my 1993 expedition to Everest, the only member of the Tenzing family to do so. Given the great risks faced over so many decades, it is not surprising that one day Chomolungma would exact a price from our clan. For those who survived, the price was too high: the mountaineering world lost in Lobsang its greatest gentleman and one of its finest climbers.

RITA GOMBU MARWAH, 1957–

The daughter of Nawang Gombu, Rita Gombu inherited her father's gutsy, shoot-from-the-hip attitude as well as his great strength and skill in the mountains. She was a pioneer of Sherpa women's climbing, and the outstanding success of Indian women mountaineers owes much to her passion for the sport and her considerable mountain skills.

Rita was born in difficult family circumstances in Darjeeling in September 1957. Her mother, Dawa Phuti, died in childbirth. Bereft, her father, Nawang Gombu, released the tiny but robust infant into the care of the nurses at the old Planters' Hospital.

Rita Gombu Marwah at Everest, 300 meters above Base Camp.

When she was six months old, Ang Lhamu and Tenzing welcomed her into the sprawling family at Ghang-La, where she remained until she was twelve years old, by which time her father had remarried. Rita called Ang Lhamu "Mummy" and was deeply attached to this warm and generous woman. So it was that Rita spent her childhood living in the midst of mountains and expeditions. It is hardly surprising that climbing became her calling, for in her mind she had climbed the great Himalayan peaks before she had even set foot on them.

Her earliest recollection of Everest is of being taken to a public reception in honor of her father when he made his first ascent in 1963. Although just five years old, she knew what this mountain was even if she didn't fully understand the significance of what Ghombu had achieved.

Educated at Loreto Convent in Darjeeling, Rita demonstrated an early natural climbing ability, which her family encouraged in their daughter—still quite unusual in those days—enrolling her in basic courses at HMI as soon as she was old enough. As Rita gained experience, her confidence in her abilities grew. Her first summit was the B. C. Roy peak, an HMI training peak that was child's play for this young

Sherpani. She was then invited to join a pre-Everest expedition to Kabru Dome (6,600 meters) and Mana (7,272 meters), training peaks in Sikkim, India. On this training expedition Rita realized that she could perform as well as if not better than most of her more experienced colleagues; Everest became a real possibility for her.

Her Everest dreams were realized when she was invited to join the 1984 Indian Everest expedition, a landmark in India since it was the country's first mixed Everest team. In India, a far more traditional nation than most, climbing was not seen as a woman's activity, although India had produced some fine women mountaineers. So when the chance for Everest came, some very determined women planned to join the expedition. They proved to be more than capable, in some instances outperforming the men.

On 9 May the first summit team set out at 7 A.M. from their South Col base: Ang Dorji, who had climbed Everest before, Phu Dorji, a mountaineering instructor, and Rita, then aged twenty-seven. Weather conditions were not good, and after an hour in the freezing conditions, Ang Dorji, who feared frostbite and also was not using bottled oxygen, turned back. For several more hours Phu Dorji and Rita continued their climb, but the wind had increased to 50 mph and clouds were moving in across the Southeast Ridge. Rita wanted the summit, but not at the cost of her life, so she made the difficult decision to retreat after having reached 8,665 meters, just 183 meters short of the summit. Phu Dorji went on to reach the summit alone that day.

Rita says she has no regrets about this decision, and that she knew she could have reached her goal had the weather cooperated. Her women's team was ultimately successful, for on the second bid Bachendri Pal reached the summit a few days later, becoming the first Indian woman to do so. For Rita, the entire experience—ferrying up and down the great Khumbu Icefall, life at Base Camp, the chance to climb high on Everest, and the honor of being part of an historic expedition—was extraordinary and gratifying.

It would be nine years before she returned to Everest as deputy leader of the first Indo-Nepalese Women's Everest Expedition. Bachendri Pal was expedition leader, and the aim of the expedition was to give the younger female climbers of India and Nepal a chance to climb Everest. Rita now had two young children and no desire to make a summit bid.

Six women on the team summited: nineteen-year-old Diki Dolma, Radha Devi Thakur, Deepu Sharma, Santosh Yadav, Savita Martoliya, and Suman Kotiyal. It was an astonishing achievement by any measure, reflecting Bachendri's and Rita's expert planning and leadership.

Lobsang's death on the mountain around this time sent a chill through the team, for he had trained many of the women. Rita, as I did, bore the deep sorrow of being a family member. She could not accept his death until she saw him herself, so Rita and her team put their Sherpas at the disposal of my exhausted crew to bring Lobsang's body down. With the end of this tragic expedition, Rita decided to close the Everest chapter of her life.

Rita is very clear about why she wanted to climb Everest: because she knew she could. Although she admits that her father's success and encouragement were positive factors, she did not feel any family pressure to climb.

Rita's life is still as busy as ever with her work as an executive with Air India and raising her two children. She no longer climbs but remains passionate about the outdoors and tries to expose her son and daughter to the mountains whenever possible. Should they wish to follow in the footsteps of their mother and grandfather she would not stop them, but she is nevertheless grateful that for the younger generations of the family climbing is now a choice, not a requirement for survival. She attributes this fortunate situation to her great-uncle Tenzing, for it was his Everest success, she believes, that gave Sherpas an identity and that changed their fortunes as a community.

JAMLING TENZING NORGAY, 1965–

Jamling, whose name means "world-renowned," was born in Darjeeling in 1965, the second of the four children of Tenzing Norgay and Daku Sherpa.

He felt a strong desire to climb from an early age and often accompanied his father on trekking expeditions into Sikkim with HMI. Although a devoted father to the four children, Tenzing was not keen for them to follow in his footsteps: when Jamling advanced the idea of attempting Everest with the 1984 Indian Women's Expedition, his father quickly quashed the plan, exhorting Jamling to get a good education so he wouldn't *have* to carry loads in the mountains, risking his life.

Educated at St. Paul's Anglican School for Boys and then Mt. Hermon School in Darjeeling, as were his brothers and sister, Jamling, like me, excelled at sport and athletics and was a fierce competitor in all fields. Almost the same age, my uncle and I reveled in competing with each other at school, and the achievements of one would spur the other on to even greater achievements. Little did we know that we would also reach the summit of Everest just one year apart. With his parents often away, Jamling grew into an independent and self-sufficient young man. Like his siblings, he attended college in the United States, and upon graduation from Northland College in Wisconsin he found little difficulty in settling into the Western way of life in the United States.

These years in the United States, however, deprived him of the final years of his parents' lives, for his father passed away in 1986 and his mother in 1992. Once married and with a young family of his own, Jamling began to feel that he was losing touch with the Himalaya, so he moved back to Darjeeling and assumed responsibility for the upkeep and preservation of his father's house, Ghang-La, which remains his home. He is currently the only child of Tenzing and Daku to live in the Himalaya.

The dream of Everest, though, burned strongly for Jamling and, despite his father's old advice against pursuing climbing, he accepted an invitation to join the 1996 IMAX Everest Expedition as climbing leader. Although he had no expedition experience, Jamling was confident that he could handle the responsibilities of leading a climbing team on a major Himalayan peak. Among his fellow climbers were Everest veterans Ed Viesturs and David Breashears, both of whom had impeccable mountaineering credentials.

Jamling decided to consult with a Buddhist lama before embarking on such a dangerous quest, traveling in January 1996 to Siliguri, West Bengal, to meet Chatral Rimpoche, a most revered lama of the Nyingma sect. Rimpoche performed a divination, declaring that conditions were not favorable. Jamling was deeply troubled by this, but by then he was committed to the Everest team and could not withdraw. Later that spring he also consulted with Geshé Rimpoche, a lama in Kathmandu, whose divinations were more cautiously optimistic. Jamling decided to continue with the expedition.

Jamling Tenzing Norgay on the summit of Everest, 23 May 1996.

Finally on the flanks of the mountain in May, the IMAX team decided to retreat to Camp II while other teams from around the world made their own summit efforts on 10 May. The weather deteriorated, and all too soon nine climbers—including expedition leaders Rob Hall and Scott Fischer—from several teams had lost their lives to Everest. Shocked and disheartened, the IMAX team wavered over the next days about whether to renew or abandon their efforts, so Jamling asked his wife by cell phone to consult Geshé Rimpoche again. The omens were good and, summoning tremendous willpower and personal courage, Jamling and his fellow climbers renewed their push up the mountain. Conditions improved markedly, and on 23 May at last Jamling stood where his father had stood in 1953. It was a profoundly moving experience for this son of Everest.

CHAPTER 10

THE NEW LORDS
OF EVEREST

●

IF SHERPAS PARTICIPATED in the modern Olympics or other physical endurance events throughout the world, the *chiyas* (tea-houses) of the Khumbu, Darjeeling, and the great Barun Valley would likely be adorned with gold medals, ribbons, and a collage of international press clippings. Yet we rarely enter such events, largely due to lack of funding but also because a Sherpa's physical stamina comes so naturally that he or she is unlikely to see it as notable.

In long-distance races in Nepal, such as the occasional Kathmandu to Everest Base Camp run, Sherpas take line honors easily. In fact, it's not uncommon for a Sherpa to run from Everest Base Camp to Lukla in a single day, a journey that generally takes Westerners three days to walk. I once made a nonstop circumambulation of the sacred peak of Mount Kailas in Tibet, which involves crossing the 5,635-meter Dolma

View of North Ridge of Everest from Pang La in Tibet. Lhotse peeks out from behind Everest, upper left.

La, in twelve hours—a total distance of 51 kilometers or thirty miles. Indeed, any non-Sherpa who has trekked with Sherpas and has asked them, usually on bended and exhausted knees, "How long to camp?" knows that the stock response from the smiling, unstrained face will be, "In Sherpa time or Western time?"

In the 1970s many Sherpas began to see mountaineering as a career rather than as a rather dangerous form of occasional employment. Coupled with this was a shift in the way Western climbers saw their Sherpa colleagues. Sherpas' strength and stamina in the mountains were almost legendary, but Western attitudes tended to preclude Sherpas from tackling technical pitches or performing lead roles on a peak. One young Sherpa was pivotal in changing this image. He possessed not only the innate abilities of his race in abundance but the desire and initiative to learn from watching his technically superior Western climbing companions and then to prove that he was up to any task on a mountain. This man was Pertemba Sherpa, the first of a new generation of Sherpas. Pertemba and other Sherpas who followed made their mark on the major peaks, and at last Sherpas began to receive well-deserved public recognition for technical climbing achievements.

PERTEMBA SHERPA, 1948–

As a highly intelligent man with some degree of education, Pertemba Sherpa could have done anything he wanted to do. But he, like Tenzing himself, is a rare Sherpa who climbs solely for the love of climbing and the joy of summiting, so mountaineering is the vocation he chose.

Pertemba was born in Khumjung village in the Khumbu in 1948. His family were farmers, and he was one of the first students to attend the newly opened Hillary School, where he was enrolled from 1962–65. Two of his older brothers had worked regularly as expedition Sherpas, so the world of mountaineering was familiar to him, and in 1966 he traveled to Kathmandu to work for Colonel Jimmy Roberts, the now legendary father of Himalayan trekking for Westerners. Roberts had established the first trekking agency in Nepal, Mountain Travel, and saw in Pertemba the makings of an excellent sirdar. Pertemba received a modest salary and free quarters in the company compound in Kathmandu when not with a trekking party in the hills.

In 1968 he gained his first taste of climbing with a large German

Pertemba Sherpa on Gauri Shankar, 1979.

trekking and climbing group in the Mardi Himal region of the Anna-purnas. He astounded the Western team members with his agility and fearlessness, despite being a novice mountaineer, and so found the direction he wished to follow in his Himalayan work. In 1970 he joined his first major expedition, a British team attempting the awesome South Face of Annapurna I (8,078 meters—in 1950, Maurice Herzog's team made this the first 8,000-meter peak to be climbed). The 1970 climb, led by Chris Bonington, was a complete success, yet equally important was the lifelong friendship that developed between the British climbing legend and Pertemba Sherpa. Bonington would later write of Pertemba in *The Everest Years: A Climber's Life*:

> Highly intelligent, good-looking, charismatic he seemed at home in any situation in the West, and yet he hadn't lost the traditional values of Sherpa society. He had that combination of twinkling humour, dignity and warmth that is one of the enduring qualities of so many Sherpas.

In 1972, with Bonington, Pertemba made the first of his two attempts at the unclimbed Southwest Face of Everest, one of the most difficult and dangerous routes on Everest—a sheer face of rock and ice requiring highly technical and skilled climbing. The team failed to summit but gained invaluable experience and knowledge of the route that would stand them in good stead when they tried again in 1975. Apart from his outstanding organizational skills as sirdar, Pertemba had proven his skill as a high-altitude mountaineer, and on 26 September he finally reached the summit of Everest with Briton Pete Boardman (who would later lose his life climbing the Kangshung Face). Although the low visibility that day meant he could see virtually nothing of the extraordinary vista below, Pertemba was overcome with emotion and excitement. He proudly tied the flag of Nepal to the old pole, now gone, left by a Chinese survey team and began the long descent.

Between major expeditions Pertemba worked with Jimmy Roberts and enjoyed the relatively easy life of a trekking sirdar, with no climbing, no risk, and lots of Sherpa staff to share the load. His work enabled him to meet a wide variety of people, which he thoroughly enjoyed, and kept him in peak condition for his next climb. It would also lay the foundations for his own business later in his career.

In 1979 he returned to Everest with a West German expedition, the first to put all its members on the summit of Everest, including Pertemba. It remains the shortest expedition on record, just thirty-two days (compared to the normal six to eight weeks) from Base Camp to summit and back to Base Camp! For Pertemba, however, the summit did not bring the euphoria of his first ascent, although the weather on this occasion was near perfect. Looking out from his perch at the top of the world, he found the view all he had hoped it would be, and he felt that now he could return to his life in trekking and put Everest behind him.

But given his great love of climbing big peaks, this was not to be, for in 1985 he was approached by a Norwegian team led by Arne Naess, which included Bonington, with whom Pertemba was by then quite close. At thirty-seven, Pertemba was already past the upper age (thirty-five) for most Sherpa mountaineers, but this was an invitation he could not refuse—he accepted the offer of work as sirdar plus a place on a summit team.

The Norwegian expedition was record-breaking in many ways; it was the first ascent of Everest by a Scandinavian team; it put a record number of team members—seventeen—on the summit; and American team member Dick Bass, at age fifty-five, became the oldest person to climb Everest and the first person to reach the highest point on all seven continents. In addition, Sherpa legends Ang Rita and Sungdare made their respective third and fourth ascents of the mountain, Ang Rita without bottled oxygen. This ascent was also Bonington's first and Pertemba's last.

Pertemba would be involved in many more attempts on the mountain, but only as sirdar. These included the successful 2000 Nepali Women's Expedition, which put four Sherpanis atop Everest.

Pertemba no longer hungers for the summit. Three ascents of Everest were enough to satiate the climber in him, and he believes that the universal obsession with Everest discourages climbers from attempting smaller, equally beautiful peaks that are as demanding—if not more so—than Chomolungma.

Now running his own trekking agency in Nepal, he teaches climbing in the Langtang and Annapurna ranges of the Nepal Himalaya, and occasionally joins one of his trekking groups to stretch his legs and meet new people. He still travels widely. He has climbed in England, Switzerland, and many other countries, has visited the Australian outback, and has scaled Mount Whitney in Alaska. He is an executive member of the Nepal Mountaineering Association and is a committee member of Edmund Hillary's Himalayan Trust as well as a member of the Kathmandu Environmental Education Project. (Founded in the late 1980s, KEEP educates both tourists and Nepalis on major environmental issues—such as deforestation, waste management, erosion, energy conservation, and wood-cutting—impacting the region.)

Mountaineering has been, he says, a "mixed blessing" for Sherpas. He believes that the intrusion of the outside world has irrevocably changed the Everest region and our Sherpa culture and that, in some ways, we have lost some precious aspects of our ancient traditions. In cultural terms his concerns are with the social-family system—the breakdown of the village network in which the old and very young were cared for. He worries about the young generations of Sherpas (like himself) who seek work that takes them away from their home village and leaves the family network lacking. He is concerned that young Sherpas are increasingly less willing to learn and speak the Sherpa language. Yet generally he believes the changes have been positive, for our people now enjoy benefits we otherwise would not have, and we have been able to absorb many positive aspects of Western life and culture, such as health and hygiene, education, and technology. Sherpa climbers, too, have become experienced, well-equipped mountaineers who are generally paid well for their work and for whom mountaineering provides more financial security than previously.

For his two young daughters, he is content in the knowledge that the education he is now able to afford for them will enable them to lead lives of their own choosing. If they want to climb he will support them, but more importantly he wants to engender in them a love and respect for nature and the outdoors, which can only help Nepal to a brighter environmental future.

DORJEE SHERPA, 1965–

In the hamlet of Thamo, a short walk from Thamey, I sometimes stop at a *chiya* (teahouse) for a glass of that sweet, milky tea so welcome on a cold Himalayan day. On a wooden bench nearby sits an uncommonly large Sherpa who looks as if he could carry a team of Western climbers to the summit of Everest with little difficulty. He is known as Lambu Dorjee, or Big Dorjee, and in early December 2000 he was on his way to Everest Base Camp to claim a prime patch of glacial moraine for his spring 2001 Everest expedition team (those who don't do this about six months before their expedition get the worst sites). Eric Shipton and his ilk, the illustrious members of the OBOE Club (the "on the back of an envelope" expedition planners) would turn in their graves at the industry that has become Everest expeditioning.

Yet for Dorjee it is simply business. Everest *is* business. And it is a business this capable Sherpa knows well, for he has climbed Everest eight times. Were he a Westerner he would be a living legend, with sponsorship offers flooding in and his financial future secure. Asked how many more times he will climb Chomolungma, he does some quick mental arithmetic before replying, "three or four." This, he says, is how much he needs to earn to buy a house and land and to educate his children, even though it will mean climbing into his early forties. It is on such occasions, when a risked life is calculated in rupees, that conflicting emotions arise: pride in the ability, courage, and simple practicality of the Sherpa people, and anger and resentment that they must risk their lives on the mountains to win the basic comforts of life.

"I don't have to climb," Dorjee says matter-of-factly. "I could work as a trekking guide or farmer if I chose to. But climbing pays far better, and I'm good at it." It is difficult to argue with this. The hard work of Dorjee, like my grandfather decades ago, has paved the way for the new generation of Sherpa climbers, myself included, to have a good life apart from mountaineering and to climb when we choose.

Dorjee, a native of Thamo, was born in 1965 and began working on expeditions in 1987 when he was hired as the mail runner on an Annapurna IV attempt. However, his chance to climb did not come until spring 1990, when he was taken on as a climbing Sherpa—whose wages far exceed those of a trekking Sherpa—on a team attempting Everest from the north. He did not summit, however, because the Chinese government at that time would not allow Sherpas above 6,500 meters or Camp II—this informal policy was enforced by Chinese liaison officers as a means of ensuring that only Chinese summited Everest from the north. Makalu followed later that year, and then in 1991 came another attempt on Everest with a Spanish team approaching from the south. But still there were no summit opportunities.

Finally, in 1992, with Todd Burleson's American Southeast Ridge team, Dorjee stood on top of the world. His unexpected exhilaration surprised him. The following year he was officially a climbing member of the Indian Women's team, reaching the summit on 10 May, and again with a British team in the autumn. Further summit success came in 1994 with the Americans in the spring and a rare, post-monsoon expedition with a British team. His next Everest climb was not until the spring 1997 British Expedition, on which Dorjee accompanied Brigitte Muir, the first Australian woman to climb Everest, to the summit. "She was a strong climber," he recalls. "She did it all by herself, but we were with her."

His seventh summit came in 1999 with American climber Pete Athans. Dorjee speaks with great respect for Athans, as indeed do all Sherpas who have climbed with him. Much of this attitude has to do with a 1991 spring Everest expedition led by Lobsang Sherpa, who was one of the first of our people to seek the recognition of Sherpa successes on Everest. With dedicated support from Athans and some of his American colleagues in raising the funds for an exclusively Sherpa assault on Everest, Lobsang's team put three Sherpas on the summit, Sonam Dendu, Ang Temba, and Apa Sherpa (for the second of his eleven ascents). In a poignant and appropriate reversal of roles, Athans and some of his American colleagues worked as "Sherpa" support climbers on this expedition, carrying loads and helping to set up the high camps, a point not lost on the Sherpa community.

Dorjee is still climbing in the new millennium, but reaching the top himself is no longer important to him, though getting the summit team to the top results in a bonus for the climbing Sherpas. He isn't disappointed if he doesn't summit—that is his karma for that climb. What has been his best expedition? "All of them," he laughs aloud. "I'm alive!" Does he experience fear on a climb? "No, not really. The only thing I worry about is avalanches. The rest is hard work physically, but not really dangerous for me."

Dorjee has no interest in climbing other Himalayan peaks: his family and their future are his priority, and, ever the pragmatist, he knows that Everest pays better, so it will remain his goal. He has no expectations of assistance from his foreign climbing colleagues. After an expedition, he says, he rarely hears from them, and certainly no one has ever offered to sponsor his children's education or support his future. Yet he is not bitter or resentful, for they always take good care of him on the mountain, ensuring he is supplied with good equipment, good food, and life insurance for the duration of the expedition. For this he is grateful. His only suggestion for improvement in his working conditions is that experienced climbing Sherpas like himself would receive far more equi-table pay if they were hired directly by the foreign climbing leader, rather than through the local trekking agent, who keeps a good chunk of the agreed wage. A reasonable request from a man who asks little of moun-taineering but who, like so many of his Sherpa climbing colleagues, has contributed such a great deal.

APA SHERPA, 1962–

The slightly built Apa Sherpa from Thamey has eyes that exude inner strength and courage. Sherpas say his nerves are as cool as the great Khumbu Icefall and that he is the best man to have around in a crisis. Apa's titanic strength lies in his will to succeed; it is a formidable force that has driven him to climb Everest no fewer than eleven times.

Apa received a basic education at the Hillary School in Thamey and is literate in Nepali and in English. As with most Sherpas, literate or not, his early career options were two: trekking or mountaineering. Although his first climbing forays were unsuccessful attempts on Anna-purna I and nearby Dhaulagiri, on those trips he learned that he needed to improve his climbing techniques and his mental attitude, which he then tackled in earnest. In 1990 his hard work reaped the reward of sum-miting Cho Oyu at the age of twenty-eight, and his extraordinary climb-ing career was under way.

Everest summits followed one after another, with seemingly effort-less climbs in ten of the eleven years from 1990 to 2000. This astound-ing record continues to escape notice both within and outside his native Nepal, perhaps because Apa is a quiet and steady achiever, not the self-promoting type who demands attention and reward. Apa denies that his Everest summit quest is motivated by a desire to break records, but his long, unofficial competition with Ang Rita—who has climbed Ever-est ten times without bottled oxygen—perhaps belies that claim. Apa has used oxygen but generally summits without it.

Both Apa and Ang Rita are professional mountaineers, working full-time at it, like so many Sherpas now. Both come from rural back-grounds—indeed, they're both from Thamey—in which climbing is a means to a financial end, not a deliberate career choice or a passion. Whatever his reasons for climbing Everest, Apa has demonstrated his

Above: Apa Sherpa in his home village of Thamey, 2000. Below: Babu Chiri Sherpa and Tashi, Khumbu, 2000.

determination and strength of spirit and body. He knows that a climber's greatest enemy lies within: if we win the battle within ourselves, in our own heads, then no mountain can defeat us and no other climber can compete with us. That awareness is his greatest strength.

BABU CHIRI SHERPA, 1966–2001

Thirty-four years old and father of six young daughters, Babu Chiri was a diminutive Hercules of the Sherpa world. Born in Takshindo in the Solu region, he began his mountaineering career as a porter at the age of thirteen and at twenty-three achieved his first summit, Kanchenjunga.

His summits include other giants of the Himalaya: Dhaulagiri, Shishapangma, Cho Oyu, and Ama Dablam. He summited Everest ten times (mostly without the use of bottled oxygen) via several routes, including the Southeast Ridge, the North Ridge, and the West Ridge, and he is the only person to have climbed Everest twice (in 1995) within a fourteen-day period. Most climbers spend just ten to fifteen minutes on the summit before cold and concern about the descent drive them down, but in 1999 Babu Chiri set up a tent there and stayed for twenty-one hours—without bottled oxygen! During his extraordinary sojourn at the summit, to keep active and alert he sang the national anthem of Nepal into a radio, while his team members at Base Camp recorded and broadcast the transmission on Radio Nepal. "I had to keep talking on my radio, because if I fell asleep I would just freeze over and never wake up," he would later recall.

One could close the record books there, but in spring 2000 he stunned the mountaineering world again by leaving from Base Camp at 5 P.M. on 20 May and reaching the summit of Everest at 9:56 A.M. the following day—a total climbing time of sixteen hours, fifty-six minutes—stopping on the 3,850-meter ascent only for a total of seventy-five minutes to rest and to change his wet socks. "I could have done it faster," he would state matter-of-factly, "had it not been for the terrible blizzard." He broke by nearly three and a half hours the speed record set in 1998 by Kaji Sherpa from Thamey. Most Western mountaineers, generally taking anywhere from two to four weeks to acclimate themselves, are dumbfounded by these records.

Asked why he performed these feats, Babu's reply was frank and uncomplicated: "It's good for my business and it's my job. It will help me build a school in my village for my children and those of my friends there who have no chance for an education." His Nepalese company, Nomad Expeditions, was doing well, but one feels that Babu's accomplishments deserve wider attention than they have so far garnered.

Babu Chiri lost his life on Everest in spring 2001. He fell backward into a gaping crevasse at Camp II while taking photographs—a tragic end to a remarkable climbing life. His body was retrieved by a team of Western and Sherpa climbers and flown to Kathmandu for a public funeral and cremation. Babu Chiri was mourned by both local and foreign climbers, for his cheerful nature and indomitable spirit in the mountains endeared him to all. He added a new dimension to Everest mountaineering and further enhanced the already prodigious mountaineering record of the Sherpas.

●

Sherpa mountaineering and climbing experience, our lifelong exposure to high altitudes, and our long cultural history of carrying and walking great distances under adverse conditions are of significant value to teams from outside our high, unique piece of the world, and Sherpas are indeed paid for our work on expedition teams. In Western eyes, that seems to make us "paid help." Perhaps that's why the majority of Western teams, on achieving their goal, simply pack up and leave without conveying to their Sherpas their gratitude for the help rendered.

There *are* foreign men and women expeditioners who take the time to get to know us and our culture and who later publicly and faithfully acknowledge the Sherpa contributions to an expedition in their interviews, books, and presentations. We Sherpas are grateful to these mountaineers, but we wish they could become the rule rather than the exception.

Given sufficient funding, technical training, and social and economic freedom, for every Messner, Hillary, Bonington, Lowe, and Boukreev there is a Sherpa mountaineer equivalent. Consider Ang Rita Sherpa, Pertemba Sherpa, Sungdare Sherpa, Apa Sherpa, Ang Dorjee, and Ang Tshering. Many other Sherpas are also multiple summiters of Everest, and there are the nameless Sherpa hundreds over the past many decades who have carried loads twice the size of Western packs to the South Col and back. When the mountaineering world truly acknowledges and appreciates the contributions of Sherpas in Himalayan climbing, a natural result will be the realization that Sherpas deserve the same benefits and provisions afforded Western team members: disability insurance, income protection insurance, and survivors' benefits. And when those securities are in place, only then will Sherpas climb as equals, with equal risks, equal protections, and equal, unfettered joy in the summit.

CHAPTER II

MORE
THAN MOUNTAINS

⬤

THERE IS NOT A SHERPA anywhere in the world who would not admit to a fairly severe pang of homesickness every time he or she hears a Himalayan flute or sees an image of those greatest of mountain peaks. The ancient bonds between these people and their vast Himalayan valleys and mountains cannot be broken in a single lifetime.

The mountaineering success of their forebears has, however, afforded many young Sherpas and Sherpanis good educations, comfortable and safe lives, and the luxury of *choosing* their futures. The transition from the old way of life to the new has been far from easy. The cultural gaps to be crossed in just one or two generations are wide, and for some Sherpas the road has proved too long and the separation from

View of North Face of Everest from Base Camp in Tibet.

Sherpa village of Phortse with Sherpani harvesting potatoes, their staple crop.

their homeland too traumatic. Yet many have traveled that road despite the difficulties.

There are now hundreds of Sherpas living abroad: those who have been invited or permitted to live and work in the United Kingdom, the United States, Australia, France, and numerous other countries, and those who live and work illegally overseas in order to make enough money to return to Nepal and establish their own business or buy land and a home. There are also Sherpas who have chosen to stay and work in Nepal and India in aid organizations, government agencies, or within the tourism industry. Their educational backgrounds vary from the most elementary schooling in a Himalayan Trust or local village school, to the highest levels of international postgraduate study and teaching.

Tenzing Norgay's eldest daughters, Pem Pem and Nima, were educated at a local Nepali school in Darjeeling before Tenzing reached the summit of Everest in 1953. Thereafter Tenzing was able to send them to the prestigious Loreto Convent School, where they learned impeccable English and were exposed to girls from many races and regions, both local and foreign. Pem Pem, my mother, married Dhendup Tshering, a local Tibetan whose family were of aristocratic stock, and went on to become matron of the Junior and Primary wings of St. Paul's Anglican School for Boys, a position she held until her retirement in 2000. Nima worked abroad for the Indian Tea Board before eventually marrying Noli C. Galang, a talented and successful Filipino graphic artist. Their children and those of Tenzing and Daku were educated at the best schools in Darjeeling and went on to careers far removed from icy, dangerous peaks and massive high-altitude loads.

Pem Pem's eldest son, my brother, Sonam Tshering, earned a law degree from the University of Delhi and practiced there for several years before returning to open his own law office in Darjeeling. He later married and migrated, with his Tibetan wife, Tseten, and two young sons, Tashi and Norbu, to Australia. Our sister Yangzen graduated as a teacher and worked at Mt. Hermon School in Darjeeling before taking up private tutoring interspersed with frequent travels abroad. I earned a bachelor's degree in sociology from the University of Delhi before becoming a Sydney-based mountaineer and businessman.

Nima's children have also followed diverse careers, with her son Palden graduating in mass communications from Wichita State University in Kansas in 1996. He now works as a media producer in Singapore, where he lives with his Javanese wife, Fira, and their daughter, Syaza. His younger sister, Pema, has a degree in journalism from the University of Minnesota and plans to work in public relations.

Tenzing and Daku's four children attended St. Paul's and Mt. Hermon Schools in Darjeeling before going to college in the United States with the help of their father's friends there. Now all, with the exception of Jamling, who returned to Darjeeling after a long period in the United States, still reside there. The eldest, Norbu, has for the past eight years been the development director of the American Himalayan Foundation in San Francisco, where he is responsible for fundraising to support the many projects in which the Foundation is involved throughout the Himalayan region. Norbu at one time considered a mountaineering career but thought that his future would be more secure in other fields. He studied for his bachelor's degree at the University of New Hampshire and followed with a course in development directorship at the Institute for Non-Profit Studies in San Francisco. Jamling, as mentioned earlier, has assumed responsibility for the family home in Darjeeling and his father's travel company, Tenzing Norgay Adventures. Deki, Tenzing and Daku's only daughter, is a graduate of the Florida International Institute and lives with her American husband, Clark, and their son, Tenzing Thinley, in Los Angeles, where she runs her own dot-com business. Damey, the youngest of the four children, graduated from Manhattanville College and is now a Hong Kong–based marketing executive for Phillip Morris.

Samden Lhatoo, the son of Dorjee Lhatoo and Sonam Doma, has excelled in the field of medicine and is an academic neurologist specializing in epilepsy. A member of the Royal College of Physicians in London, his research has been recognized by the American Epilepsy Society. He lives in Bristol, England, with his Tibetan wife, Sonam, and their children Karchen and Rigzin, and is a veritable treasure trove of Himalayan mountaineering history and lore. I feel sure that beneath all that medical research and academic paperwork there is a Himalayan climber struggling to get out.

Sammy's younger brother Yonden is a senior anchor and assistant editor for Asia Television in Hong Kong, and another brother, Lhari, works in the Indian Police Service Cadre as assistant superintendent, a prestigious post. Contemplating his sons' achievements, Dorjee must reckon that every night spent in an icy mountain camp and every life-risking pitch on the great Himalayan peaks was well worth the cost.

Nawang Gombu's daughter Rita is an executive with Air India, while son Phinjo is a staff reporter with the *Toronto Star* in Canada. His second daughter, Yangdu, and her Ladakhi husband, Motup Goba, run the successful Rimo Expeditions in Delhi, while youngest daughter Ongmu is an executive with Gillette International in Boston.

Fiji seems an unlikely home for a Thamey Sherpa, but it was there that Kami Temba studied for several years until he could return to Nepal to practice medicine. Kami is one of the great success stories of Sir Edmund Hillary's Himalayan Trust. One of the problems the trust has faced since its establishment in the early 1960s has been the unwillingness of some of the Sherpas whom it has trained abroad in various fields, notably medicine, to return to the Khumbu to bestow the benefit of that training on their people. Educating students in Nepal rather than abroad has improved this in recent years, an option made possible by the improving facilities in Kathmandu. However, there was never a moment when Kami did not consider returning to the Khumbu. His wife and children still live in Thamey, running the Valley View Lodge, and he now has a much-respected position at the Khunde Hospital. Kami Temba represents the future of Solu Khumbu, a future that Sherpas must dream and plan for themselves. Outsiders may help, but the drive must come from within, and Sherpas like Kami Temba have shouldered this responsibility willingly.

There are others. Royal Nepal Airlines now has four Sherpa commercial pilots, including Ang Jangbu and Ang Gyalzen. Sherpas now own more than one-third of the trekking and mountaineering agencies in Kathmandu, and there are dozens of successful Sherpa restaurants and hotels in Kathmandu, Solu Khumbu, and around the world.

The twenty-six schools of the Himalayan Trust have spawned and nurtured hundreds of young Sherpa careers. Some have gone on to enter the travel and tourism field in varying capacities—hoteliers, mountain and trekking guides, travel office administrators—while others have attained scholarships and grants for higher study. Ang Rita, chief administrative officer of the Himalayan Trust in Kathmandu, is one such Sherpa. He was one of the scruffy and illiterate forty-seven students who comprised the very first class at the Hillary Primary School in Khumjung. Ang Rita recalls his first day of formal schooling as being a lark. The headmaster, Tem Dorji Sherpa, began to write on the blackboard the letters of the English and Nepali alphabets, and for some inexplicable reason the children found it outrageously amusing. Not so Tem Dorji, who made it clear to the children that they had been blessed with a unique opportunity. Of these forty-seven students, three would secure the first Hillary Scholarships for secondary school study in Kathmandu, and one of them was Ang Rita.

At the final secondary examinations in 1969, Ang Rita placed at the top of the nineteen thousand students taking the National Examination of School Leaving Certificate. He earned two degrees, one in intermediate science in 1973 and one in public administration in 1976. Ang Rita's contribution over the years to the Himalayan Trust has been invaluable, and Sir Edmund and his colleagues feel justifiable confidence in the future security of this exceptional organization when it is in the hands of such capable and responsible people.

The second scholarship went to Mingma Norbu Sherpa. Mingma studied in New Zealand for his forestry doctorate before returning to take up a post as warden of the Sagarmatha (Everest) National Park, where he remained for many years. He now represents Nepal and Bhutan for the World Wildlife Fund.

Lhakpa Norbu, awarded the third scholarship, was for a time mayor of Khumjung district. He completed a doctorate on Sherpa life and traditions, studying Thamey and surrounding villages. Today he holds a highly respected position among his Sherpa people in regard to cultural and religious issues.

Perhaps one of the most endearing and inspiring success stories is that of Lhakpa Sonam Sherpa from Namche Bazaar.

Lhakpa Sonam is the son of Sonam Girmi, a renowned Sherpa mountaineer from Namche. His mother was a close friend of the Tenzing family, and she spent many years in Darjeeling helping Ang Lhamu with her duties at Ghang-La before returning to settle with her husband in Namche. In 1969 Lhakpa Sonam's father joined an expedition to Tukche Peak in the Annapurnas led by Swiss alpinist and photographer Ruedi Homberger. The climb was a success, making the first ascent of this peak, and Homberger and Sonam Girmi became firm friends.

Several years later Ruedi went to Namche to meet Sonam Girmi and his young family. Lhakpa was a student at the Hillary School at Khumjung and later won a Himalayan Trust scholarship for further study at Saleri in Solu. But when Homberger returned again to Namche in 1982, he was devastated to find that young Lhakpa (now aged twenty) had contracted meningitis and became profoundly deaf. Undaunted by his disability, Lhakpa set about gathering records, statistics, and literature of Sherpa mountaineering for a Mt. Everest Documentation Centre and Sherpa Culture Museum in Namche, for which Homberger raised funds in Switzerland. Homberger also tried to help Lhakpa regain his hearing, but Swiss doctors could not help him.

The center is currently compiling a complete record of Sherpa mountaineering, including photographs of all those who have climbed Chomolungma. The museum, meanwhile, with its small but beautifully displayed artifacts, offers a glimpse of a traditional life now fading in the upper Khumbu valleys.

Lhakpa manages both establishments and is making plans for several other small projects, such as the extension of the photo gallery in the center, the building of a large Buddhist *stupa* and copper prayer wheel within the building complex, and the construction of a formal library to house his growing collection of mountaineering literature.

In many ways, Lhakpa Sonam epitomizes the ideal for the new generation of Sherpas. Educated and well-traveled, he is still deeply moved by the strength and tradition of his own culture and, in particular, its mountaineering lore. He understands and accepts the changes that the wider world has brought to the Khumbu but has managed to weave them into his traditional society. He is a remarkable man undertaking a task that will be appreciated and treasured by generations of Sherpas to come.

– CHAPTER 12 –

CHANGE AND
THE FUTURE

●

HE SHERPAS' WORLD has changed profoundly since those
first tentative steps toward the summit of Everest, taken by the
gentleman adventurers of the early twentieth century. Local
politics, global economics, and technology, as well as internal politics
and rivalries between Sherpa communities have all contributed to
change. The Sherpas have managed to ride the waves and, for the most
part, reap the benefits of change, though they have paid a high price
for their newfound prosperity and prestige, one not uncommonly
exacted from a people undergoing great change. The opening of the
borders has resulted in an influx of unwanted elements: drugs in the
bright lights of Kathmandu, for example. However, mountaineering and
tourism have been mostly a blessing for the Sherpas. Before the 1950s,
the infant mortality rate was very high; even in Tenzing's family, only six

Sherpa children in Khumbu, 1953.

of fourteen children survived infancy. Modern medical facilities didn't exist, and folk medicine and mystic beliefs stood in for modern treatment and even basic hygiene. Subsistence farming in the climatically inhospitable region resulted in unreliable food sources.

The Solu Khumbu region holds the key to the future of Sherpa culture and way of life by virtue of the fact that the majority of Sherpas and Sherpa institutions (monasteries, museums, tea shops) are in this small region. Sherpas live in Kathmandu, the Helambu region of Nepal, and Darjeeling, as well as abroad, but the true heartland of the culture is still very much in Solu Khumbu. Largely thanks to the work of the Himalayan Trust, no other region in the Himalaya can boast the same number of schools, hospitals, and health posts. On the other hand, the halcyon days of the Darjeeling Sherpas are long over: the community there is dwindling as mountaineering employment shifts inexorably to Nepal. Unless one is involved with HMI, whose clientele is now primarily Indian, or with some form of private business, there is little opportunity for employment for a Sherpa in Darjeeling, where positions of power are still held primarily by Bengalis. Many of those who remain are retired climbers; their well-educated offspring generally live abroad and visit the region only occasionally.

For many years after the first ascent of Everest in 1953, the Western influx was restricted to mountaineering expeditions, mostly in spring, the optimum climbing season; hence few outsiders came to Solu Khumbu the rest of the year. Then came the work of Sir Edmund Hillary and the Himalayan Trust in the early 1960s. As a result of the trust's efforts, many Sherpas were receiving a basic education before mass tourism came to the region, giving the populace a measure of breathing space in which to prepare mentally and culturally for the ways of the West. This was because Hillary did not see his role and that of the Himalayan Trust as one of "handing out and doing all" for the Sherpas. He approached the project with his characteristic common sense and honesty, encouraging the Sherpas to ask for what we needed, how we thought we would get it, and what we would personally contribute to achieve our goals. He continues to help us develop and fine-tune this plan. Consequently, we learned a great deal about planning and finance, which were new concepts to a culture used to relying primarily on subsistence farming. By putting responsibility largely onto us and empowering us to make our own decisions, the Himalayan Trust also began to enable us to exercise some self-determination—also a new concept.

Although the future of the Sherpas is no longer solely based on mountaineering and guiding, a great many Solu Khumbu Sherpas still make their livelihoods in these two fields. Hence changes in mountaineering, in particular commercial expeditions, will continue to affect Sherpa society. With rare exceptions Sherpas climb for money, and for those with little or no education (and there are still many) mountaineering provides a lucrative, if dangerous, career. A climbing Sherpa can earn in two months what it might take a trekking sirdar a year or more to earn. Great prestige, too, is attached to mountaineering success—especially an Everest summit—among the Sherpa. Not only does an Everest summit virtually ensure future expedition work, it earns the respect of one's village and community.

The endless debate over commercial climbing expeditions—wherein anyone with the money and determination to climb a major Himalayan peak, generally Everest, can join an organized team of experienced Western and Sherpa climbers—is purely academic to the Sherpas. Commercial expeditions bring more work, and hence more income. Still, even after years of involvement with foreign expeditions, Sherpas continue to marvel at the seemingly endless finances those from abroad have at their disposal for this extraordinarily arduous and unlikely quest. But whoever comes to Everest and regardless of whether they summit or even climb to Camp I, wages for Sherpas remain constant (notwithstanding summit bonuses) and can be applied to the construction costs of a house or to school fees.

On the other side of commercial expeditions is the change in the professionalism of foreign team members themselves: it seems to Sherpas that any foreigner with enough money is eligible to be dragged up a mountain. Sherpas who have worked with world-class mountaineers and climbers and are themselves consummate professionals are sobered by the amateurishness of some team members and by the occasional blindness of foreign team leaders to the dangers presented by ill-prepared clients. They also privately express great amusement at the antics and unrealistic hopes of many who come to climb.

Indeed, mountaineering ethics do not yet really concern most Sher-

View of the north ridge of Ama Dablam from the trail above Pheriche village.

pas. It is irrelevant who comes to climb or why they do so. They are all too aware, however, of the increased risks climbers are taking on Everest. Queuing beneath the Hillary Step for an hour or more concerns them greatly, not only for their own safety but also because, when disaster strikes, it is they who are most often called upon to rescue foreign climbers. They accept this with typical pragmatism as a condition of modern-day Everest mountaineering and feel powerless, even reluctant, to change it, because any threat to the numbers coming to Everest is a threat to their livelihood. With the climbing peak royalty for Everest now a staggering $75,000 U.S. per expedition (with a maximum of seven summiters) and ever-increasing numbers of mountaineers and would-be summiters clamoring for permits, it is unlikely the Nepalese government will reduce its own income by reducing the number of climbers permitted on the mountain each season. That constant number means that Sherpas with the courage—or more accurately, the lack of alternative career options—can expect to be hired by expeditions for the foreseeable future.

The road to Everest has also brought wealth, prosperity, and a much brighter and more comfortable future to nonexpedition Sherpas, who do not have to contend with the risks and uncertainty of mountaineering or climbing. For Sherpas in the major villages on the way to Everest and for those who early on commanded sufficient capital and business savvy to invest in tourism, the rewards over the past quarter century have been great. Villages such as Lukla, Phaphlu, Tengboche, and, in particular, Namche Bazaar, have boomed, while more remote hamlets such as Phortse and Thamey have experienced a much slower rate of change and significantly lower levels of development and prosperity.

In addition, Sherpas have become a trekking industry elite and are much sought after as sirdars and guides. The reasons for their popularity are simple: they generally speak some English, which they've learned at Himalayan Trust schools or through Kathmandu trekking agencies; they learn other languages quickly and easily; they accept responsibility and show considerable initiative in a crisis; and they are, after all, Sherpas—famous to Westerners who have been raised on tales of Everest and who lump Sherpas into a sort of "faithful native" category.

The newfound prosperity of the Sherpas is generally easily identifiable. In the old days, wealth was not immediately obvious: the poor lived and looked just as the rich did, and only local knowledge about land and yak ownership differentiated the haves from the have-nots. Today, however, affluent houses and lodges and the general absence of young children (attending good schools in Kathmandu) clearly identify the nouveau riche of the Sherpa world.

This economic transformation of Sherpa society has not been trouble-free. The general effects of inflation and tourism are the same as elsewhere. Tourism drives up local prices and puts pressure on the poorer families, who then pay higher prices for basic items such as rice, oil, and clothing. Goods traditionally traded from Tibet and the upper Khumbu valleys can now be purchased far more cheaply in Kathmandu, thus threatening the livelihoods of Sherpas who have relied on trade and handicrafts for an income. This problem is further exacerbated by the closing of Tibet in 1959 and the increased limits on free movement by Tibetans and Sherpas over the old trade route across the Nangpa La from Tibet into Khumbu.

Sherpas, too, have little tradition of banking savings in the form of cash deposits in an actual bank. Spare funds are commonly channeled into real estate or durable goods: into house or lodge maintenance or into the purchase of jewelry, an age-old symbol of wealth and social prestige. Thus there is little liquid cash to see them through hard times. Fortunately, Nepal has enjoyed a long run of political stability and economic growth since its opening in 1950, and the exponential growth of tourism each year in the absence of the disruptive influences of war, political upheaval, or spiraling depression means the Sherpas have not had to change their way of saving.

Other issues threaten the fabric of Sherpa society and its environment. These have been mostly disregarded by the Sherpas themselves, for their detrimental effects are not obvious and do not immediately threaten incomes.

Village after village in Solu Khumbu is eerily devoid of young, working-age folk. The aged and frail are cared for by siblings or female relatives who have chosen to remain in the harsh environment of the high Himalayan villages. Their offspring visit occasionally from Kathmandu or farther afield, and the wealthier ones take their parents and elderly relatives away with them for the winters or when they can no longer manage alone in their villages. The potato and barley fields lie fallow, the laboriously built stone farmhouses and field walls often in a state of disrepair or total collapse. This flight is because young Sherpas reject the backbreaking grind of farming life when they can make money in trekking and climbing or when they choose a better education, with its opportunities for many careers in the city.

This mass flight of the younger folk from rural to urban areas is the most significant result of the infusion of expedition and tourism monies, because it is ultimately transforming the entire culture. Old crafts such as carpet weaving, *thangka* painting, wool spinning, and traditional carpentry are disappearing in the face of readily available and lower-priced imported goods. There is also good money to be made in selling to unsuspecting tourists cheap, mass-produced "Tibetan and Sherpa" curios from Kathmandu and India rather than making them.

Tibetan Buddhist monasteries have also suffered. The wealth and prestige assured a family whose son rose up through the monastery ranks, especially if he were a significant reincarnation, can now be attained in other ways, primarily through careers in tourism and mountaineering. So, whereas once almost every Solu Khumbu family would have installed a son into a monastic life, today few do so, and the numbers of monks have consequently dwindled. Some in the Sherpa community see fewer monks as an opportunity for Tibetan Buddhism as practiced by the Sherpas to return to a purer form, studied and practiced by those who have a true calling to lead the monastic life and to devote themselves faithfully to the study of the ancient texts and teachings.

The other area of great concern for the future of the Sherpas is the fragile and increasingly threatened ecology of the Khumbu. Apart from a handful of Sherpas, some of whom have witnessed the inevitable impact of greatly increased human activity on other environments around the world, there is little awareness on the part of the Sherpas or their non-Sherpa neighbors of the mounting environmental disaster. For the three thousand Sherpas and two hundred non-Sherpas in the region, tourists are a convenient scapegoat for these difficulties: the twenty thousand tourists to the Khumbu each year contribute immensely to the pressure placed on the Himalayan ecosystem. It is clear that more efficient methods are needed for managing wood usage, trash disposal, and the huge annual influx of tourists and expeditioners.

The high demand for wood has resulted in deforestation and erosion, and foreign supporters are working with increasing numbers of local Sherpas educated in various fields of ecological study to tackle these serious problems. Sagarmatha National Park was established in the 1970s, thus beginning not only a process of reforestation but also of education of the Sherpas in the absolute priority of this program. The long-standing practice in Solu Khumbu of wood-cutting for cooking and heating, however, is not easily discouraged when the alternatives—oil- or kerosene-driven generators—are expensive, inconvenient, and inadequate. Projects such as the Austrian hydroelectricity scheme in Khumbu and the successful Swiss hydro project in Solu have helped alleviate pressure on the forests, but these do not yet fully meet the needs of the region, particularly in peak tourist season. Sherpa lodge owners are reluctant to institute strict and unpopular restrictions on lighting, heating, and hot showers even if it contributes to a sustainable forest environment. The demand for the wood is irrefutable and growing, and while there is wood to burn, the ravaging of Solu Khumbu's natural resources will continue.

One immediate result of the commercialization of expeditions is a corresponding increase in the amount of debris—particularly non-biodegradable debris—abandoned on the slopes and high camps of the Khumbu. Foreigners' cleanup expeditions to Everest are admirable, and incentive schemes, whereby expedition Sherpas receive a redemption fee for each discarded oxygen bottle they bring down to Base Camp, are helpful. The problems, however, extend far beyond litter on a single peak.

It will take nothing less than a wide-ranging, educated, and concerted effort by both Sherpas and tourists/expeditioners to minimize the grave impact that human activity—both resident and transient—has on the region.

＊

The future of the Sherpa people, their traditions, their homeland, their culture and spirituality, is in the hands of the new Sherpa generations. They face significant obstacles, not least of which is the increasingly volatile nature of Nepalese politics, which could once again slam shut

Tenzing Norgay, May 1973.

the door on all tourism and expeditioning. Still, Sherpas today possess more power than any generation before them to preserve and protect their homeland, with its unique culture and society. They have also inherited an extraordinary strength, determination, and love for the mountains. If they are able to remain grounded in this great legacy and augment it with education and wisdom in this new millennium, then the safe and prosperous future of the Sherpa people and their beloved Himalaya is assured.

For inspiration they need go no further than that most famous of Sherpas—Tenzing Norgay—for he, in one amazing lifetime, forged the path the next generations of his people are now navigating. His life and achievements have been the bridge his Sherpa people have crossed from their isolated, subsistence existence of almost a century ago to the relative affluence and sophistication they enjoy today. His ability to retain his faith in his Sherpa traditions and in himself throughout his whirlwind Everest years stand as testimony to the depth and strength of his Sherpa culture. The drastic changes in his life and his homeland exacted a toll on him personally, there can be no doubt, yet the Tenzing of Everest and of his later years still embodied the pride and dignity of his race, and he remains the symbol of all that Sherpas are and will continue to be: adaptable, strong, and deeply committed to all that their Himalayan Buddhist traditions instill in them.

May the blessing of Jomo Myolangsangma go with them.

SHERPA ASCENTS OF EVEREST

1953—2000

Date of Summit	Name	Village	Climbing Route	Expedition Nation	Details
29/05/53	Tenzing Norgay	Darjeeling	Sth Col	United Kingdom	Died 09/05/86
01/05/63 20/05/65	Nawang Gombu	Darjeeling	Sth Col Sth Col	United States India	
22/05/65	Sonam Gyatso	Darjeeling	Sth Col	Italy	
24/05/65	Ang Kami	Darjeeling	Sth Col	India	Died 06/70
29/05/65	Phu Dorje	Khumjung	Sth Col	India	Died 10/69
12/05/70	Chotare	Namche	Sth Col	Japan	Died 01/94
05/05/73	Lhakpa Tenzing	Namche	Sth Col	Italy	
05/05/73 28/08/85	Tamang Shambhu	Reshango	Sth Col Nth Col	Italy Spain	
07/05/73	Sonam Gyaltsen	Taksindo	Sth Col	Italy	
16/05/75	Ang Tshering	Namche	Sth Col	Japan	
26/09/75 01/10/79 21/04/85	Pertemba	Khumjung	SW Face Sth Col Sth Col	United Kingdom United States Norway	
15/09/77	Pemba Norbu	Namche	Sth Col	South Korea	
03/05/78 15/05/79	Ang Phu	Khumjung	Sth Col W Ridge	Austria Yugoslavia	Died Everest 05/79
16/10/78 23/04/90	Ang Kami	Tsermadingma, Khumbu	Sth Col Sth Col	West Germany Nepal	
16/10/78 23/05/84	Ang Dorje	Thamo	Sth Col Sth Col	West Germany India	No oxygen No oxygen Died Everest 10/84
16/10/78	Mingma Nuru	Khumjung	Sth Col	West Germany	No oxygen
01/10/79	Lhakpa Gyalzen	Phortse	Sth Col	West Germany	
02/10/79	Ang Jangbu	Pangboche	Sth Col	West Germany	
02/10/79	Ang Phurba	Namche	Sth Col	West Germany	

Date of Summit	Name	Village	Climbing Route	Expedition Nation	Details
02/10/79 21/10/81 05/10/82 29/04/85 10/05/88	Sungdare	Pangboche	Sth Col Sth Pillar Sth Col Sth Col Sth Col	West Germany United States Canada Norway Japan/China/Nepal	Died 10/89
14/05/80	Pasang Temba	Lhawa/Ghat	Sth Col	Spain	
24/10/81	Young Tenzing (Yong/Yung Tenzing)	Namche	Sth Pillar	United States	
05/10/82 15/05/91	Lhakpa Dorje	Kunde	Sth Col Nth Col	Canada United States	
07/10/82 29/04/85 26/09/88	Pema Dorje	Khumjung	Sth Col Sth Col Sth Pillar	Canada Norway South Korea	
07/10/82 23/05/97 27/05/98 21/05/00	Lhakpa Tshering	Kunde	Sth Col Sth Col Sth Col Nth Col	Canada Canada/United States United States China	
07/05/83 15/10/84 29/04/85 22/12/87 14/10/88 23/04/90 15/05/92 16/05/93 13/05/95 23/05/96	Ang Rita	Yelanjung, Thamey	Sth Col Up Sth Pillar, down Sth Col Sth Col Sth Col Sth Col Sth Col Sth Col Sth Col Nth Col Sth Pillar	United States Czechoslovakia Norway South Korea Spain Nepal Chile Spain Russia Sweden	
14/05/83	Lhakpa Dorje	Phortse	Sth Col	United States	
16/12/83	Nawang Yonden	Lukla	Sth Col	Japan	
09/05/84	Phu Dorje	Darjeeling	Sth Col	India	Died 05/87
23/05/84	Dorjee Lhatoo	Darjeeling	Sth Col	India	
23/05/84	Sonam Paljor	Darjeeling	Sth Col	India	
21/04/85	Lhakpa Dorje (Ang Lhakpa, Ang Lhakpa Dorje)	Kunde	Sth Col	Norway	Died Everest 12/88
21/04/85	Dawa Norbu	Yelangjung, Thamey	Sth Col	Norway	Died Everest 10/86
29/04/85	Chowang Rinzing	Namche	Sth Col	Norway	

Date of Summit	Name	Village	Climbing Route	Expedition Nation	Details
30/4/85 05/05/88 16/05/93	Ang Phurba	Thamey Og	Sth Col Up Sth Col, down Nth Col Sth Col	Norway Japan/China/Nepal Spain	
28/08/85	Ang Karma	Dhorbu, Solu	Nth Col	Spain	
28/08/85	Shrestha, Narayan	Dhulikel	Nth Col	Spain	Died Everest 09/87
05/05/88 24/05/89	Lhakpa Nuru (Ang Lhakpa)	Kunde	Up Nth Col, down Sth Col Sth Col	Japan/China/Nepal United States	Died 12/89
05/05/88	Lhakpa Sona	Phortse	Nth Col	Japan/China/Nepal	
10/05/88	Tamang Padma Bahadur	Ramechap	Sth Col	Japan/China/Nepal	
10/05/88	Tshering Dorje	Chinese	Nth Col		
26/09/88 10/05/89	Ajiwa	Thamey	Sth Col Sth Col	France Yugoslavia	Died 09/89
26/09/88 10/05/89 12/05/92 04/10/92 22/04/93	Sonam Tshering	Beding	Sth Col Sth Col Sth Col Sth Col Sth Col	France Yugoslavia New Zealand Germany Nepal	No oxygen Died Everest 04/93
26/09/88 13/05/94 11/05/96	Pasang Tshering	Beding	Sth Col Sth Pillar Nth Col	France Japan Japan	
29/09/88	Pasang Gyaljen	Thumbuk	Sth Col	United States	
02/10/88 10/05/90 25/05/97 18/05/99	Nima Tashi	Pangboche	Sth Col Sth Col Sth Col Sth Col	United States United States United States United States	
02/10/88	Dawa Tshering	Rimijung	Sth Col	United States	
02/10/88 16/05/89	Phu Dorje	Pangboche	Sth Col Sth Col	United States U.S./Mexico	Died Everest 05/89
13/10/88	Lhakpa Sonam		Sth Col	France	Died 10/88
14/10/88 23/10/89 15/05/95 20/05/98	Nima Rita	Thamey	Sth Col W Ridge from Sth Sth Col Sth Col	Spain South Korea United States United States	No oxygen

Date of Summit	Name	Village	Climbing Route	Expedition Nation	Details
16/05/89	Ang Dannu	Kunde	Sth Col	United States/Mexico	
24/05/89 05/10/90 08/05/91 10/05/93 09/05/94	Sona Dendu (Sonam Dendu)	Khumjung	Sth Col Sth Col Sth Col Sth Col Sth Col	United States France Nepal/United States South Korea United States	
13/10/89	Chuldin Dorje	Khumjung	Sth Col	Japan	
13/10/89	Tchiring Chumbi Lama (Tchiring Thebe, Tshering Tshemba Lama)	Nupri, North of Gorkha	Sth Col	Japan	Died 12/89
23/10/89	Nuru Jangbu	Ghat	W Ridge	South Korea	
23/04/90	Pasang Norbu	Namche	Sth Col	Nepal	
23/04/90	Khatri Top Banadur	Jhubung, Gulmi	Sth Col	Nepal	
07/05/90 28/05/99	Gyalbu	Lhasa	Nth Col Nth Col	China	
10/05/90	Ang Jangbu	Phortse	Sth Col	United States	
10/05/90 08/05/91 12/05/92 09/10/92 10/05/93 10/10/94 15/05/95 26/04/97 20/05/98 26/05/99 24/05/00	Apa Sherpa	Thamey Og	Sth Col Sth Col Sth Col Sth Col Sth Col Sth Col Sth Col Sth Col Sth Col Nth Col Sth Col	New Zealand United States/Nepal New Zealand United States/Mexico United States Japan United States Indonesia United States United States United States	
10/05/90 10/05/93	Dawa Nuru (Danuru, Da Nuru)	Phortse	Sth Col Sth Col	United States United States	
10/05/90	Wangyal		Nth Col	China/United States/USSR	
05/10/90	Ang Temba	Beding	Sth Col	United States	
05/10/90	Nawang Thile (Pemba Dorje, Ang Nawang)	Beding	Sth Col	France	

Nawang Thile *continues*

Date of Summit	Name	Village	Climbing Route	Expedition Nation	Details
22/04/93	Nawang Thile *continued*		Sth Col	Nepal	
17/05/00			Nth Col	International	
06/10/90	Babu Tshering	Taksindu,	Sth Col	France	
22/05/91	(Babu Chiri or	Solu	Nth Col	United Kingdom	
10/10/93	Ang Babu)		Nth Col	United Kingdom	
14/05/95			Nth Col	United Kingdom/France	
26/05/95			Nth Col	United Kingdom/France	
23/05/96			Sth Col	France	
21/05/97			Sth Col	United Kingdom/Iceland	
6-7/05/99			Sth Col	Sweden	Stayed 21 hours on summit; no oxygen
26/05/99			Sth Col	Sweden	No oxygen
21/05/00			Sth Col	Nepal	Died Everest 4/01
06/10/90	Dawa Sange	Chaurikarka	Sth Col	South Korea/Japan	Died 09/91
06/10/90	Pemba Dorje	Pangboche	Sth Col	South Korea/Japan	
07/10/90	Lhakpa Rita (brother of Kami Rita of Yilajung)	Thamey	Sth Col	Yugoslavia	
15/05/92			Sth Col	United States	
13/05/94			Sth Col	United States	
25/05/97			Sth Col	United States	
07/10/90	Ang Phurba	Beding	Sth Col	France	
07/10/90	Phinzo	Beding	Sth Col	United States	
16/05/93			Sth Col	United States	
16/05/95			Nth Col	United States	
07/10/90	Nima Dorje	Beding	Sth Col	France	
27/05/91	(Dorje)		Nth Col	Japan	
16/05/93			Sth Col	India	
08/05/94			Sth Pillar	Japan	
11/05/95			NE Ridge	Japan	
13/05/96			Nth Col	Japan	
08/05/91	Ang Temba	Kunde	Sth Col	Nepal/United States	
15/05/91	Ang Dawa	Lumsa	Nth Col	United States	
12/05/92	Tapting	Solu	Sth Col	New Zealand	
10/05/93			Sth Col	South Korea	
15/05/91	Gyalbu	Beding	Nth Face	Sweden	
06/10/93			Sth Col	France	
18/05/96			Nth Col	Norway	
23/05/97			Sth Col	Canada/United States	

Date of Summit	Name	Village	Climbing Route	Expedition Nation	Details
15/05/91	Mingma Norbu (Mingma Nuru)	Beding	Nth Face	Sweden	Died 09/94
22/05/91 10/05/93	Chuldin Temba	Namche	Nth Col Sth Col	United Kingdom United States	
27/05/91 19/05/98	Phinzo Norbu	Beding	Nth Col Nth Col	Japan India	
12/05/92 10/05/93 09/05/94 10/05/96 23/05/97 21/05/00 07/10/00	Ang Dorje (Chuldin)	Pangboche	Sth Col Sth Col Sth Col Sth Col Sth Col Sth Col Sth Col	New Zealand New Zealand New Zealand New Zealand New Zealand Canada Slovenia	
12/05/92	Ang Gyalzen	Namche	Sth Col	United States	
12/05/92	Lobsang	Darjeeling	Sth Col	India	
12/05/92	Nima Temba	Beding	Sth Col	Netherlands	
12/05/92 17/05/96 28/05/99	Sange	India	Sth Col Nth Col East Face	India India India	
12/05/92 14/10/95 10/05/96 23/05/97 20/05/98 27/05/98 17/10/98 22/05/00	Tashi Tshering	Pangboche	Sth Col Nth Col Sth Col Sth Col Sth Col Sth Col Sth Col Sth Col	New Zealand South Korea United States Canada/United States United States United States Nepal United States	
12/05/92	Wangchuk	Makalu Barun	Sth Col	India	
12/05/92 22/04/93 06/10/93 13/05/94 17/05/96 18/05/98	Dawa Tashi	Beding	Sth Col Sth Col Sth Col Sth Pillar Nth Col Nth Col	Netherlands Nepal France Japan Norway India	
12/05/92 11/10/94 23/05/97 26/05/99 20/05/00	Dawa Temba	Thamo	Sth Col Sth Col Sth Col Sth Col Sth Pillar/SE Ridge	United States United Kingdom Malaysia Sweden Denmark	
15/05/92	Ang Phuri	Sailung, Beni Solu	Sth Col	Chile	

Date of Summit	Name	Village	Climbing Route	Expedition Nation	Details
15/05/92 28/09/92 22/04/93 09/10/93 08/05/94 01/05/95	Lhakpa Nuru	Karikhola	Sth Pillar Sth Col Sth Col Nth Col Sth Pillar NE Ridge	Spain Italy Nepal United Kingdom Japan Japan	Died Everest 09/95
15/05/92 22/04/93	Pemba Norbu (Nuru)	Monjo Chaurikarka	Sth Pillar Sth Col	Spain Nepal	
15/05/92 10/05/93 07/10/93 13/05/94 11/10/94 27/05/97 05/05/99 17/05/00	Dorjee (Lambu Dorjee, Big Dorjee)	Thamo	Sth Col Sth Col Sth Col Sth Col Sth Col Sth Col Sth Col Sth Col	United States India United Kingdom United States United Kingdom United Kingdom United States International	
15/05/92 13/05/94 26/05/99	Tamang, Man Bahadur (Gopal)	Jangding, Salleri	Sth Col Sth Col Nth Col	United States United States Georgia	
09/10/92 16/05/93 14/05/95 26/09/96 17/10/98	Kaji (Pasang Kami, Pasang Kazi)	Loding, Junbesi	Sth Col Sth Col Nth Col Nth Col Sth Col	United States/Mexico South Korea United States Indonesia Nepal	Speed ascent without oxygen
13/04/93	Ngati	Phortse	Up Nth Col, down Sth Col	South Korea	Died 03/97
22/04/93	Mrs Pasang Lhamu	Lukla	Sth Col	Nepal	Died Everest 04/93
10/05/93	Ang Chumbi	Unknown	Sth Col	New Zealand	
10/05/93	Ang Tshering	Kunde	Sth Col	South Korea	
10/05/93	Gurung, Motilal	Sedua	Sth Col	United States	
10/05/93 17/05/96 25/05/98 28/05/99	Kusang Dorje	Darjeeling	Sth Col Nth Col Sth Col E Face	India India United Kingdom India	
10/05/93	Lobsang Tshering Bhutia	Darjeeling	Sth Col	Australia	Died Everest 10/05/93

Date of Summit	Name	Village	Climbing Route	Expedition Nation	Details
10/05/93	Na (Nga) Temba	Sikli, near	Sth Col	India	
16/05/93		Karikhola	Sth Col	India	
07/10/93			Sth Col	United Kingdom	
09/10/93			Sth Col	United Kingdom	
08/05/94			Sth Pillar	Japan	
17/05/96			Nth Col	Japan	
23/05/97			Sth Col	Malaysia	
18/05/98			Nth Col	Japan	
05/05/99			Sth Col	United States	
10/05/93	Norbu	Beding	Sth Col	New Zealand	
09/10/93	(Nuru)		Sth Col	France	
09/05/94			Sth Col	New Zealand	
10/05/96			Sth Col	New Zealand	
27/05/98			Sth Col	United States	
18/05/00			Nth Col	Japan/Austria	
10/05/93	Ongda Chiring	Dinching, Sedua	Sth Col	India	
07/10/93	(Wangda Tshering)	(Makalu area)	Sth Pillar	Spain	
14/05/95			Nth Col	United States	
10/05/93	Pemba Temba	Pangboche	Sth Col	United States	
10/05/93	Rinzin	Tapting, Solu	Sth Col	South Korea	
16/05/93	Dorje	Tapting, Solu	Sth Col	United States	
16/05/93	Jangbu	Lumsa, Salleri	Sth Col	Spain	
16/05/93	Lobsang Jangbu	Sangbu, Beding	Sth Col	India	
09/05/94			Sth Col	United States	No oxygen
07/05/95			Sth Col	New Zealand	No oxygen
10/05/96			Sth Col	United States	No oxygen Died Everest 21/09/96
16/05/93	Nima Norbu Dolma	Darjeeling	Sth Col	India	
16/05/93	Durga Tamang	Unknown	Sth Col	United States	
16/05/93	Tenzing	Thamey	Sth Col	India	
09/10/93			Sth Col	United Kingdom	
10/05/96			Sth Col	United States	
23/05/97			Sth Col	United Kingdom	
12/05/99			Sth Col	United Kingdom	
18/05/00			Nth Col	Japan/Austria	
17/05/93	Ang Pasang	Pangboche	Sth Col	United Kingdom	
25/05/97			Sth Col	United States	

Date of Summit	Name	Village	Climbing Route	Expedition Nation	Details
18/05/00	Ang Pasang *continued*		Sth Col	Nepal	
17/05/93	Kami Tshering	Pangboche	Sth Col	United Kingdom	
23/05/97	(Ang Tshering)		Sth Col	Canada/United States	
22/05/00			Sth Col	United States	
06/10/93	Panuru	Phortse	Nth Col	South Korea	
11/10/96			Sth Col	South Korea	
27/05/98			Nth Col	United States	
07/10/93	Pasang Kami	Karikhola	Sth Col	United Kingdom	
11/05/95			NE Ridge	Japan	
11/05/96			Nth Col	Japan	
18/05/98			Nth Col	Japan	
09/10/93	Ang Pasang	Karikhola	Sth Col	United Kingdom	
09/10/93	Lhakpa Gelu	Ruptsa,	Sth Col	United Kingdom	
24/05/95	(brother of	near	Nth Col	United Kingdom	
	Dawa Norbu)	Karikhola			
19/05/96			Nth Col	United Kingdom	
23/05/97			Sth Col	United Kingdom	
24/05/98			Nth Col	South Africa	
13/05/99			Sth Col	United Kingdom	
17/05/00			Sth Col	International	
09/10/93	Nima Gombu	Beding	Sth Col	France	
09/05/94	(Gombu)		Sth Col	New Zealand	
10/05/96			Sth Col	Taiwan	
25/05/98			Sth Col	United Kingdom	
12/05/99			Sth Col	United Kingdom/United States	
24/05/00			Sth Col	International	
08/05/94	Dawa Tshering	Beding	Sth Pillar	Japan	
11/05/95			NE Ridge	Japan	
17/05/96			Nth Col	Norway	
13/05/94	Chuwang Nima	Thamey	Sth Col	United States	
10/10/94	(Chhewang Nima)		Sth Col	Japan	
13/05/96			Nth Col	Japan	
26/09/96			Nth Col	Indonesia	
19/05/98			Nth Col	Japan	
05/05/99			Sth Col	United States	
18/05/99			Sth Col	United States	
23/05/00			Sth Col	United States/Canada	
13/05/94	Kami Rita	Yilajung,	Sth Col	United States	
25/05/97	(Topke)	near Thamey	Sth Col	United States	
15/05/98			Sth Col	Singapore	
13/05/99			Sth Col	United Kingdom	
23/05/00			Sth Col	United States/Canada	
13/05/94	Nima Temba	Lukla	Sth Pillar	Japan	

Date of Summit	Name	Village	Climbing Route	Expedition Nation	Details
10/10/94	Dawa Tshering	Thamey	Sth Col	Japan	
13/05/96			Nth Col	Japan	
26/09/96			Nth Col	Indonesia	
19/05/98			Nth Col	Japan	
13/09/99			Sth Col	Japan	
12/05/95	Lhakpa Dorje	Kurima,	Nth Col	Taiwan	
23/05/96		Solu	Sth Col	United States	No oxygen
12/05/95	Tenzing Nuru	Yilajung,	Nth Col	Taiwan	
25/05/97		near Namche	Sth Col	United States	Died Everest 25/05/97
12/05/95	Mingma Tshering	Beding	Nth Col	Taiwan	
10/05/96			Sth Col	Taiwan	
23/05/97			Sth Col	New Zealand	
19/05/98			Nth Col	Japan	
05/05/99			Sth Col	Sweden	
17/05/00			Nth Col	Japan/Austria	
15/05/95	Arita	Thamey	Sth Col	United States	
20/05/98	(brother of Apa Sherpa)		Sth Col	United States	
24/05/00			Sth Col	United States	
16/05/95	Jangbu	Changba	Nth Col	United States	
23/05/96		Tapting, Solu	Sth Col	United States	
23/05/97			Sth Col	United States	
16/05/95	Musal Kaji Tamang	Gorakhani, Solu	Nth Col	United States	
24/05/95	Tshering Dorje	Karikhola	Nth Col	United Kingdom	
13/05/99			Sth Col	United Kingdom	
26/05/95	Karsang	Thamey	Nth Col	United Kingdom	
25/05/98	(Ang Rita's son)		Nth Col	New Zealand/Japan	
27/05/99			Nth Col	New Zealand	
26/05/95	Lama Jangbu	Karikhola	Nth Col	United Kingdom	
25/05/96			Sth Col	South Africa	
24/05/98			Nth Col	South Africa	
29/05/99			Nth Col	South Africa/United Kingdom	
16/05/00			Sth Col	United Kingdom	
26/05/95	Lobsang Temba	Khumjung	Nth Col	United Kingdom	
27/05/99			Nth Col	New Zealand	
14/10/95	Keepa (Kipa)	Hille, near	SW Face	South Korea	
11/10/96		Karikhola	Sth Col	South Korea	
27/05/97			Sth Col	United Kingdom	
14/10/95	Ang Dawa Tamang	Gorekhani,	SW Face	South Korea	
11/10/96	(Dawa)	Solu	Sth Col	South Korea	

Date of Summit	Name	Village	Climbing Route	Expedition Nation	Details
07/05/97	Ang Dawa Tamang *continued*		Nth Col	South Korea	
14/10/95	Zangbu	Nele, near Paphlu	Nth Col	South Korea	Died Everest 14/10/95
10/05/96	Dorje Morup	Darjeeling	Nth Col	India	Died on 05/96
10/05/96 19/05/00	Nawang Dorje (Da Nawang Dorje)	Rolwaling	Sth Col Nth Col	United States Japan/Austria	
10/05/96	Tsewang Paljor	Darjeeling	Nth Col	India	Died Everest 10–11/05/96
10/05/96	Tsewang	Smanla	Nth Col	India	Died Everest 10–11/05/96
11/05/96 26/09/96 18/05/98	Ang Gyalzen	Wong, Thamey	Nth Col Nth Col Nth Col	Japan Indonesia Japan	
17/05/96	Pemba Tsering	Thamo	Nth Col	Japan	
17/05/96	Nadra	India	Nth Col	India	
19/05/96	Mingma Dorje	Karikhola	Nth Col	United Kingdom	
19/05/96	Phur Gyalzen	Karikhola	Nth Col	United Kingdom	
23/05/96 21/05/97 06/05/99 26/05/99 21/05/00	Dawa	Taksindo	Sth Col Sth Col Sth Col Sth Col Sth Col	France United Kingdom Sweden Sweden Nepal	
23/05/96 23/05/97 25/05/98 05/05/99 17/05/00	Dorje	Nunthala, Solu	Sth Col Sth Col Sth Col Sth Col Sth Col	United States United States Singapore Canada International	
23/05/96	Jamling Tenzing Norgay	Darjeeling	Sth Col	United States	
23/05/96	Muktu Lhakpa	Tashigaon, Makalu	Sth Col	United States	
23/05/96	Thilen (brother of Muktu Lhakpa)	Tashigaon	Sth Col	United States	
25/05/96	Ang Dorje	Tate, Khumbu	Sth Col	South Africa	
25/05/96 25/05/97 29/05/99	Pemba Tenji (Tenjee, Pekka Tenja)	Chatu, Solu	Sth Col Sth Col Nth Col	South Africa United States South Africa	

Date of Summit	Name	Village	Climbing Route	Expedition Nation	Details
26/09/96	Gyalzen	Loding	Nth Col	Indonesia	
23/05/97			Sth Col	Malaysia	
20/05/98			Nth Col	Japan	
05/05/99			Sth Col	United States	
27/04/97	Dawa Nuru (Norbu)	Thamey	Sth Col	Indonesia	
18/05/98			Nth Col	India	
21/05/97	Danuri (Danu)	Simigaon, Rolwaling	Sth Col	Nepal	
23/05/97	Ang Phuri Gyalzen	Sikli, near Karikhola	Sth Col	Malaysia	
23/05/97	Dawa (Datenzi)	Karikhola	Sth Col	United Kingdom	
20/05/98			Sth Col	Iran	
23/05/97	Kami	Pagam, Kerung	Sth Col	United States	
05/05/99			Sth Col	Sweden	
23/05/97	Fura Dorje	Sotang, Solu	Sth Col	Malaysia	
25/05/98			Sth Col	Singapore	
27/05/99			Nth Col	Mexico	
23/05/97	Tashi Tenzing	Darjeeling	Sth Col	New Zealand	
25/05/97	Mingma Chhiri (Tshering)	Thamey	Sth Col	United States	
26/05/99			Sth Col	Mexico	
27/05/97	Dawa Sona	Pangboche	Sth Col	United Kingdom/United States	
27/05/98			Sth Col	United States	
18/05/99			Sth Col	United States	
29/05/97	Tenzing Dorje	China	Nth Col	China	
18/05/98	Ang Mingma	Yilaung, near Thamey	Nth Col	Japan	
18/05/00			Sth Col	Nepal	
18/05/98	Nawang Tenzing (Tenzing)	Beding	Nth Col	India	
18/05/98	Thomting	Beding	Nth Col	India	
19/05/98	Nima Gyalzen	Beding	Nth Col	India	
13/05/99			Sth Col	United Kingdom	
17/05/00			Nth Col	Japan	
19/05/98	Pasang Kitar	Beding	Nth Col	Japan	
13/06/99			Sth Col	United Kingdom	
19/05/00			Nth Col	Japan/Austria	
19/05/98	Tshering Dorje	Rolwaling	Nth Col	Japan	

Date of Summit	Name	Village	Climbing Route	Expedition Nation	Details
20/05/98	Ang Pasang	Thamey	Sth Col	United States	
20/05/98	Chuldim	Khumjung	Sth Col	Iran	
20/05/98	Chuldim Nuru	Phute, near Thamey	Sth Col	United States	
20/05/98	Gyalzen	Phute, near Thamey	Sth Col	United States	
20/05/98 24/05/00	Pemba Norbu	Namche	Sth Col Sth Col	United States United States	
20/05/98 13/05/99	Pemba Rinzi (brother of Tshering Dorje)	Karikhola	Sth Col Sth Col	Iran United Kingdom	
22/05/98	Dawa	Loding	Nth Col	Japan	
25/05/98	Dawa Nuru	Phortse	Nth Col	United States	
25/05/98	Lhakpa Rita	Phortse	Nth Col	United States	
25/05/98	Nawang Phurbu	Beding	Sth Col	Singapore	
25/05/98 06/05/99 26/05/99	Nima Dorje (Bocha Lama)	Makalu-Barun	Sth Col Sth Col Sth Col	United Kingdom Sweden Sweden	
25/09/98 13/05/99	Nima Wangchu	Kamujung	Nth Col Sth Col	United Kingdom Japan	
26/05/98 05/05/99	Pasang Tshering (Ang Tsering)	Pangboche	Sth Col Sth Col	United Kingdom United Kingdom	
26/05/98 13/05/99	Pasang Dawa (Pa Dawa)	Pangboche	Sth Col Sth Col	United Kingdom United Kingdom	
05/05/99	Ang Chiri	Beding	Sth Col	Sweden	
05/05/99	Chhongra Nuru	Taka, Solu	Sth Col	Canada	
05/05/99 22/05/00	Phu Tashi	Pangboche	Sth Col Sth Col	United States United States	
12/05/99 22/05/00	Chewang Dorje	Thamey	Sth Col Sth Col	Georgia United States	
12/05/99 19/05/00	Nawang Tenzing	Phortse	Sth Col Nth Col	Georgia Japan	
13/05/99 17/05/00	Dawa Nurbu (Damuru, brother of Lhakpa Gelu)	Karikhola	Sth Col Sth Col	United Kingdom International	

Date of Summit	Name	Village	Climbing Route	Expedition Nation	Details
13/05/99 24/05/00	Nawang Wangchu (Ngawang Wangchuk)	Chaplung, Chaunrikarka	Sth Col Sth Col	Japan International	
13/05/99	Tamang, Krishna Bahadur (Jeta)	Kanku, Solu	Sth Col	Japan	
26/05/99	Lhakpa Nuru	Thamey	Sth Col	Mexico	
26/05/99	Nanda Dorje (Nawang Chumbi)	Khumjung	Nth Col	United States	
26/05/99	Samdu	Arun, Makalu	Nth Col	Italy	
27/05/99	Phurba Tashi	Khumjung	Nth Col	New Zealand	
28/05/99	Pemba Tashi	China	Nth Col	China	
28/05/99	Tashi Tshering (Zhgshiciren)	Tibet	Nth Col	China	
16/05/00	Thamting		Sth Col	Spain	
16/05/00	Nima Nuru		Sth Col	Spain	
16/05/00	Pemba Gyalzen		Sth Col	United Kingdom	
17/05/00	Phinzo		Nth Col	Japan	
17/05/00	Palden Namgye		Nth Col	Japan	
17/05/00	Pemba Gyalzen II		Nth Col	Japan/Austria	
17/05/00	Pemba Dorji II		Nth Col	Japan	
18/05/00	Lhakpa Sherpa		Sth Col	Nepal	
18/05/00	Ang Phurba		Sth Col	Nepal	
19/05/00	Pemba Doma		Nth Col	International	
19/05/00	Gyalu Lama		Nth Col	Japan	
19/05/00	Pasang Kami		Nth Col	Japan	
20/05/00	Dawa Chiri		Sth Pillar SE Ridge	Denmark	
21/05/00	Nima Dawa		Sth Pillar SE Ridge	Denmark	
21/05/00	Lhakpa Tshering II		Sth Col	Canada	

Date of Summit	Name	Village	Climbing Route	Expedition Nation	Details
21/05/00	Mingma Tenzing		Sth Col	Canada	
21/05/00	Mingma		Sth Col	Canada	
21/05/00	Tenzing Dorje		Sth Col	Canada	
21/05/00	Nuru Wangdi		Sth Col	Canada	
21/05/00	Karchen Dawa		Sth Col	Canada	
22/05/00	Pasang Tshering III		Sth Col	Poland	
23/05/00	Mingma Chiri		Sth Col	United States/Canada	
24/05/00	Lhakpa Tshering III		Sth Col	United States	
24/05/00	Kami Rita II		Sth Col	United States	
24/05/00	Pemba Tshering II		Sth Col	United States	
24/05/00	Pemba Chuti		Sth Col	United States	
24/05/00	Pasang Tharke		Sth Col	United States	
24/05/00	Nima (Ang Nima)		Sth Col	United States	
24/05/00	Dawa Jangbu		Sth Col	United States	
26/05/00	Mingma Nuru II		Sth Col	International	
27/05/00	Lhakpa Gyalzen II		Nth Col	Spain/Argentina	
07/10/00	Pasang Tenzing		Sth Col	Slovenia	

A total of 489 Sherpa/Nepali summits out of 1,318 total Everest summits.

This list was compiled by Elizabeth Hawley, Kathmandu, for the period 1953–1999, with records for 2000 by Peter Gillman. This list also includes those non-Sherpa Nepalis who have reached the summit of Everest as they were working in the role of "Sherpa."

BRIEF
BIBLIOGRAPHY

Alpine Club. *The Alpine Journal* (London), various years.

Bonington, Chris. *The Everest Years: A Climber's Life.* New York: Viking, 1987.

Chua-Eoan, Howard. "Heroes and Icons." *Time* 68 (14 June 1999).

Fisher, James F. *Sherpas: Reflections on Change in Himalayan Nepal.* Berkeley: University of California Press, 1990.

Fürer-Haimendorf, Christoph von. *The Sherpas of Nepal: Buddhist Highlanders.* Berkeley: University of California Press, 1964.

Groom, Michael. *Sheer Will: The Inspiring Life and Climbs of Michael Groom.* Milsons Point, N.S.W.: Random House Australia, 1999.

Hillary, Sir Edmund. *High Adventure.* London: Hodder & Stoughton, 1955.

Hillary, Sir Edmund. *The View from the Summit.* London: Doubleday, 1999.

Himalayan Club. *The Himalayan Journal* (Bombay), various years.

Hunt, John Baron. *The Ascent of Everest.* New York: Dutton, 1954.

Norgay, Tenzing, and Malcolm Barnes. *After Everest: An Autobiography.* London: G. Allen & Unwin, 1977.

Norkey, Tenzing, and James Ramsey Ullman. *Man of Everest: The Autobiography of Tenzing.* Rev. ed. London: Severn House, 1975.

Norkey, Tenzing, and James Ramsey Ullman. *Tiger of the Snows: The Autobiography of Tenzing of Everest.* New York: Putnam, 1955.

Ortner, Sherry. *Life and Death on Mt. Everest: Sherpas and Himalayan Mountaineering.* Princeton: Princeton University Press, 1999.

Shipton, Eric Earle. *That Untravelled World: An Autobiography.* London: Hodder & Stoughton, 1977.

Thapa, Vijay Jung. "Lords of Everest." *India Today,* 7 July 1997.

Tilman, H. W. *The Seven Mountain-Travel Books.* Seattle: Mountaineers, 1983.

Unsworth, Walt. *Everest: The Mountaineering History.* 3rd ed. Seattle: Mountaineers, 2000.

Younghusband, Sir Francis. *The Epic of Mount Everest.* London: E. Arnold, 1926.

A NOTE FROM
THE WRITER

PAHAR KHOTI—A NAME SO ALIEN to a girl raised in a traditional Australian Catholic family, yet a name that awakened some distant spirit or memory—if one believes in such things. Pahar Khoti was an old house in the Blue Mountains near Sydney—a rundown, ramshackle place we had rented for a vacation when I was ten years old—architecturally from the "early modern broken period," as one friend later put it!

Yet in this house in the cold and mists of our tiny mountains was the spirit of the Himalaya. Or perhaps the spirit of the Himalaya was in me, and this house was the catalyst for freeing it. There were only two books on the shelves in the sitting room. One was *Seven Years in Tibet*, by Heinrich Harrer, and the other was *Man of Everest*, the autobiography of Tenzing Norgay Sherpa as told to James Ramsey Ullman. At that young age I knew scarcely anything of India, Nepal, Tibet, the Himalaya, or Mount Everest. I barely knew of their existence. Yet in that house those two titles drew me like a magnet despite the great pile of reading material I'd lugged along with me—*Collected Ghost Stories, Jane Eyre, Wuthering Heights, On Windycross Moor.* The titles of those two books had the same effect on me as the name of the house. Even now when I think of that day I can feel and smell the cool, clear whisper of a Himalayan wind that blew through my mind and, ultimately, changed my life.

Exotic "Tibet" in the Harrer title enticed me to read that book first. It's a wonderful tale of an extraordinary land and people. But it only sharpened my desire for the Everest story and my curiosity to find out who this "Sherpa Tensing," as my parents referred to him, really was. I read *Man of Everest* in one sitting. I pored over the black-and-white photographs. I reread the account of the final summit climb many times. I was there with them—every step. Suddenly the Brontë sisters' Yorkshire moors paled into insignificance!

I was terrifically impressed by Tenzing's humor, his courage, and his genuine humility. Everyone I had ever known was so "safe" and predictable. Yet here was a young, illiterate man who dreamed of the ultimate, who broke free from his quiet and secure life and went for the dream. Perhaps it was the dawning of the idea within me that I could be more—do more, discover more about myself than I had hitherto thought possible. Perhaps Tenzing's Everest was my personal Everest—I don't know. But I was so moved by his account of his life that at the tender age of ten I wrote to him, c/o the Himalayan Mountaineering Institute in Darjeeling (wherever that was!). In childish and awkward words I told him that I liked him and admired him—and that I had come, through his story, to love "his mountain," Everest. I wrote that one day I would come and see Everest for myself—this coming from a kid who abhorred all sports and who wouldn't walk around the block to save her life!

The Himalayan passion born at Pahar Khoti eventually wove its way into the fiber of my life. And Everest became the focal point of this passion. I read everything I could get my hands on about the history of Everest mountaineering, and I became a trekking and mountaineering guide in the Himalaya. I loved to listen to the Sherpas talk of their climbs and their Western colleagues who had such a different attitude toward the Himalayan peaks. I learned a great deal from the Sherpa people—about Everest, about mountains, yes . . . but also about life in general.

They are such positive and clear-thinking people. The word "simple" describes them well but has some negative overtones. They are simple in every positive sense of the word—life is simple, and if it's not simple for you, then it should be! This is how Tenzing felt, and it was so much a part of his strength. However, there were many who used his simplicity to deceive him and confuse him. These people hurt him deeply, as I came to realize years later, after I had married into his family.

But before that time, when I was working as a guide in the Himalaya in 1983, I had the honor of meeting Tenzing in his home in Darjeeling (I now knew where it was!). We sat and had tea and chatted about work, mountains (not Everest), his dogs, and Australia. He had a keen and curious mind and an easy manner. I had been so excited at the prospect of meeting him that I feared I would babble. But I simply felt relaxed and enjoyed his company in the same way I would when I first met his eldest daughter, Pem Pem, many years later. After our second cup of tea, I mentioned to Tenzing that I had written to him as a child. That famous smile lit the room, and he crossed his legs. "Oh, yes. I remember that letter." Of course he didn't, but it was kind and gracious of him to say so. It was a wonderful, memorable day for me.

I was camped on the banks of the Trisuli River in central Nepal in 1986 when Radio Nepal broke the news that Tenzing Norgay had died in his home in Darjeeling. Although I hadn't even met my husband yet, the news struck me as if a member of my own family had died. Around me no one spoke—the Sherpas, the local villagers, the Indian truck drivers who had joined us for tea. Silence. We all knew him. A great man—a man of the people like all of us—had gone. It was so very sad. I am told that in India the response was the same.

This book is for Tenzing and for all his Sherpa people. It is for his children and his grandchildren—and his great-grandchildren, my children. In a small way, although he never knew it, his Everest was my Everest. My spirit was freed by his, and by his written words, and I will be always grateful to him for this.

JUDY TENZING
OCTOBER 2001

ART
CREDITS

·

graphical Society; 29: J. B. Noel/Royal Geographical Society; 31: E. Smythe/Royal Geographical Society; 33: J. B. Noel/Royal Geographical Society; 37: Royal Geographical Society; 40 (top): Courtesy J. Jackson; 40 (bottom): Tashi Tenzing Photo Library; 44 (both): Royal Geographical Society; 47: L. V. Bryant/Royal Geographical Society; 49: Royal Geographical Society; 55: Courtesy J. Jackson; 58 (top 2): A. Gregory/Royal Geographical Society; 58 (bottom): Royal Geographical Society; 60: Courtesy Annelies Sutter; 64 (both): Tashi Tenzing Photo Library; 67: H. Bury/Royal Geographical Society; 71: Royal Geographical Society; 72: Courtesy C. Wylie; 76, 77, 78, 80: Courtesy Annelies Sutter; 83: Courtesy Tenzing Family Collection; 84: Courtesy Norman G. Dyhrenfurth/Swiss Foundation for Alpine Research; 90 (top left and top right): Royal Geographical Society; 90 (bottom): Tashi Tenzing Photo Library; 91 (top), 93: Courtesy Norman G. Dyhrenfurth/Swiss Foundation for Alpine Research; 94: NASA; 98 (both), 101, 103, 104 (top): Courtesy Norman G. Dyhrenfurth/Swiss Foundation for Alpine Research; 104 (bottom): Tashi Tenzing Photo Library; 106: Courtesy Norman G. Dyhrenfurth/Swiss Foundation for Alpine Research; 112 (top and bottom): A. Gregory/Royal Geographical Society; 115: A. Gregory/Royal Geographical Society; 116 (top): C. Wylie/Royal Geographical Society; 116 (bottom): W. Noyce/Royal Geographical Society; 120 (top and bottom): A. Gregory/Royal Geographical Society; 121 (top): A. Gregory/Royal Geographical Society; 121 (bottom): J. Hunt/Royal Geographical Society; 122 (clockwise): Royal Geographical Society; Royal Geographical Society; A. Gregory/Royal Geographical Society; Royal Geographical Society; map courtesy *Tiger of the Snows* (Tenzing); 123: Royal Geographical Society; 124 (top and bottom): A. Gregory/Royal Geographical Society; 125 (top and bottom): A. Gregory/Royal Geographical Society; 127: Royal Geographical Society; 129: A. Gregory/Royal Geographical Society; 130: E. Hillary/Royal Geographical Society; 132: Royal Geographical Society; 133: G. Band/Royal Geographical Society; 136 (top and bottom): A. Gregory/Royal Geographical Society; 140: Courtesy Tenzing Family Collection; 143: Courtesy D. Reist; 153: Courtesy M. Feuz; 154 (top): Courtesy M. Feuz; 154 (bottom): Courtesy D. Reist; 155 and 156: Courtesy M. Feuz; 157, 159, 160, 162 (top and bottom): Courtesy Tenzing Family Collection; 167: Courtesy Pem Pem Tshering; 168 (top): Courtesy Tenzing Family Collection; 168 (bottom) and 171: Courtesy Nima Tenzing Galang; 172: Courtesy George Lowe; 174: Courtesy Peter Friedli; 178, 181: Courtesy Tenzing Family Collection; 184, 187, 188 (top and bottom), 192, 193: Tashi Tenzing Photo Library; 195: Lobsang Tshering Bhutia; 203: Tashi Tenzing Photo Library; 205, 206 (top and bottom), 209, 212, 213: Tashi Tenzing Photo Library; 216: Courtesy Norman G. Dyhrenfurth; 222 (top and bottom): Courtesy Norman G. Dyhrenfurth; 227, 233: Tashi Tenzing Photo Library; 237: Jamling Tenzing Norgay Collection; 238: Tashi Tenzing Photo Library; 241: Chris Bonington Picture Library; 248 (top and bottom): Tashi Tenzing Photo Library; 252, 254: Tashi Tenzing Photo Library; 260, 264: Tashi Tenzing Photo Library; 269: Bob McKerrow/Hedgehog House Photographic Library.

TASHI TENZING, GRANDSON OF TENZING NORGAY SHERPA, was born and raised in the Himalaya and educated in Darjeeling and Delhi. He worked as a trekking and mountaineering guide in the Himalaya before meeting and marrying his Australian-born wife, Judy Pyne. Judy had spent over a decade in the Himalaya and India as one of the region's first female mountain guides. In 1990 they settled in Australia and established their own specialist Himalayan travel agency, Tenzing's Himalayan Travel Centre.

Tashi and Judy have two children, Pasang and Dechen, and return regularly to the Himalaya for work and rejuvenation. Tashi lectures on the history and climbing of Everest, and Judy, a graduate in South Asian history, teaches courses on the cultures and history of the Himalayan kingdoms and India. They collaborated on *Tenzing Norgay and the Sherpas of Everest*: Tashi as voice and memory, Judy as writer.